MANAGEMENT OF BEHAVIOUR IN SCHOOLS

Other books edited by Ved P. Varma

Stresses in Children (1973) London: University of London Press.
Advances in Educational Psychology Vol. 1 (1973) (co-editor
Professor W.D. Wall), London: University of London Press.
Psychotherapy Today (1974) London: Constable
Advances in Educational Psychology Vol. 2 (1974) (co-editor Mia
Kellmer Pringle), London: Hodder and Stoughton.
Piaget, Psychology and Education (1976) (co-editor Professor Phillip
Williams), London: Hodder and Stoughton.
Anxiety in Children (1984) London: Croom Helm/Methuen.
Advances in Teacher Education (1989) (co-editor Professor V. Alan
McClelland), London: Routledge.
*The Management of Children with Emotional and Behavioural
Difficulties* (1990) London: Routledge.
Special Education: Past, Present and Future (1990) (co-editor Peter
Evans), Lewes: Falmer Press.
The Secret Life of Vulnerable Children (1991) London: Routledge.
Truants from Life: Theory and Therapy (1991) London: David
Fulton.
Prospects for People with Learning Difficulties (1991) (co-editor
Professor Stanley Segal) London: David Fulton.
Resilience and Vulnerability in Human Development (1992) (co-
editor Professor Barbara Tizard) London: Jessica Kingsley.
Coping with Unhappy Children (in press) London: Cassell
Educational,
How and Why Children Fail (in press) London: Jessica Kingsley.
How and Why Children Hate (in press) London: Jessica Kingsley.

Management of behaviour in schools

Edited by Ved P. Varma

LONGMAN
London and New York

Longman Group UK Limited
Longman House, Burnt Mill,
Harlow, Essex CM20 2JE, England
and Associated Companies throughout the world

*Published in the United States of America
by Longman Publishing, New York*

© Longman Group UK Limited 1993

First published 1993
ISBN 0–582–07572.6

British Library Cataloguing-in-Publication Data

A catalogue record for this book is
available from the British Library

Library of Congress Cataloging-in-Publication Data

Management of behaviour in schools / edited by Ved P. Varma.
        p.   cm.
    Includes bibliographical references and index.
    ISBN 0–582–07572–6
    1. Classroom management 2. School discipline
    3. Problem children – Education
  I. Varma, Ved P.
  LB3013.M324 1993
  371.1′024′0973 – dc20   92–5637
                                                  CIP

Set by 9 in 9½ on 11¼ Times

Transferred to digital print on demand 2001

Printed and bound in Great Britain by Antony Rowe Ltd, Eastbourne

This book is dedicated, with affection and esteem,
by the Editor to Professor V. Alan McClelland,
Dean, School of Education, The University of Hull.

CONTENTS

CONTRIBUTORS

Philip Barker, Professor, Departments of Psychiatry and Paediatrics, University of Calgary, Canada.

Tim Brighouse, Professor of Education, University of Keele.

Loraine Corrie, Edith Cowan University, Western Australia.

Audrey Curtis, Department of Child Development and Primary Education, University of London Institute of Education.

Harry Daniels, Department of Special Educational Needs, University of London Institute of Education.

Jim Docking, formerly Head of Education at Whitelands College and Chairman of School of Education at the Roehampton Institute, London.

V. John Furlong, Professor, Department of Education, University College, Swansea.

Gerry German, Principal Officer, Commission for Racial Equality, London.

Clive R. Hollin, School of Psychology, University of Birmingham and Glenthorne Youth Treatment Centre, Birmingham.

Michael J.A. Howe, Professor, Department of Psychology, University of Exeter.

David Jones, Department of Psychology, Birkbeck College, University of London.

Mick McManus, Course Leader of the BEd degree at Leeds Polytechnic.

Robert Povey, Educational Psychologist and formerly Principal Lecturer, Christ Church College, Canterbury, Kent.

Robert Richardson, Headteacher, William Penn Secondary School, London 1968–83.

Derek Wright, Emeritus Professor of Education, Leicester University.

FOREWORD

Concern about pupil behaviour in school is a worldwide phenomenon. Children have relatively few years of compulsory schooling, and if they are to benefit fully from these, then they will need to spend as much time as possible on the tasks in hand, and do so in as attentive a way as is possible in the circumstances.

The management of pupil behaviour lies, therefore, at the very heart of the teacher's repertoire of professional skills. If the thousands of hours spent in school are badly managed, then children simply do not devote sufficient time to learning all that is required of them in the complex world of the late 20th century. If they always have to be told exactly what to do, they never learn the independence of judgment about their own and other people's behaviour that is an essential component of responsible citizenship.

Behaving sensibly, however, is also a considerable responsibility for young people themselves. On the one hand they do need to learn, and appreciate in many cases the importance of schooling. On the other hand the social pressures from their peers, the apparent pointlessness of some of what they are asked to learn, and the sheer inconsistency, from their point of view, of much of adult life, brings its share of inter-personal and personal problems. As one perplexed eight year old told a researcher during the Leverhulme Primary Project, 'We're not allowed to muck about, we're not allowed to fight, and we're not allowed to yell at the top of our voices, and a few other things which I can't remember. We've got quite a lot of rules – loads'.

This book performs a valuable service in bringing together under one cover some of the work on pupil behaviour management. It is a book which should be read by all those who seek to understand better what is involved by probing behind the superficiality of much of the discussion on the topic.

Professor Ted Wragg

EDITOR'S PREFACE

The management of children with emotional and behavioural difficulties has always been a source of worry and anguish for those who
have to deal with them. Their unpredictable behaviour can make us
feel quite helpless. The problem is as old as education itself and is
never far from teachers' minds. In the 1890s a government report
concerned itself with the rising crime rate amongst young people, and
a century later the Elton Committee pronounced on the matter of
school discipline.

The Elton Committee showed themselves to be realists: 'We
conclude that any quest for simple or complete remedies would be
futile' (para. 6, p. 12); 'Reducing bad behaviour is a realistic aim.
Eliminating it completely is not' (para. 2/29, p. 65). The report makes
138 recommendations addressed to over a dozen groups with an
interest in education – from pupils to the Broadcasting Standards
Council. Such a comprehensive sweep makes for difficulty in identifying a particular Elton theme: the report's own summary occupies
eight pages. It would not be too gross an exaggeration to say that the
report was born, acknowledged and then largely ignored: such is the
reward of being reasonable and judicious, a fate shared with so many
of the children who are the subject of this present book. The money
allocated to post-Elton in-service training through the Local Education Authorities' Training Grant Scheme was withdrawn in April
1992.

If Elton can be said to have a theme, it is that discipline in schools
is a broadly based responsibility. Teachers must be good classroom
managers; headteachers must take the lead in developing whole-
school policies; schools must foster shared values; pupils must be
given responsibility and have their differing achievements recognized;
parents must be socially responsible; and police, governors, broad-
casters, employers, Local Education Authorities and the government
must all contribute. Those involved in the pre-service and in-service
training and guidance of teachers were the subject of 13 recommendations in the Elton Committee's report. One result is that teacher
training courses now have clearly identifiable elements concerned
with the management of pupil behaviour; another is the continuing
need to ensure that research and good practice are widely
disseminated.

This present book is written by 14 leading and practising educationalists, psychologists, a sociologist and a child psychiatrist, whose views command respect, examination, scrutiny and study. Trainee teachers beginning their studies will find it invaluable and the more experienced teachers will also find it of use. My selection for this volume is based upon the following factors: to illustrate what can be done to alleviate behavioural problems in schools; to show a range and variety of work in the area, which is both practical and applied; and to include the work of key names in the field.

Ved. P. Varma
London

ACKNOWLEDGEMENTS

We are indebted to the following for permission to reproduce copyright material:

Croom Helm for an extract from *Preventing Classroom Disruption: Policy, Practice and Evaluation in Urban Schools* by D. Coulby and T. Harper (1985); Pergamon Press Plc for an extract from an article by M. Rutter, 'A children's behaviour questionnaire for completion by teachers: preliminary findings' from the *Journal of Child Psychology and Psychiatry* Vol. 8 (1967); Hodder and Stoughton Limited for Figure 14.1 on pages 228 and 229 from *You and Your Community* by M. McManus (Foundation for Life Series) (1991).

PART ONE

Reasons of and treatments for behaviour problems

CHAPTER 1

Psychodynamic thinking and discipline

DEREK WRIGHT

The question this chapter addresses is whether, and if so to what extent, the psychodynamic way of thinking has relevance to the problem of discipline in schools. To ask the question is at once to focus upon discipline as an interpersonal transaction rather than as an institutional problem. The adult person in the role of teacher has the responsibility to see that learning takes place in other persons in the role of student or pupil. The problem of discipline arises when student-persons, apparently deliberately, set about frustrating teacher-persons from achieving the task for which they are employed. They do this, of course, by being inattentive, covertly or overtly disruptive of other students, disobedient, rude, and threaten to push the situation out of the teacher's control. Beyond their responsibility for learning teachers are also held to have some responsibility for the moral development of students such that, if possible, they become law-abiding citizens. This means that within the school community teachers are expected to respond in a controlling fashion to violations of the institutional rules of the school and those forms of behaviour like theft, bullying and vandalism which take us more firmly into the moral domain.

There are, of course, teachers who believe that their task is only to teach, and that issues of discipline as defined should be taken out of their hands by the system. As they see it their response to disruptive and rule-breaking students should be the minimal one of passing them over to others, usually higher in the hierarchy, whose specific responsibility is to deal with them. However, they cannot usually leave the matter there. They expect, even demand, that the response of the system is in some way punitive. If it is not they are apt to feel undermined, let down, and perhaps a little demoralized. In short, they have a personal involvement in the impersonal response of the institution.

And surely this is true of all of us, as teachers, in some degree. We need to know we have behind us the authority and power of the institution. The question we have to deal with is how often we openly invoke this. In greater or lesser degree we need to be able to identify with the institution, and if, as it seems, the institution lets us down, we are left, as persons, with a reduced sense of our own potency. At the heart of it is the need we feel, on occasion, that as teachers we are somehow bigger and more powerful than we are as persons.

The more that teachers identify with the relatively impersonal authority and power of the institution, the more their interpersonal relationships with students will be characterized by what Piaget has called 'unilateral respect', that is control and constraint on the one hand, and fear and powerlessness on the other. There are certain sorts of adult personality structure which find security within a stable system of relationships of this kind. But there are many other teachers, perhaps all at some time or another, who are most personally fulfilled in their professional role only within relationships of 'mutual respect', as Piaget has called them, that is relationships characterized by reciprocity and cooperation. Such teachers are apt to find the disciplinary confrontation as a tiresome diversion from that more personal interaction with students as equals. They find no particular personal satisfaction in the assertion of authority and power. They look for a way through the problem of rebellious and difficult students that does not require them to move into the power assertion mode. Is this possible? Clearly it would seem so because some teachers manage it, more or less. If the psychodynamic way of thinking has value it would seem to lie in the invitation to us to look at the unilateral, power assertive relationship in order to understand a little more clearly what is going on in it, and thereby enable us to move more towards a relationship of mutual respect which yet does not mean relinquishing our responsibilities for discipline and the creation of a positive learning atmosphere.

The psychodynamic way of thinking originated, as is well known, with Freud and has since been elaborated in a number of different directions. Its natural home, we might say, is in psychotherapy. Some contemporary psychoanalysts define the therapeutic process as one of the 'narrative reconstruction' of the patients' histories, relationships, inner problems, and so on, and in particular of the relationships between patients and therapists. When patients are enabled to reconstrue their lives and situations, new meanings are realized, attitudes and feeling patterns are modified, and possibilities of a more fulfilling life emerge. The process of narrative reconstruction itself involves the bringing into awareness of a psycho-logic which was underlying the patients' way of living and which hitherto was unrecognized.

Teachers are not therapists, but their relationships with their students can have at times, if not most of the time, an element of the therapeutic for both themselves and their students. Indeed, it could be argued that for teachers to develop as persons within their professional role, and not be held static by them, this element must be present. Within the psychodynamic understanding of the therapeutic process, the therapeutic element in the teacher–student relationship would involve the teacher in the process of realizing the underlying psychologic of self and other and helping the other to share a little in the process. It could be argued that it is precisely in the disciplinary confrontation that the therapeutic element is most needed for both parties so that the subsequent modifications of attitude and feeling can so change the relationship that the disciplinary issue can be resolved in a more creative, mutually respectful way.

Before going further, and in order to earth the discussion, I want to recount an event that occurred in my second year of teaching in a Grammar School. There is nothing special about it except that for me it was a significant learning moment. Many teachers can recount their own stories of a similar kind. In a third year class, Peter was continually disruptive of the class and aggressively disobedient towards me. Although I knew he was like this with other teachers, it felt very much like a personal attack. Naturally I felt my authority as a teacher threatened and responded with punitive anger: I put him in detention. Fortunately, in that school we were expected to carry out the punishment ourselves. It was the third detention in so many weeks. Sitting there with Peter in an otherwise empty classroom, the minutes ticked by in silence. Impulsively, I went and sat on the floor with my back to the wall and invited him to join me. Rather warily, he did. I expressed my feeling that the whole business was pointless and daft, and asked him what he felt was wrong. For the next hour he poured it out, how much he felt frustrated by school, and how lonely and despairing he was, and how unfair the whole world was to him. It was the last time I ever put him in detention. He was never easy to deal with but we were connected now at a more personal level, and I took time every now and again to keep that personal connectedness alive. I never saw him again as disruptive and disobedient (though both words could still have been used) but as a deeply unhappy boy clogged up with his own disturbing, inward agenda which I now had some insight into.

The point of this simple and ordinary experience is that it led me to begin a narrative reconstruction of Peter, my relationship to him, and to just a little extent, of me. Looking back now I would want to take the process further. The original construction in my mind was that here was a student (not yet Peter in any significant sense) who was behaving badly, who was doing things he ought not to be doing, and that my own anger was righteous. I was responding to him less for what he was, as a person, than for what he stood for, a bad student – and of course students should be good, well behaved, and keen to learn.

In retrospect it is clear that the personal psycho-logic of my response involved a fear of my own impotence and what is called 'identification with the super-ego', itself a defence against that fear. People in authority over the young are, it seems, particularly vulnerable to the mechanism of identification with the super-ego. In brief, it is the process whereby the conscience which normally inhibits our own behaviour is turned outwards towards someone else so that for a while we are our consciences regarding the other, and that conscience is less effective in controlling us. Hence the powerful desire to punish and the moralizing that goes with it. It is while we are identified with our super-egos that we are wholly unable to see that 'there but for the grace of God go I', or, perhaps more relevantly in this context, 'there despite the grace of God went I'.

The more we are aware of this psycho-logic in us, the less we are likely to be taken over by it and the more likely we are to retain a degree of objectivity in the situation. But going with this, and helped by it, is a reconstruing of the recalcitrant student. To take a simple example. I can see a student, moralistically, as lazy, and thereby putting his failure to learn entirely across in him. Equally accurately I can see him as preoccupied with his own agenda, or, perhaps most usefully, as someone I have not yet succeeded in interesting in what I have to teach. These ways of construing him bring with them different attitudes and responses in me. More deeply, it has been said that the antisocial act is an expression of hope. With young people this is not too hard to see. For to protest, however inarticulately, is still to hope that things might be better, and the individual has not yet withdrawn into hopelessness. Working for some years with delinquent adolescents taught me that, as well as other inner conflicts, most of them suffered from a deep, primitive and inarticulate sense of having been treated unfairly all along the line, and their delinquent acts were at least partially an expression of this. To use the psychodynamic term they were 'acting out' a sense of injustice they did not understand.

Clearly, to narratively reconstruct the behaviour of disruptive students involves seeing something of the psycho-logic which underlies their disruptive behaviour. And this means listening to them and helping them towards clearer articulation and some beginnings of understanding of what is going on inside them. In psychodynamic terms it is forstalling acting out by enabling the student to communicate in words. How much better if, before setting fire to the head's study, students were able to communicate their frustrations and be listened to and responded to in a way which respects how frustrated they feel. For this to happen, the head, or other teacher, would need to move somewhat from a unilateral respect relationship to one closer to mutual respect.

I am aware that some teachers will see what I have been saying as 'going soft'. I would reply by saying it is rather becoming more human. Certainly it may require of the teacher the discovery of an inner personal strength which is not dependent upon identification with institutional power, though that will never disappear. And it does not necessarily mean the abandonment of sanctions. In general young people do not resent sanctions when they see them as fair and necessary. But for this to happen they need to feel that they have been fully heard, and that the response has taken into account what they have said.

CHAPTER 2

Sociological perspectives on disaffection from school

V.JOHN FURLONG

In this chapter I want to discuss disaffected or deviant behaviour at school – specifically that means focusing on the issues of classroom disruption and truancy. In Britain the most common way of understanding such behaviour is still in terms of a 'medical' model (Ford et al. 1982). Children who reject their schooling are seen as suffering from some form of pathology – they are *mal*adjusted to the world of school. The focus of the explanation as well as the strategies designed to effect a 'cure' are firmly directed at the individual.

This individualized approach remains dominant despite the fact that since the 1960s educational surveys have repeatedly shown that the incidence of disruption and truancy in British schools is patterned in significant ways. There are, for example, well-established correlations between disruption, truancy and age (Davie et al., 1972; Mitchell and Shepherd, 1980; Sammons and Mortimore, 1990); gender (Davies, 1984; DES, 1989); region (DES, 1973); school organization (Rutter et al., 1979; Mortimore et al., 1988); educational achievement (Tyerman, 1968; Fogelman, 1978; Croll and Moses, 1985); and class (Davie et al., 1972; Rutter et al., 1975; Farrington, 1980; Sammons and Mortimore, 1990). These correlations first began to be revealed from the 1960s onwards and they forced academics if not practitioners to reassess the explanations most frequently advanced. If deviant behaviour was patterned in these ways then explanations could not entirely be located within the individual pupil; indeed the concept of maladjustment as an individual pathology could be quite misleading. The hunt for sociological explanations was on.

In the search for sociological explanations, sociologists of education, like criminologists before them, turned to the work of Durkheim (1951, 1966). Durkheim's essential contribution to the establishment of criminology was to suggest that crime and deviant behaviour were not pathological but were essentially 'normal'. Crime, Durkheim suggested, may certainly be unacceptable but rather than understanding it as a pathology it should be looked at as behaviour designed to respond to particular social circumstances. Through this assertion he instantly shifted the focus for theorizing and research from the individual to the social context in which crime takes place. Instead of exploring the individual's psychology, Durkheim's theory suggests that the proper objective is to study the social circumstances that criminals face; it is because groups of people face similar social pressures that the incidence of crime is patterned. It is this line of argument that has been adopted by most of those working on the sociology of school deviance. During the last 25 years a wide variety of studies have been undertaken in which disruption and truancy are seen as 'rational' and 'normal' responses to the social circumstances young people have to come to terms with.

The sociological approach is still best illustrated in classic books such as Hargreaves' (1967) study of Lumley Secondary Modern School or Lacey's (1970) study of Hightown Grammar and Ball's (1981) work on Beachside Comprehensive. All three books adopt an unequivocally social interpretation of deviance, documenting the development of pupil subcultures amongst educationally unsuccessful groups of pupils. Other researchers have studied the impact of teachers' labelling on pupils' deviant 'careers' (Sharp and Green, 1975; Bird, 1980). More recently interest has focused on the relationship between disruption and truancy and a variety of social and cultural factors: race (Fuller, 1983; Furlong, 1984; Walker, 1988; Mac an Ghaill, 1988); working-class culture (Willis 1977; Brown, 1987); masculinity and femininity (McRobbie, 1978; Connel et al., 1982; Walker, 1988). Despite important theoretical differences, the underlying thrust of much of this body of work follows Durkheim's suggestion that we should explore the social circumstances that lead young people to act in unacceptable ways rather than seeing them as maladjusted or pathological. In this sense, sociologists working in this area are all Durkheim's children.

The sociology of school deviance is then, despite its current neglect, a rich and diverse field – at least in academic circles. Yet even at its height it made relatively little impact on policy. Presumably there are many reasons for this failure. Tomlinson (1982) and Ford et al. (1982), for example, suggest that the reason that the psychological perspective is so dominant in Britain is because it has become institutionalized through the Schools Psychological Service; promoting an individualistic approach is in their interest. Yet I would suggest that part of the problem also lies in the weakness of the sociological research itself. At first sight the arguments may seem convincing, but the underlying analysis in such studies is often simplistic. For example, researchers often focus on the influence of one aspect of the social world at a time (school organization, working-class culture) thereby denying the multiplicity of factors that may influence children in their rejection of schooling. Moreover, they frequently adopt a highly simplified view of social structure, analysing complex issues such as social class or teachers' expectations in a one dimensional, 'categorical' manner. Finally, in their enthusiasm to explore the social dimensions of deviance, sociologists seem to deny that there are important psychological questions to be addressed as well.

Emotion and the hidden injuries of schooling

The starting point for the reconstruction of a sociological perspective on deviance must be at a psychological and particularly at an emotional level. All sociological theories have within them – sometimes explicitly, but usually implicitly – a model of how individuals function at a psychological level (just as all psychological theories trade, often implicitly, on sociological assumptions). It may be by default rather than by design, but I would argue that the psychological model implicit in sociological research in this field is often the same and is frequently inadequate. In almost every case young people are seen as rational and knowing individuals. The implicit assumption seems to be that they logically and rationally appraise the situation that they are in and then devise an appropriate strategy whether that be deviance or conformity.

I want to suggest that this rationalist view of human action is far too limited for the task of understanding why pupils reject school. Rejecting schooling is nearly always a strongly emotional experience. Even the most hardened pupils will experience intense and often contradictory emotions when they are challenging school. Feelings of anger, fear, frustration, elation and guilt may all be present. In the classroom the peer group may be shown the more positive side when feelings of bravado and elation may be to the fore (Furlong, 1976) while in the privacy of the headteacher's office the same pupils may express guilt and remorse at their actions. The truth is that all of these different feelings are experienced by disruptive and truanting children in contradictory and often confusing ways.

Rather than ignore this emotional level I believe that sociologists should use it as a starting point. If emotionality is inherently bound up with school deviance then what we need to construct is a 'sociology of emotion'. We must ask why is it that some pupils express such strong emotional reactions to school. Specifically, that means disentangling two very different things. We must recognize that for some pupils their emotionality will be a product of their educational experience; schools make all sorts of demands on pupils and for some this can result in 'hidden injuries' (Sennett and Cobb, 1977) that are the basis of disaffection. However, we must also recognize that for other pupils, school may not be the primary cause of their emotional difficulties; it may merely be a 'site' where they give vent to an emotionality that has quite different roots (see, e.g. Mongon and Hart, 1989). Clearly though these two are interconnected. It is because school is so often a demanding experience that children who are already emotionally vulnerable choose to reject it. Even when the initial cause of emotional disturbance is clearly outside the school – for example, in the family – there remain important questions to be asked about why school does indeed become a focus for the expression of their hostility.

A fuller sociological analysis of school deviance must therefore begin by making a more complete analysis of what the emotional demands of schooling actually are, how they can result for some pupils in 'hidden injuries' and how pupils deal with the emotional consequences. As I will argue below, that means looking again at the impact of educational structures and particularly power in schools. It also means taking unconscious motivation and repression more seriously than sociologists have in the past.

Structure, power and disaffection

Central to all existing sociological studies of pupils' disaffection is a concern with social structure and power. The argument within such studies has been that deviance at school is to be understood as a way in which pupils come to terms with social and especially educational structures. Put in less sociological terms, disruption and truancy are ways in which young people respond to the demands of school and other social pressures. This for example is the argument in Hargreaves' classic study of Lumley School. The boys in the bottom stream, 4D, were coming to terms with the structure of the educational system that was divided between high status grammar schools and low status secondary moderns; they were also responding to the internal structure of the school – its streaming system. It was the impact of these social structures that resulted in the 'hidden injuries' of school for the boys of 4D.

If we are to understand school deviance in sociological terms we therefore need to locate our analysis within a debate about the impact of social structure; it is here that we will find the key to the social dimension of emotion at school. However, for the most part, the way in which social structures are understood in the sociological literature seems quite inadequate; too often they become crude and one-dimensional. Children do not reject school simply because they are working class or because they find themselves in a particular type of school; both of these factors, and many others besides (peer group pressure, the local job market, personal relationships within the home) may be significant at the same time. What is more, pupils do not reject abstract social structures, they reject real teachers going about the day-to-day business of schooling.

Part of the problem with existing studies therefore concerns the way in which social structures themselves are understood. But what then are social structures? Perhaps the best way of explaining them is to quote from Connell (1987) who describes the constraints of structures as 'the experience of being up against something; of limits on freedom' (p. 92). Structures are constraints on the way we act; they may even be constraints on the way we think. Such constraints can be material, or financial but in education the most frequent constraints that pupils run up against are political. When we think of political constraints it is to recognize that in some situations other people have the power to determine how we act, however we think.

What is distinctive about the use of power in education is that it is used to do more than merely secure conformity. When we as teachers use our power in school, when our actions become part of the political structure for the pupils that we teach, then what we are trying to do with our power is to change our pupils in very fundamental ways. Through our power, we attempt to get children to accept certain values, to aspire to certain futures for themselves and to accept and understand their own strengths and limitations. Educational structure – the power of education – is used not just to impose certain sorts of behaviour but to construct young people in particular ways. We do not use our power simply to force children to act in these ways. Rather we insist that they come to see themselves and organize their lives in these ways.

Education then is about changing people and this is why it is potentially such a strong emotional experience. Once they have gone through school young people are different, they have been constructed by the school and they are also expected to construct themselves, both objectively and subjectively, in ways made available through school. To say this is not to make a value judgement about whether this process is good or bad, merely to show that it is inherent in what education is. As such it will, on some occasions and for some pupils, be a highly positive experience and for others a negative one. However, what I want to suggest is that it is only by developing a deeper understanding of the way in which we are constructing young people, it is only by disentangling the ways in which, through schooling, we use our power to change young people and to insist that they change themselves, that we can start to understand the roots of disaffection. The demands that we make on young people are for some the cause of 'hidden injuries'; for others who are already emotionally vulnerable they can become the focus of conflict.

If we want to understand what it is about schools that encourages some children to reject their education then we must ask more carefully than we have in the past what the structures of education are. What is it that pupils 'fetch up against'; in what ways do we use our power to try to change young people and get them to change themselves? Disaffection is one way in which pupils come to terms with these demands.

Before trying to set out some of the structures of schooling that I think are important I want to make three preliminary points about the nature of educational structures. The first point is to emphasize that education is not a single structure, rather it is made up of a number of different structures. As such, many of these educational structures, many of the ways in which power is used in school, will be in tension or contradiction. Different structures will offer pupils different constraints and opportunities in how to construct themselves.

The second point is that the structures that young people meet within school are, like all structures, human products. As human products, they have a history; they themselves are the object of political debate and struggle within the teaching profession and, increasingly, elsewhere. As a result, the educational structures that impose on young people change over time and different structures will change at different rates which can add to the contradictions.

The final point to note about structures is that children are not necessarily fully aware of them when they are young, rather they are 'emergent' in children's consciousness. It is only as they grow up and particularly as they became teenagers that the 'contradictions hard edges, relations with other dimensions of present and future life become clear' (Connell, 1987).

With these preliminary points in mind, I now want to begin the process of setting out what I see as the most important structures in education, the most significant ways in which we use power to construct young people at school. I say 'begin the process' because I do not assume that the structures that I am going to discuss are the only ones that there are within education; I merely offer them as a starting point.

The production of ability

The first structure or complex of structures that I want to discuss concerns the production of ability. At first sight this may seem a rather odd idea. How, you might ask, is ability 'produced' through schooling and how can it be seen as a structure in the way that I have described it above? I want to argue that ability is essentially a social construct which is produced mainly through the process of schooling. When I say that ability is a social construct that is not to deny that children come into the school system with different intellectual capacities and talents – of course they do. However, by the time they leave school, young people have more than different capacities, they have different abilities. Through the process of schooling they 'receive' an ability (it is an active process) they are 'abilit*ied*'. Differences between pupils are *accentuated*, (even the most minor differences can land pupils in a different class or set) certainly differences between pupils are *legitimated* (by the time they leave school some have certificates and some do not) and those differences are *lived*. I suspect that for all of us the view that our teachers had of our ability has become part of our subjective view of ourselves.

The production of ability in these terms is a product of schooling. But how does the structure of schooling contribute to the production of ability as a public and personal fact?

At one very general level, differences in ability are enshrined in and indeed produced by the organization of schooling itself. This of course varies historically. If we go back between the wars when my father was at school, then by and large those in Britain who could not pay for it did not receive a secondary education. In the 1950s and 1960s when I went to secondary school there was a tripartite system with grammar schools, secondary moderns and a few technical schools. Today, the majority of young people in Great Britain spend their secondary education within a comprehensive school. What is significant about this rather obvious history is that depending on which historical period one went to school in, ones' ability, in both a public and personal sense, would have been constructed differently. The very organization of schooling therefore becomes a structure that influences the production of ability in the broadest of terms.

However, ability as a social construct is not only produced through the influence of organizational factors such as those described above. It is also produced by more fine-grained educational factors. Here, following Bernstein's (1971) lead, it is sensible to examine the *curriculum* (what counts as knowledge), *pedagogy* (how knowledge is communicated) and *evaluation* (how knowledge is assessed). These three factors also vary over time and establish a complex pattern of positive and negative opportunities for the construction of ability.

I can perhaps make the point clearer by giving some examples. First, curriculum. If one looks carefully at the physical education curriculum in schools over the last few years one can see something of a 'quiet revolution' has taken place. Today in many schools, competitive team sports have been marginalized and instead the curriculum is made up of a wide variety of individually based sporting activities – sailing, golf, horse riding. The hope is that by providing a very different curriculum a much wider range of pupils can experience success in physical education than before. The changing nature of the curriculum has set up a different pattern of possibilities for success and failure.

The nature of pedagogy is also highly significant in the construction of ability and that too changes. There is in many British primary schools an emphasis on non-didactic methods, on adapting the content to the interests and 'needs' of the individual child. As children are only too well aware, the pedagogical style adopted in many secondary schools is rather different – it is less person centred. In moving from the primary to the secondary school children move between different pedagogical regimes and these regimes have profound effects on the production of success or failure. Because of the reduced emphasis on the individual the differences between the two states – success and failure – is more sharply focused.

Finally, if we look at forms of evaluation – how knowledge is assessed – we can see that these too have a very significant influence on the production of ability. At present in Britain it is possible to point to two different trends which work in different directions in the production of ability. On the one hand, recent years have seen the development of profiling which encourages a broadly based view of achievement and in some schools even allows the participation of pupils in the selection of criteria against which they are to be judged. At the same time, through the National Curriculum, nationally defined targets of achievement seem likely to sharpen the demarcations of ability. Once nationally defined assessment targets are in place, teachers will have to use their power in the detailed construction of ten levels of pupils' ability in each of the major subject areas.

The curriculum, pedagogy and assessment structures – and they are structures because they are the way in which teachers use their power – have their own history and are subject to political struggle and change. Because of their complexity they also offer differing and sometimes contradictory opportunities for the social production of ability as a public and personal product. For some children they will offer affirmation while for others the experience will be largely negative. Because of the highly personal nature of the experience the complex way in which one's ability is 'produced' through school will always be highly emotionally charged and have a major impact on the degree of one's attachment to education.

The production of values

The production of ability is the prime responsibility of the school. As such, its influence reaches right back to the earliest days of a child's career as a pupil. However, the production of ability is not the only 'structure' of schooling that is significant in relation to deviance; it is not the only source of 'injuries'. Schools attempt to 'produce' pupils in other ways too. Here we must examine the values enshrined in formal schooling; values about knowledge, values about behaviour and values about aspirations for the future. Although these values may appear more diffuse than the concern with ability, they too become structures for pupils; they become constraints that young people 'fetch up against'. As such they are particularly important in relation to the differentiation of pupils in terms of class, race and gender. I think that the experience of each of these structures can be linked to disaffection through an emergent sense of difference and exclusion.

It is clear that schools have a position on values concerned with their central activities. For example, as teachers we value certain sorts of knowledge, largely still liberal academic knowledge. Schools also value certain sorts of behaviour. Indeed schools have a very clear moral code on what is appropriate behaviour, though there are often important differences in what is thought to be acceptable for boys and girls, older and younger pupils, and so on. Finally, it is also clear that teachers subscribe to common values about what are appropriate aspirations for boys and girls in relation to their future schooling and working lives. In relation to all of these areas – knowledge, behaviour and aspirations – schools have a value position. Once again, we must recognize that these values change over time. Nevertheless, despite such variation the values presented in school are clearly those of a particular group, the educated white middle class.

But as with other aspects of schooling, these values are not held neutrally by teachers, rather they themselves become structures. Through the day-to-day minutiae of school life there is an attempt to 'produce' young people in these ways. We as teachers try our hardest to encourage young people to value certain sorts of knowledge (indeed it is enshrined in the curriculum); to believe certain forms of behaviour are appropriate (codified in part in school rules); to aspire to certain futures (often exemplified in careers advice). As 'structures' these values are more diffuse and less tangible than those concerned with ability but nevertheless highly influential. Once again, though, young people will experience them as both an opportunity and as an exclusion. However, as an opportunity, they will be more readily grasped by some children than others.

Pupils who are different will only very slowly come to understand that they are excluded, separate. Probably the reason is that teachers try very hard to conceal the fact that certain pupils do not conform to these central values. Very often I would suggest pupils only develop a sense of 'difference' and 'exclusion' by noticing how other pupils are 'included'. For the most part, pupils are not 'made' at school; in almost every area apart from ability, the home is far more significant. Throughout their lives in school, pupils live in a family culture which has its own values. These values may well vary from those held by the school in terms of class and race, as well as in more idiosyncratic ways. Particularly powerful will be differences between families in how young people are constructed as male and female. The opportunities held out by the school in relation to its central values will therefore be differently received. For some pupils they will be a source of differentiation and rejection.

The production of occupational identity

The structures that I have discussed so far – ability, the development of certain value positions in relation to knowledge, behaviour and aspiration – are all central to the activity of the school. However it is also apparent that factors outside the school are highly significant too. Particularly important is the employment structure. Again, I want to emphasize that the reason it is so important is because it is part of the way young people are 'produced'. When young people negotiate with an employment structure they are not merely 'getting a job'; rather they are negotiating an occupational identity.

Clearly, employment structures vary historically. If we compare the 1960s with the 1990s or one region of the country with another we can see that for some school pupils there may be plenty of jobs while for others in a different historical period or in a different region, there may be very few jobs. Therefore the employment market imposes constraints on the development of an occupational identity at the simplest level of whether jobs are readily available or not. However the employment market is also influential in more detailed ways too. Specific training opportunities, entrance qualifications, the possibilities for upward or lateral mobility – all of these features of the employment structure are highly influential on the way in which young people negotiate an employment identity. What is significant about this process for the understanding of deviance at school is that pupils' ability to negotiate the structure that faces them is in part determined by their educational qualifications. Formal educational qualifications are one of a number of 'resources' that they bring to negotiate that structure. Formal schooling helps provide some pupils with invaluable resources in this negotiation process while for others it will be a source of exclusions. The significant point is this – formal schooling is not the only resource available for entering the employment market. Family contacts, even family capital, can also be highly significant. The perceived utility of schooling will vary both in relation to young people's perception of the employment opportunities available to them as well as their view of the relative significance for them of formal schooling in that negotiation process.

If we are to understand deviance in older pupils we need to spend a great deal more time documenting their emerging sense of employment opportunities and the role of education in that process as well as developing a greater understanding of the role that other factors play in the achievement of an occupational identity.

In all of these ways then – in the production of ability, in the production of an occupational identity and in the development of certain value positions in relation to knowledge, behaviour and aspiration – the school is involved in producing young people. Constructing their subjectivity as well as their public identity, their 'legitimate' differences, and in each case there are positive and negative opportunities. Through interacting with these structures, pupils can come to feel valued, have a sense of achievement and a sense of inclusion. Alternatively, they can feel excluded, devalued and feel a sense of loss. Schools, though, are highly complex places and these different structures may offer competing or even contradictory opportunities. Pupils may succeed on the sports field but fail in maths, and so feel excluded. Alternatively, they may fail in both sports and maths but because they have a similar underlying sense of values to their teachers they still feel included despite their failure.

Existing research does not plot in any detailed way how these structures impose on pupils in their daily lives.

It is because schooling is about changing young people and offering them the opportunities to change themselves that it is potentially such an emotional experience. In the final section of this chapter I want to return to this issue of emotionality in order to outline the model of human personality that is necessary for such an understanding of deviant behaviour.

Repression and contradiction

As I suggested above, most sociological accounts see pupils in a very one-dimensional fashion. They are seen as cool, rational and calculating in their behaviour, logically adapting it to the social situations that they face. I want to argue that if we want to understand the emotional dimension of schooling then we need a more complex view of human personality.

In this task I would suggest that there are two important principles that need to be addressed. First, we must view the human personality as operating at more than one level. We need to see human behaviour as motivated both by consciousness as well as by unconsciousness. Juliet Mitchell in her book *Psychoanalysis and Feminism* (1975) suggests that most social science is not anti-Freud, rather it is pre-Freud. It has not taken on board the idea that there is such a dimension of the human personality as the unconscious that is significant in the motivation of behaviour. I would suggest that some recognition of the unconscious is necessary in understanding deviance because with such a notion comes the idea of repression. The 'injuries of schooling', the emotional feelings that arise from the complex experiences of being excluded and devalued need not be dealt with immediately; those feelings can be repressed. I would suggest that for those pupils who are excluded and devalued, disruption and truancy involves giving vent to those long repressed feelings. It is no coincidence that pupils often turn to each other for support when they are breaking the moral code of the school. It has long been recognized by group psychologists (Bion, 1948–51) that groups can encourage people to get in touch with emotional feelings that would normally be held in check.

The second feature necessary for a reconceptualization of personality more appropriate for an understanding of deviance is a sense of contradiction and ambivalence in our behaviour. Most of us, when we pause for thought, recognize that we have highly complex emotional lives and this in part derives from the fact that our social world often makes contradictory emotional demands on us. Schools as I have suggested are highly complex and often contradictory places in the demands they make on young people. Teachers offer affection, approval and a sense of achievement – all at a price of course. However pupils have to learn to live with the fact that those same teachers at other times can be a source of exclusion, devaluation and loss.

Given the cross cutting demands and opportunities of schooling, pupils' feelings will inevitably be contradictory. Even the most conformist groups will sometimes give vent to hostility while hostile groups may often feel remorse and guilt.

Conclusion

My argument therefore is that schooling is a highly demanding experience which inevitably gives rise to many emotional injuries. Most children live with these 'injuries' – they repress the emotion and carry on with the business of schooling, perhaps finding another more acceptable outlet for their feelings. There will be two groups of pupils though for whom this will not be the case. Those pupils who are particularly injured by their school experience will on occasion give vent to their aggression and challenge those in authority. Because the expression of such emotions is forbidden it is more likely that such pupils will draw on their friends for support and oppose schools as a group. There will, however, be other pupils who are already emotionally vunerable. For these pupils, even the most mundane demands of school may be too much and may become the focus of conflict and rejection Phtiaka (1988).

However, it is also apparent that deviance does not always stay at this highly emotional level. The majority of pupils who suffer 'injuries' at school find a way of coping with them. They evolve a subculture; in other words they evolve a social solution to their psychological problem.

The form that these subcultures take can vary enormously depending on the cultural resources to hand. They may involve the development of physical masculinity or of an emphasized femininity (Willis, 1977; McRobbie, 1978; Walker, 1988); different racial groups may well have their own 'solutions' (Furlong, 1984; Mac an Ghaill, 1988). What these subcultures do is to give pupils a rationale, a philosophy, a way of explaining and dealing with their experience of schooling. By taking part in a subculture they may be able to find legitimate reasons for valuing different knowledge, for aspiring to different futures and for valuing different ways of behaving. The problem for the school is that once pupils have evolved such subcultures, once they have a rationale for rejecting school then they are much more difficult to bring back into line.

Of course, it is here, at the end of the line that sociologists have come in. It is these groups where the pupils can espouse a philosophy and answer the researcher's questions readily that are so frequently documented in the literature. However, if we really want to understand what gives rise to deviant behaviour then we must probe beneath the surface of what pupils tell us to the complex pattern of injuries that schooling can produce as well as the emotional difficulties that follow.

References

Apple, M. (1982) *Education and Power*, London: Routledge and Kegan Paul.

Ball, S. (1981) *Beachside Comprehensive*, London: Cambridge University Press.

Bernstein, B. (1971) 'On the classification and framing of educational knowledge' in M.F.D. Young (ed.) *Knowledge and Control*, London: Macmillan.

Bion, W.R. (1948–51) 'Experiences in Groups', *Human Relations*, Vols 1–7.

Bird, C. (1980) 'Deviant labelling in schools – the pupils' perspective', in P. Woods (ed.) *Pupil Strategies*, London: Croom Helm.

Brown, P. (1987) *Schooling Ordinary Kids*, London: Tavistock.

Connell, R.W. (1987) *Gender and Power*, London: George Allen and Unwin.

Connell, R.W., Ashendon, J., Kessler, S. and Dowsett, G. (1982) *Making the Difference*, London: George Allen and Unwin.

Croll, P. and Moses, D. (1985) *One in Five: the Assessment and Incidence of Special Educational Needs*, London: Routledge and Kegan Paul.

Davie, R., Butler, N. and Goldstein, H. (1972) *From Birth to Seven*, London: Longmans.

Davies, L. (1984) *Pupil Power; Deviance and Gender at School*, Lewes: Falmer.

Department of Education and Science (DES) (1973) *Survey of Violence, Indiscipline and Vandalism in Schools*, London: DES.

Department of Education and Science (DES) (1989) Discipline in Schools, Report of the Committee of Enquiry chaired by Lord Elton, London: HMSO.

Durkheim, E. (1951) *Suicide*, Glencoe, Ill.: Free Press.

Durkheim, E. (1966) *The Rules of Sociological Method*, Glencoe, Ill.: Free Press.

Farrington, D. (1980) 'Truancy, delinquency, the home and the school', in L. Hersov and I. Berg (eds) *Out of School*, London: Wiley.

Fogelman, K. (1978) 'School attendance, attainment and behaviour', *British Journal of Educational Psychology*, 48: 148–78.

Ford, J., Mongon, J. and Whelan, M. (1982) *Special Education and Social Control; Invisible Disasters*, London: Routledge and Kegan Paul.

Fuller, M. (1983) 'Qualified criticism, critical qualifications', in L. Barton and S. Walker (eds) *Race, Class and Education*, London: Croom Helm.

Furlong, V.J. (1976) 'Interaction sets in the classroom', in M. Stubbs and S. Delamont (eds) *Explorations in Classroom Interaction*, London: Wiley.

Furlong, V.J. (1984) 'Black resistance in the liberal comprehensive', in S. Delamont (ed.) *Readings in Classroom Interaction*, London: Methuen.

Furlong, V.J. (1985) *The Deviant Pupil; Sociological Perspectives*, Milton Keynes: Open University Press.

Grioux, H. (1982) *Theory and Resistance in Education: a Pedagogy for the Opposition*, Massachusetts: Bergin and Garvey.

Hargreaves, D. (1967) *Social Relations in a Secondary School*, London: Routledge and Kegan Paul.

Lacey, C. (1970) *Hightown Grammar*, Manchester: Manchester University Press.

Mac an Ghaill, M. (1988) *Young Gifted and Black*, Milton Keynes: Open University Press.

McRobbie, A. (1978) 'Working-class girls and the culture of the femininity', in Centre for Contemporary Cultural Studies (CCCS) Birmingham University, *Women Take Issue*, London: Hutchinson.

Mitchell, J. (1975) *Psycholanalysis and Feminism*, London, Harmondsworth: Penguin.

Mitchell, S. and Shepherd, M. (1980) 'Reluctance to go to School', in A. Litterson and I. Berg (eds) *Out of School*, London: Wiley.

Mongon, D. and Hart, S. (1989) *Improving Classroom Behaviour: New Directions for Teachers and Pupils*, London: Cassell.

Mortimore, P., Sammons, P., Stoll, I., Lewis, D. and Ecob, R. (1988) *School Matters: the Junior Years*, London: Open Books.

Phtiaka, H. (1988) *An Evaluation of the Division Between Mainstream and Special Education at Secondary Level with Special Reference to Deviant Behaviour; a Critical Analysis of Two Case Studies*, Unpublished Ph.D thesis, University of Cambridge.

Rutter, M., Cox, A., Tupling, C., Berger, M. and Yule, W. (1975) 'Attainment and adjustment in two geographical areas. I: The prevalence of psychiatric disorder', *British Journal of Psychiatry*, 126: 493–509.

Rutter, M., Maughan, B., Mortimore, P., Dunston, J. and Smith, A. (1979) *Fifteen Thousand Hours: Secondary Schools and their Effects on Children*, London: Open Books.

Sammons, P. and Mortimore, P. (1990) 'Pupil achievement and pupil alienation in the junior school', in J. Docking (ed.) *Education and Alienation in the Junior School*, Lewes: Falmer.

Sharp, R. and Green, A. (1975) *Education and Social Control*, London: Routledge and Kegan Paul.

Sennett, R. and Cobb, J. (1977) *The Hidden Injuries of Class*, Cambridge: Cambridge University Press.

Tomlinson, S. (1982) *A Sociology of Special Education*, London: Routledge and Kegan Paul.

Tyerman, M. (1968) *Truancy*, London: Ward Lock.

Walker, J.C. (1988) *Louts and Legends: Male Youth Culture in an Inner City School*, London: George Allen and Unwin.

Willis, P. (1977) *Learning to Labour*, Farnborough: Saxon House.

CHAPTER 3

Behavioural approaches to the management of difficult behaviour

DAVID JONES

The terms behaviour therapy and behaviour modification still give rise to feelings of suspicion and disbelief among many teachers and parents. An even more hostile reaction is often forthcoming from therapists, counsellors and other professionals versed in more psycho-dynamically based methods of intervention. There seems to be a general fear that in some way attempts to change behaviour will interfere with human dignity and freedom of action. It is suggested that such an approach is both too mechanistic and too materialistic. At best, the critics claim, behaviour modification may make life in the classroom a little more bearable for teachers but only by imposing change and conformity on difficult children without improving their academic achievements. Futhermore, the accusation is repeated over and over again that behaviour modification fails to address the underlying turmoil and distress in the child which is the cause of the difficult behaviour and that only treatment of the basic personality problems will result in lasting improvement.

These anxieties about the methodology of behaviour modification and the criticisms of the theoretical bases of the approach are largely unfounded and reveal a lack of understanding of the paradigm shift which has taken place in recent years with the merging of cognitive and behavioural methods of intervention. To a much greater extent than other therapeutic methods cognitive behaviour therapy sets the specific goals of trying to improve the quality of life for identified problem children and consequently also for those who interact with them, whether at school or in the home. The principles of learning theory still retain a central part in the design of behavioural techniques but much greater attention than in the past is paid to the cognitive, social and emotional characteristics of the disturbed child. In particular, it has been recognized that disobedient, impulsive and aggressive children often have low self-esteem relative to others in their peer group. This is not the cause of the behaviour difficulties but rather a symptom or consequence of adverse experiences. A well-designed behavioural intervention will attempt to modify both some of the overt behaviour difficulties which may be causing distress to others as well as providing direct training to help the child or adolescent develop better feelings about the self and better social skills. Such an intervention is not a 'cure' of an illness. It is not claimed to be powerful enough to overcome longstanding cognitive or personality difficulties of constitutional origin. Quality of life is improved to the extent that conflict with others may be reduced and to the extent that negative feelings and anxieties may be replaced by positive ones.

The starting point for all behavioural techniques is a careful and detailed assessment of the current problem. The term 'applied behavioural analysis' is often used to describe the evaluation procedure. Many attempts at behaviour change in the classroom have failed because this initial assessment stage has been neglected or treated superficially. Although behavioural analysis is rightly considered to involve scientific methodology the whole procedure depends upon the acquisition of an adequate data base to allow the generation of valid hypotheses on how best to bring about behaviour changes. It is this problem-solving phase in the design of intervention programmes which requires the greatest skill and experience. All too often teachers and parents have become disenchanted with behaviour modification techniques because they have experienced failure in the execution of inadequately designed interventions.

Assessing difficult behaviour

An essential first step in the behavioural analysis is to determine who is giving rise to the problem behaviours and who is affected by them. This is rarely as simplistic a process as it might appear to be at first sight. Even in cases where there seems to be a clearly identified problem child whose behaviour is said to be disrupting the work of the class there is often a need for an evaluation of group dynamics. A child having once been identified as a trouble maker can become the scapegoat for a wider range of difficulties. There is good evidence from social psychology that in group situations individuals may indulge in more extreme and risky activities than they would on their own. This can be particularly true in bids for leadership and dominance in the classroom and playground.

Determining who is affected by the difficult behaviour is not always straightforward. A teacher may feel threatened or challenged by confrontational behaviour from a child, but in most cases the teacher's main concern will be the reduced time available for instructing the class. It may become clear that some teachers are able to contain the difficult child whereas others feel unable or unwilling to do so. When the difficult behaviour involves aggression or dangerous activities other children or their parents may be complaining to the school and some form of disciplinary action may have become unavoidable.

The assessment phase will usually have two further distinct components. First, there is a need for history recording: the final disruptive event which may have precipitated the request for help or action may in itself be relatively trivial and in such cases it is important to catalogue the range of concerns about the child and the duration of the worries. The second phase is to establish properly documented baselines of the difficult behaviour.

A decision on whether or not to seek help when a child's behaviour is giving rise to relatively minor problems can be much more difficult than in cases where there are clear violations of acceptable norms. In the absence of a supportive consultation system which allows early discussion of behaviour problems the child passes up the school accumulating a reputation of difficulty and experiences of negative reactions from adults in positions of authority. Sadly, the majority of adolescents showing more extreme conduct disorders are found to have a long history of disruptive behaviour which was somehow tolerated and contained until someone reached breaking point. Intervention and the training of social skills behaviours are much more likely to be effective if initiated at an early stage in the child's school career.

Establishing baseline frequencies for behaviours is an essential part of the scientific methodology of behaviour modification (Gelfand and Hartmann, 1984; Sambrooks, 1990). Without measurement the process of change and possible improvement cannot be adequately documented. This approach contrasts markedly with psychotherapy and other interventions where intensive and expensive treatment is often continued until the child or parent stops asking for help. The choice of baseline measures will be dependent upon the type of problem. In many cases it is appropriate to record not only the frequency but the actual time of disruptive events. Just occasionally patterns emerge which invite further investigation. For example, several teachers in a large comprehensive school had noted in a particular second year class occasional experiences of uncooperative behaviour which were out of character. Subsequent record-keeping showed that the problem always occurred early in the afternoon sessions and never in the mornings. A little further investigation revealed that there were occasional lunch-time trips by this group to a local supermarket to purchase cans of lager. The quantities of alcohol involved were quite small but sufficient to cause the observable behaviour changes in these young adolescents. In this instance there was more detective work done than behaviour therapy but the solution depended upon accurate baseline recording. Many teachers will quote similar examples of moodiness and lethargy in children at particular times of day, usually after a break period, and the subsequent discovery of glue-sniffing or other forms of substance abuse.

The major problem with baseline record-keeping is that the recording process must be kept sufficiently simple to prevent it interfering with classroom activities. Nevertheless, well-designed record sheets make it possible to get measures of both problem behaviours and instances of cooperation and social conformity. The goals of most interventions will be to increase positive behaviours as well as to reduce negative behaviours. Baseline measures are more of a problem when the difficult behaviour occurs relatively infrequently. This can be the case with children who have occasional temper outbursts in the classroom and may be model pupils for most of the rest of the time. In these instances it is necessary to gather as much background information as possible relating to each incident noting which other children are involved.

The initial analysis of the problem will usually lead to the formulation of preliminary hypotheses on what, if anything, the child may be gaining from the difficult behaviour. Underlying this assumption that at some level there are payoffs and benefits to the child despite all the negative reactions from teachers and sometimes parents are the learning theory principles that behaviours which are repeated over time are maintained by reinforcement. Whilst the importance of reinforcement on learning can be readily demonstrated under controlled conditions in simple experiments involving either animals or children, it is much more difficult to identify the hierarchy of reinforcers which may be involved in maintaining the behaviour patterns of a difficult child. All therapeutic models have to wrestle with this problem of explaining the formation and continuation of symptoms. In learning theory terms the principles involved are the same as for other behaviours. Since all children experience different reactions to their behaviours from an early age they all to some degree develop different expectations of the outcome of actions and in many cases complex reinforcement and punishment networks may support the development of antisocial or difficult behaviour. A separate section will be devoted to the analysis of reinforcement hierarchies and the selection of reinforcers to bring about behaviour modification.

Assessing the difficult child

A further dimension to the behavioural analysis assessment is a consideration of factors intrinsic in the child who has been identified as behaviourally difficult. First, there is a need to consider the cognitive and linguistic development of the child. If the child is attending a mainstream school it will be necessary to evaluate his or her academic record and if there is evidence of under-achievement a full cognitive assessment may be indicated. A consideration of the child's profile of abilities rather than an overall estimate of general intelligence gives better insight into the pattern of the child's cognitive development. Children whose intellectual abilities are in the borderline learning difficulties range are particularly vulnerable to feelings of bewilderment and alienation if their needs and capabilities have not been adequately recognized at school. Repeated experiences of failure in the classroom situation will quickly destroy motivation to learn. This may be particularly true of children in the low ability group who also come from home backgrounds which place a minimal value on doing well at school. The school system should not be surprised to find that many children with behaviour difficulties of the acting out type are in this category of borderline abilities. There is a considerable burden of responsibility on teachers to avoid labelling children as stupid when they are functioning to the best of their ability. Behaviour modification programmes for children in this category will need to include giving the child appropriate experiences of success in learning situations by identifying and developing their strengths.

A similar problem arises with children of average or above average abilities who have undetected specific learning difficulties, particularly in the area of literacy skills. These children may have been frequently criticized for the poor quality of their written work or openly ridiculed for mistakes in their reading. Even when the problems of these children are fully recognized and allowed for at school the handicap can have severe effects on self-esteem and motivation generally with subsequent expressions of difficult behaviour in the classroom. Once again a sensitive and understanding approach to behavioural difficulties is necessary. Inattentiveness and occasional expressions of anger are a consequence of frustration rather than direct oppositional behaviour. Teaching these children involves the double challenge of facilitating their learning in other areas despite the literacy problems and at the same time helping them to sustain the motivation necessary to continue with formal and informal remedial work.

Children with learning difficulties are not the only group to experience feelings of inadequacy in the school situation. A not insignificant number of children of average or above average ability levels find themselves in very competitive high ability teaching groups. This situation arises sometimes as a consequence of parental pressures and partly because of the advantages of receiving intensive education during their early years at school. It is important to carry out comprehensive cognitive assessment when a child or adolescent in a high ability group is resorting to disruptive or difficult behaviour. If the child is functioning below the level of the group then a transfer to a broader educational band is indicated but every attempt should be made, preferably with supportive cognitive therapy, to help the child to identify the long-term advantages of the change.

On other occasions, cognitive assessment of difficult children may confirm that they are of exceptionally high intellectual abilities. The verbally fluent child who constantly interrupts with questions and insists on trying to correct the teacher can be as difficult a management problem as the obstinate or disinterested child. These verbally assertive children are rarely popular with their peer group and in some cases may be being bullied or teased outside the classroom. The intervention approach here is likely to need to focus on the development of age appropriate social skills. They can be exceptionally demanding children to work with even in individual cognitive therapy. Sometimes they can be helped by being shown video recordings of themselves interacting in a social situation so that they can gain insight into how their behaviour appears to others.

Cognitive assessment of behaviourally difficult children frequently indicates that they are impulsive and have short attention spans. This is an important observation because it draws attention to the possibility that at least some of these children may have intrinsic cognitive difficulties. Recognition that there are considerable individual differences in self-control and impulsivity removes some of the blame from the difficult child. Perhaps the most common criticism of all made by teachers of children is that they do not pay enough attention. Inattention in itself is not always immediately recognizable but when it is accompanied by hyperactivity or motor restlessness then it becomes one of the most frequent causes of pupil-teacher conflicts in the classroom. So much of what is regarded as difficult behaviour falls into this category that the topic merits further discussion in a separate section.

A comprehensive cognitive assessment will include measurement of the child's personality characteristics. Sullen but aggressive children can often be depressed or anxious and these characteristics can be quickly investigated using self-report questionnaires. These aspects of assessment are discussed in more detail in Jones (1990). It is also valuable to use standardized behaviour checklists to obtain ratings of the child from teachers and parents. The Conners' Teacher Rating Scale has been widely used to obtain information on the child's group participation, classroom behaviour and attitude towards authority as well as giving an estimate of hyperactivity (Goyette et al., 1978). Rutter's Children's Behaviour Questionnaire (Rutter, 1967) allows teachers to record their impressions of difficulties very quickly. At the other extreme Achenbach's Child Behaviour Checklist (Achenbach, 1979) can be used to collect extensive information from parents.

Hyperactivity and attention disorder

It is sometimes claimed that there is at least one hyperactive child in every class. This highlights some of the problems of definition. All too often labels are applied to children who happen to differ from the norm for their peer group. There has been considerable debate and controversy around whether hyperactivity should be considered to be a separate diagnostic category with the status almost of an illness or disability. In the past terms like minimal brain damage and hyperkinetic disorder were applied to children who were excessively fidgety, easily distractible and impulsive in their actions. The implication was that some degree of central nervous system involvement was responsible for the problems. There was always some uncertainty about how much significance should be attached to the motor activity since the problem seemed to be most noticeable in formal situations like sitting at a desk in the classroom or at the table at mealtimes but did not always extend to situations in which the children were actively engrossed. North American studies seem to attach greater clinical significance to the symptoms of hyperactivity than British studies and quote higher incidence figures sometimes of the order of 5 to 10 per cent for school-age populations (Barkley, 1981). Both parents and teachers seem to report a higher incidence of restlessness and distractibility in boys than girls.

The American Psychiatric Association (1980) in its Diagnostic and Statistical Manual of Mental Disorders (DSM-III) defined a condition referred to as 'attention deficit disorder' (ADD) which could occur with or without hyperactivity. The hyperactivity was defined in terms of excessive and inappropriate motor activity for the child's age but the emphasis was on the presence of the symptoms of difficulty in sustaining attention and impulsive behaviour. Inclusion in this ADD category also required the child to have shown the symptoms for more than 6 months with an onset before 7 years of age.

The intention was to exclude transitory behaviour disturbances and children who develop restlessness during the school years as a consequence of learning disorders. Barkley (1981) proposed an even stricter diagnostic category for hyperactivity than DSM-III with the suggestion that the problems as reported by the parents should have been present by 6 years of age. It is interesting to note that in DSM-III-Revised (APA, 1987) which was published by the American Psychiatric Association in 1987 hyperactivity has been returned to the name of the disorder, now referred to as 'attention-deficit hyperactivity disorder' (ADHD).

Teachers will not necessarily be impressed by the complexities of where distracting motor restlessness fits into psychiatric classification systems but there are important pointers which may influence the design of behavioural control programmes. When the problems are longstanding in the child it is likely that the cognitive difficulties of inattentiveness and impulsivity will need addressing. It can also be useful to consider whether the hyperactivity is a problem both at home and at school, pervasive hyperactivity, or whether the problem is limited to one of these environments, situational hyperactivity. Schachar, et al. (1981) in a survey of 10 to 11 year-old children on the Isle of Wight reported that parents identified 9.9 per cent of the children as hyperactive and teachers identified 8.3 per cent. However, agreement between the ratings was low and only 2.2 per cent of the children were rated as overactive by both parents and teachers. The study also showed that the pervasively hyperactive group were much more likely than the situationally hyperactive group and the other children to have persistent behavioural difficulties and cognitive impairments.

Behavioural and cognitive-behavioural methods of intervention with hyperactive children have recently been the subject of a great deal of research activity. Detailed accounts of the methodology have been reviewed by Barkley (1981), Kendall and Braswell (1985), Yule (1986) and Hughes (1988). The earlier attempts at behaviour change concentrated on trying to increase the amount of time hyperactive children spent 'on task' by the administration of rewards. Typically these rewards would be tokens or points for on-task behaviour which could be changed at some later time for a more tangible reward or prize or the opportunity to take part in some chosen pleasurable activity. The choice of target behaviours needs to fit in with current teaching requirements and the award of reinforcers should be a fair and relatively unintrusive procedure. It is important to note that administering these programmes did not involve teachers in spending increased time interacting with disruptive pupils as they were able to reduce the amount of time usually spent on negative methods of control. There was even evidence in some studies of vicarious learning to the extent that other children in the class were reported to spend increased time on appropriate task-oriented behaviours. With proper management a token system can be employed for the whole class rather than for individuals with the same sorts of on-task criteria and a points system of reinforcement combined with appropriate use of verbal praise. The social pressure of the group situation can have a powerful short-term influence to assist in bringing about an increase in positive behaviour. The initial goals must always be both modest and attainable.

A second type of behavioural intervention which has been employed to modify hyperactive behaviour in the classroom is training in self-control procedures. The first phase involves training the children in self-observation and monitoring. In cognitive terms it can be argued that improving the child's self-awareness may in itself result in some behaviour change. Next the children are trained in self-evaluation or standard-setting followed by training in how to administer self-instructions. The work tasks involved need to be fairly straightforward and training usually involves modelling of the required behaviours by an adult. Token reinforcers can be administered by the teacher although some studies have involved self-reinforcement by the child actually recording responses and keeping totals of points earned. There is good evidence that administering self-instructions by speaking aloud can have a powerful directing effect upon behaviour. The full sequence of training for verbal control begins with the adult modelling the task performance and giving self-instructions aloud. Next, the child practises the task with the support of instructions spoken by the adult. The child then performs giving self-instructions aloud and, finally, if possible the child is encouraged to perform giving silent self-instructions.

Self-control and self-monitoring procedures have also been used in an effort to control impulsive behaviour in simple problem-solving situations. The evidence here is less clear-cut since it seems that although children can use self-instruction to be less impulsive and performance levels improve for simple tasks, the improvement does not always generalize to greater accuracy on more complex tasks. It is possible that the performance of some hyperactive children is limited by intrinsic cognitive factors.

At a more mundane level, room management and environmental control procedures used to be recommended as an attempt to reduce the number of distracting stimuli for hyperactive children. Current opinion throws doubt on the usefulness of these procedures as most hyperactive children are now regarded as under-aroused rather than over-aroused. In these terms restlessness is considered as part of stimulus-seeking behaviour rather than representing over-responsiveness to stimulation. Removal from stimulation and social activity can be a very effective negative reinforcer for hyperactive children, particularly if they are being challenging or have frequent temper outbursts. (More will be said about the use of time-out procedures generally in the section on reinforcement.)

More ambitious intervention programmes like the work described by Kendall and Braswell (1982, 1985) indicate that combining intensive self-control training and modelling with cognitive therapy can be more effective than behavioural training alone. Such additional techniques as encouraging hyperactive children to role play and training them in the use of coping strategies when they experience failure are worthy of much wider use in the future.

Influencing children with conduct disorders

The distinction between hyperactive children and children with conduct disorders is not always an easy one to make. Many hyperactive children may have aggressive or destructive tendencies and be confrontational with teachers. The boundaries between what might be considered to be the acceptable extremes of normal childhood and adolescent behaviour and unacceptable deviant behaviour become blurred when one considers psychiatric classification systems. The American Psychiatric Association (1987) in DSM-III-R drew a distinction between conduct disorder and oppositional disorder. In this revised nomenclature a major feature of the conduct-disordererd child or adolescent is identified as 'a persistent pattern of conduct in which either the basic rights of others or major age-appropriate societal norms or rules are violated'. Within the category of conduct disorder there are three suggested sub-types: group, solitary and undifferentiated. There are strong similarities between this new solitary aggressive sub-type and the undersocialized aggressive category which had been identified in DSM-III (APA, 1980). The distinction between conduct disorder and oppositional disorder is not easy to follow. The child with oppositional disorder is described with such labels as defiant, disobedient, quarrelsome, having tantrums and generally disagreeable and unpleasant to others. A detailed comparison of the categorization of conduct disorders in DSM-III-R and the International Classification of Diseases (ICD-10) together with an account of earlier classification systems is provided by Robins (1991).

Educational psychologists and teachers rarely use the terminology of the psychiatric classification systems but they will not fail to be distressed by the gloomy predictions in the psychiatric literature of poor prognosis for functioning in adult life for children with conduct disorders and similar conditions. Many of these children would have been labelled as maladjusted in the past if it had been felt that their behaviour could not be contained in mainstream classrooms. Current terminology in education uses the category emotional and behavioural difficulties to include children with conduct disturbances as well as emotionally withdrawn and anxious children. Also there are considerable pressures for conduct disordered children to remain integrated in mainstream schools if possible to reduce the damaging effects on self-esteem of segregation and labelling.

The evidence from longitudinal studies as, for example, those reported by Olweus (1979) is that aggressive behaviour tends to be persistent over time. There is also evidence that aggressive children are not popular with their peer groups and there is often a correlation between aggression and poor academic attainments. It would be an over-simplification to offer a single learning theory explanation for aggressive behaviour in children. Nevertheless there is evidence that aggressive children tend to come from families in which the parents frequently use such aversive methods of control as hitting and threatening the children, and these parents also tend to be inconsistent in their expression of control. Thus at least in part learning of inappropriate physical and verbally aggressive behaviour may have been influenced by having less than ideal role models. Since the aggressive behaviour is shown by conduct disordered children from an early age they will also tend to have experienced rejection from other children from as early as their playgroup or nursery school and will have been prevented from becoming fully integrated with a peer group and learning the normal range of social behaviours. In some cases aggressive behaviour will have been reinforced by the power and control achieved over other children. In other cases the aggression may reflect impulsivity and a tendency to over-react and perceive others as more threatening than they actually are. This difficulty in understanding the intentions of others is possibly a defect in social awareness and may be a consequence of underlying cognitive difficulties. Behavioural interventions for conduct disordered children need to take account of the complexity of their individual past histories but generally fall into two main categories: first, reducing the frequency of maladaptive behaviours, particularly aggression and challenging behaviour, and second, providing training for the acquisition of deficient behaviours, particularly in the area of social interaction. Both Herbert (1978) and Hughes (1988) give detailed summaries of interventions involving children with conduct disorders.

One behavioural approach to controlling aggressive children is to give them self-instructional training (SIT) in an attempt to reduce their impulsivity. As with hyperactive children they may be trained in giving themselves instructions to avoid immediate action and to cope with minor upsets and insults. Unfortunately, this sort of training is not always successful in inducing behavioural control of these children. More elaborate techniques have been employed to try to train children in anger management. Direct training in self-control is combined with cognitive therapy to improve self-esteem and facilitate the development of social problem-solving skills.

Case example
Robert was a 12-year-old boy in the second year of a large comprehensive school. He was small in build but was quite strong and fearless. Mostly he was sullen to teachers but not hostile and he was given the nickname of 'brains' by his classmates because of his glasses and studious appearance. Approximately once a month he would over-react to some trivial incident in the classroom such as being jostled or teased by another boy. Robert would explode in fury, throwing chairs, over-turning tables and swearing loudly. On one occasion it took three teachers to hold him down until his fury subsided. He was initially quite depressed when seen on his own and revealed that he had felt unwanted at home since his mother had re-married and he had moved with her into his step-father's flat. He shared a bedroom with two elder step-brothers who often ganged up against him and both parents occasionally hit him. Despite all the adversities he cooperated well on anger control training and his self-esteem improved considerably with cognitive therapy. He was able to complete his schooling without further incidents although the home situation continued to deteriorate and on leaving school at 16 he moved away to live with a distant relative in another part of London and had to terminate therapy. Unfortunately, my next contact with him was not until two years later when I was asked on his behalf to provide a Report to the Magistrates' Court as he had seriously injured someone in a fight.

This example draws attention to the need for cognitive therapy to continue after difficult children leave school although for practical reasons it had not been possible in this case.

Children with conduct disorders and other behavioural difficulties are sometimes helped by participating in social skills training (SST) working in small groups. Groups usually function more efficiently when two trainers are involved and there are initial sessions allowing ample time for instruction and discussion. Components of the training are usually modelling of the deficient or required behaviours, practice sessions, role play, feedback and generalization techniques to extend the behaviour to other situations. Practice is important in both the giving and receiving of social reinforcement. If these techniques are successful it is sometimes possible to move the group or specific individuals on to contingency contracting which allows the child to negotiate for privileges or choice of activities in return for periods of cooperative behaviour or demonstrations of self-control. This level of intervention needs to be handled with caution as misunderstandings can so easily precipitate confrontational responses.

Reflections on reinforcement and punishment

It has not been the intention of this chapter to attempt a systematic review of all the different aspects of learning theory which might be applied in behavioural intervention programmes. This task has been more than adequately carried out on a number of occasions (Yule, 1986; Herbert, 1978; Hoghughi, 1988). One thing which quickly becomes clear when analysing difficult behaviour is that there will almost invariably seem to be more than one way to try to change the situation. The law of parsimony might suggest that in such situations we should choose the simplest explanation but that falsely presupposes our ability to discern which relations between stimulus events in the environment and the child's responses are simple and which are complex. We have seen that in many cases difficult and challenging behaviours are longstanding features of the child's behavioural repertoire by the time intervention is sought. Socially maladaptive behaviours have emerged from the child's innate responsiveness to stimulation by some combination of the processes of classical and operant conditioning, exposure to variable positive and negative reinforcement, sometimes exposure to inadequate models and sometimes to periods of deprivation and stress. It would be misleading to give the impression that such behaviours are easy to modify.

For a variety of ethical reasons as well as sound psychological reasoning society has come to recognize that harsh coercive methods are both ineffective and not acceptable methods for controlling children. The threat of physical punishment was rarely a serious deterrent for the frequent offender and yet it caused terror and anxiety in untold numbers of children who rarely committed a serious transgression. As in so many areas of psychology there is a problem over how to interpret individual differences. Perhaps there are 'augmenters' and 'reducers' for pain perception. Perhaps the suggested pattern of underarousal in some hyperactive children is an explanation. Perhaps frequent early exposure to physical punishment in the home has resulted in a degree of habituation to the pain response in some children. Whatever the explanation, we are left with the observation that physical punishment and fear of punishment affect some children more than others and that this level of aversive stimulation was not a particularly effective deterrent. There is also the possibility that uncertainty about being caught and punished is arousing and that achieving increased levels of arousal is a reinforcement for some children.

What of other methods of punishment? Being shouted at and verbally abused may have become aversive through having been associated with physical punishment and painful stimulation in the past. They may even be innately frightening since there is evidence that loud noises cause distress from a young age. For most children the main effect will be in the signalling of social disapproval. Again we have the problem of understanding individual differences in responsiveness to disapproval. Certainly in some children past experiences will have resulted in habituation of responsiveness to being shouted at. Other relevant factors which are much more difficult to quantify are the amount of respect the child may have for such an authority figure as the teacher and the child's perception of the teacher's power. Sadly again the impression is that verbal criticism is not a significant deterrent for difficult children and they may even find the attention gained in the interaction to be a positive reinforcement. Other children in the class may be distressed by the haranguing. There is anecdotal evidence that many children develop an aversion to language classes because they perceive the verbal corrections of their performance by the teacher as verbal criticism. On balance then verbal criticism by teachers would seem to be an effective control for the majority of children, but not for difficult children.

A great deal has been written about time-out procedures as a behavioural control for attention seeking or disruptive behaviour. This type of intervention has had some success with acting-out children at home and in schools. If it is to be used effectively at school there must be a convenient safe place where the child can be placed and the teacher must have sufficient authority to ensure that the removal can be achieved with the minimum of effort and disruption. Properly used the time-out procedure should always be quite short and not a means of keeping the child out of the classroom. It is essential that the procedure is only used if there is a suitable room or cubicle area for the child to be placed in. Removal to a corridor or common user space where the child has the reinforcement of attracting attention and comments from others is unsatisfactory. Leaving the child alone for too long invites further misbehaviour. It is debatable whether a properly managed time-out procedure sometimes actually applies positive reinforcement by removing the child from a distressful conflict situation without the use of punishment. This latter explanation might account for some quite difficult children being ready to accept the intervention.

A further approach to discipline in the classroom has been the removal of privileges following misbehaviour. There is little in the way of experimental evidence to allow evaluation of the procedure. The practice of depriving the whole class of privileges because the culprit of some misdemeanor will not own up comes dangerously close to providing children with a modelling experience by the teacher of the misuse of power and should be avoided. Carefully designed token economy schemes with tokens earned for on-task behaviour and removed for lapses in cooperation have been shown to be effective providing that the child has a reasonable chance of finishing with some tangible gains. If not it is likely to provoke further disruption. Yet another form of discipline which offends in terms of learning theory principles is giving the child extra academic work as a punishment. Under these conditions schoolwork can very quickly acquire negative associations by classical conditioning.

On balance then it would seem that punishment in whatever form does not have a major part to play in the effective modification of difficult behaviour. The short-term gain of immediate containment of problem activities has to be balanced against the longer term negative effects on the child's motivation to learn. The behavioural analysis should attempt to identify positive reinforcements which may be maintaining difficult behaviour. The teacher who has to issue 'desist' instructions frequently is not in control and is often reinforcing the interruptions. Equally important other children must be prevented from reinforcing the problem children and joining in the distractions. Good room management allows troublemakers and leaders to be isolated and frequent variation in the teaching position reduces the number of 'blind-spots' in the classroom.

The prime objective in behavioural intervention as in good teaching practice is to achieve control by prevention of difficult behaviour. As far as possible reinforcement should be used to increase the frequency of cooperative and on-task behaviour and to promote the development of pro-social behaviour. Good behaviour should be rewarded with praise, quickly and spontaneously. Beyond this it is necessary to be both analytical and practical about the selection of reinforcers.

Early studies using behaviour modification often used rewards such as small quantities of appetizing food or sweets and some of the findings were encouraging. However, inducers of this sort are of doubtful value as methods for achieving long-term control of difficult children. The novelty effect of such methods can be used but the reinforcers used can quickly become distractors in themselves and also there is increasing concern over the violation of dental hygiene if sweet substances are administered frequently. Many studies have reported that tokens as reinforcers which can be exchanged for rewards or the right to choose activities can improve cooperation with groups of younger children or in starting behaviour change with older difficult children. A properly run token economy system can be very difficult to maintain and its success depends in part upon the appropriateness of the rewards selected for the target children. Teachers and therapists who come to know the children well enough to get this selection right are also likely to be giving the children social reinforcement and good modelling experiences.

One of the most important sources of reinforcement in any school learning situation and also in social interactions is self-awareness of success. This intrinsic reinforcement for the child comes from making a discovery or experiencing success, however trivial it may seem to others. In social interactions the reinforcement comes from the child being able to feel listened to or respected as an individual. Cognitive therapy should be aimed at facilitating the development of self-esteem and should also be used to provide information to guide the structuring of teaching situations which begin to give the child experiences of success. Once success has been perceived in a number of areas it is possible for learning to move to a higher level and in addition to individual acts of pro-social behaviour the response of cooperating in new situations becomes more likely. A final word of caution, replacing difficult behaviour by selective reinforcement of positive behaviour and withdrawal of attention from negative behaviour does not produce instant solutions to long-term problems. The process of change is gradual.

References

Achenbach, T.M. (1979) 'The child behavior profile: an empirically based system for assessing children's behavioral problems and competencies', *International Journal of Mental Health*, 1: 24–42.

American Psychiatric Association (1980) *Diagnostic and Statistical Manual of Mental Disorders (DSM-III)*, Washington: American Psychiatric Association.

American Psychiatric Association (1987) *Diagnostic and Statistical Manual of Mental Disorders (DSM-III-R)*, 3rd edn, revised, Washington: American Psychiatric Association.

Barkley, R.A. (1981) *Hyperactive Children: a Handbook for Diagnosis and Treatment*, New York: Guilford.

Gelfand, D.M. and Hartmann, D.P. (1984) *Child Behavior Analysis and Therapy*, 2nd edn, New York: Pergamon.

Goyette, C.H., Conners, C.K. and Ulrich, R.F. (1978) 'Normative data on revised Conners parent and teachers rating scales', *Journal of Abnormal Child Psychology*, 6: 221–36.

Herbert, M. (1978) *Conduct Disorders of Childhood and Adolescence: a Behavioural Approach to Assessment and Treatment*, Chichester: Wiley.

Hoghughi, M. (1988) *Treating Problem Children: Issues, Methods, and Practice*, London: Sage.

Hughes, J.N. (1988) *Cognitive Behavior Therapy with Children in Schools*, New York: Pergamon.

Jones, D. (1990) 'Psychological assessment and the management of children with emotional and behavioural difficulties', in Varma, V.P. (ed.) *The*

Management of Children with Emotional and Behavioural Difficulties, London: Routledge, pp. 79–95.

Kendall, P.C. and Braswell, L. (1982) 'Cognitive-behavioral self-control therapy for children: a components analysis', *Journal of Consulting and Clinical Psychology*, 50: 672–89.

Kendall, P.C. and Braswell, L. (1985) *Cognitive-behavioral Therapy for Impulsive Children*, New York: Guilford.

Olweus, D. (1979) 'Stability of aggressive patterns in males', *Psychological Bulletin*, 86: 852–75.

Robins, L.N. (1991) 'Conduct disorder', *Journal of Child Psychology and Psychiatry*, 32: 193-212.

Rutter, M. (1967) 'A children's behaviour questionnaire', *Journal of Child Psychiatry and Psychology*, 8: 1–11.

Sambrooks, J.E. (1990) 'Behavioural approaches to the management of children with emotional and behavioural difficulties', in V.P. Varma (ed.) *The Management of Children with Emotional and Behavioural Difficulties*, London: Routledge, pp. 41–57.

Schachar, M., Rutter, M. and Smith, A. (1981) 'The characteristics of situationally and pervasively hyperactive children', *Journal of Child Psychology and Psychiatry*, 22: 375–92.

Yule, W. (1986) 'Behavioural treatments', in E.A. Taylor (ed.), *The Overactive Child*, Oxford: Spastics International Medical Publications, 219–35.

CHAPTER 4

Discipline: an anti-racist perspective

GERRY GERMAN

Schools may not be able to change the world but they can go a long way towards changing themselves. And even where there are obvious limits on the extent to which changes can be introduced, teachers and pupils as well as the parents can be brought to an understanding of the system's shortcomings as well as its potential for progress. Inequalities nationally as well as within institutions can be demonstrated with the intention that sound, up-to-date knowledge may enable young people as well as adults to challenge the perpetuation of injustice as far as educational opportunities are concerned.

Some of those injustices are the result of racism. On the one hand, there is evidence of widespread racial harassment at all ages and stages of education. Perpetrators include teachers and parents as well as young people in schools and colleges. Racial abuse and name-calling, graffiti and bullying and violence are a feature not only of the inner cities where there are large concentrations of ethnic minorities but also of the more remote rural areas where there are only small numbers of people visible by the colour of their skin. Even in schools in what might be called all-white areas there is evidence of strong racial prejudice being vigorously brought to the surface in times of religious controversy or military conflict.

On the other hand, there are more subtle manifestations of racial discrimination which have been brought into the open through determined investigation and painstaking research.

The Inner London Education Authority looked at the discrepancy between Verbal Reasoning Test (VRT) performance and the allocation of primary school pupils to bands for the purpose of transferring a balanced intake to secondary schools. It was found that Afro-Caribbean pupils in particular were allocated to bands lower than their VRT score merited (Mortimore, 1988). The ILEA findings were borne out by the work of Cecile Wright in schools in the East Midlands where she suggested that a combination of negative prejudice, destructive stereotyping and low expectations affected assessment upon transfer from primary school to secondary school as well as in selection for examination entry and at other times when crucial decisions would be taken which affected a child's future treatment and life-chances (Wright, 1985).

An examination by the Berkshire Local Education Authority of its grammar school selection procedures revealed a discrepancy between the pool of ability (measured by the gaining of five good O Levels or their equivalents in all schools) and the numbers selected for grammar school education. The findings suggested that Asian pupils in particular might be experiencing discrimination at both 11 and 13 when transfers were carried out (BCRI, 1989). Further research has been promised but its findings are not yet known.

There seems to be evidence here to suggest that, despite their best academic efforts, young black pupils are experiencing unfair treatment. Would it be wrong to suggest that the issue is really inequality resulting from the misconduct of the institution rather than a question of discipline and order involving pupils in the first place? In the case both of the Berkshire and the ILEA pupils' merit or promise of performance went unrewarded. There seem to be grounds for belief that the Berkshire selection tests were unfair *in the first case*. As far as the ILEA pupils were concerned it seems that the School Heads' stereotypes of Afro-Caribbean pupils in particular were stronger than the evidence of the system they themselves had developed to determine allocation to bands.

Is discipline the question to start with? Or are there a range of issues that need to be considered first or possibly simultaneously? Or is discipline in ordinary and professional discourse too fixed a concept anyway to be capable of releasing individual and community potential?

Let us take the ultimate disciplinary sanction as far as the educational institution is concerned – permanent exclusion. It is subject to a strict disciplinary procedure laid down in the Education (No. 2) Act 1986. Head, governors and local education authority have clearly defined rights and responsibilities, and even the Department of Education and Science may be involved.

The black communities are concerned at the rate of black exclusion, not only from secondary and further education institutions but from primary and infant schools as well. In 1985 the Commission for Racial Equality published a report of its formal investigation into the suspensions policy of the Birmingham Local Education Authority. It found that black pupils were four times more likely to be suspended than white pupils, at a younger age, for fewer offences and for less serious offences as well as less likely to be readmitted to school (CRE, 1985).

The statistics formed a significant pattern suggesting the possibility of racial descrimination. And while it is now possible to argue that administrative procedures have been strictly followed, there are still some disturbing reports of the mistreatment of black pupils in various parts of the country. A black parents group with children at a voluntary maintained denominational school in an Inner London borough have complained about the exclusion of their children based on their stereotyping, the humiliating treatment of their parents and the possible victimization of families. A boy in his final year at a comprehensive school in a southern English county has been deprived of full-time education for over a term and a half while the Head, allegedly with the full knowledge of the Divisional Education Officer, has ignored the provision of the 1986 Act.

The latter case involved a black pupil who adopted the Rastafarian faith and grew his hair in locks accordingly. The school had strict rules about hair style and length, and a pupil could be sent home for hair that was either too long or too short! In this case it appeared that the school was ignoring both education and race relations legislation. It is by no means an isolated case, and in addition to rules about hair, rules about dress have also been invoked to exclude Muslim girls desiring to wear a costume in keeping with the rules of modesty of their religion, even when tastefully done in school colours so as not otherwise to clash.

What is disappointing is the fact that schools invoke a system of rules and discipline which ignore the inalienable rights of individuals before the law. In 1983 the House of Lords finally decided on the Mandla v. Dowell-Lee Case and established the factors to be considered in deciding whether a particular group was a racial group within the meaning of the Race Relations Act 1976 and what constituted indirect racial discrimination. The Mandla boy had been excluded from a private school because of his conscientious refusal to remove his Sikh turban and wear the school cap stipulated by the school rules. The father's contention that his son had been discriminated against on racial grounds was confirmed by the House of Lords judgement. While physically he could comply with a school rule requiring pupils to wear a school cap, on religious grounds he could not so comply.

One of the problems with systems of discipline is the conviction held by many teachers (largely supported by parents) is that no exceptions can be made to the rules: 'If you make allowances for one, then you will have a flood of requests for exemption from the rules.' This point of view is at odds with the law of the land in the first place where an admission of guilt in a court of law may be accompanied by reference to mitigating circumstances. Second, it is not borne out by the experiences of reasonable people about the sense of equity shown by most young people who recognize, understand and respect different needs and life-styles if they are given the chance.

We need to ensure that young people are given the space to draw our attention to what they consider to be unfair in our comments, judgements or decisions. Dealing with a class or group in school or college inclines the teacher or lecturer to inject an element of sameness into her/his concept of equality whereas the principles of justice and equity demand that s/he makes a full enquiry into all the relevant circumstances before prescribing the solution. Where individual attitudes and institutional procedures are influenced (as perforce they must be, albeit at various points on a continuum) by racism, it is inevitable that stereotyped responses will perpetuate injustice and division.

'Discipline in Schools', the Report of the Committee of Enquiry chaired by Lord Elton, (DES, 1989) makes a number of recommendations aimed at promoting respect for different cultures and creating congenial circumstances in which all children will be encouraged to learn and be themselves. 'Headteachers and staff should work to create a school climate which values all cultures, in particular those represented in it, through its academic and affective curricula.'

It draws the attention of teachers to 'the potential for injustice and the practical dangers of stereotyping certain kinds of pupils as troublemakers'.

In addition to her work for the Eggleston Report (Wright, 1985), Cecile Wright carried out an ethno-graphic study in a small number of infant and primary schools in a local education authority in the North of England, (Wright, 1989) where similar influences were identified in the classroom interaction between teachers and children: the less favourable treatment accorded to black children, Asian and Afro-Caribbean, was recognized by the pupils and must have affected their performance academically and behaviourally. The teachers' inconsistent responses to black and white pupils led to the alienation of the former, some withdrawing to the silence of the sidelines and others uttering more vigorous protests and thus contributing to the downward spiral of under-performance and unacceptable standards of behaviour.

The Elton Report also recommends 'that teachers should guard against misinterpreting non-verbal signals and speech patterns of pupils from different cultural backgrounds'. While Elton calls for sensitivity on the part of the teacher in responding to such differences, we would go further and suggest that the learning institution needs to embark on dismantling the racist framework that inspires impatience, condescension or hostility in the first place.

The Report also recommends 'that teachers should avoid modelling any kind of insulting or discriminating behaviour' such as deliberately mispronouncing pupils' names for the amusement of other members of the class and thereby reinforcing the attitudes of those pupils most likely to be involved in racial harassment.

That is the kind of professional indiscipline that leads to Elton's next recommendation 'that LEAs and governing bodies which employ school staff should regard the racial harassment of pupils or colleagues by teachers or other staff as a disciplinary offence'. Until those in authority over young people in schools and colleges accept such a far-reaching and radical recommendation, however, disciplinary systems will remain woefully inadequate and militate against the interests of black and white as well as teachers and taught alike. The anti-racist position demands that such offences will be viewed seriously and lead to serious disciplinary consequences.

Such sanctions would need to be known to the pupils as well as to the parents and the teachers, of course. And while they would be discussed, negotiated, understood and agreed, it would need to be stated from the outset that the process nevertheless began from a position that was not negotiable – namely, the complete unacceptability of racial harassment and racial discrimination both on legal as well as moral grounds. However, the record of local education authorities and institutions is by no means impressive in this respect. For a variety of reasons, not least concern about public image and the possible response of governors and council members to a delicate matter, the majority have failed to confront the issue.

Countless claims might be made to justify such inertia: it might stir up unnecessary controversy; it could aggravate a situation that was not really all that serious at present; the time was not yet right to debate such an issue; and so on. In such circumstances, the message being transmitted by the authorities is that it is all right to neglect the welfare of young black people along with that of black parents and black teachers so long as one avoids public political controversy.

What kind of ethos is this to encourage the highest standards of self-discipline, mutual respect and cooperation among young people? Ethos is a term that is often vaguely invoked to explain what institutions are trying to do to develop those qualities of life that are not enumerated in their curriculum statements. It is also referred to as the hidden curriculum, and while the curriculum is quite clear and explicit for the most part, the former is rarely spelt out in sufficient detail to foster the education and development of the feelings and emotions as well as the spirit – qualities that are indispensible if one is to live a balanced life as a whole person.

An interesting piece of research was carried out for the Macdonald Inquiry into the Burnage High School. (Kelly, 1989) Elinor Kelly surveyed three high schools in Manchester, two coeducational and one boys' school. She identified a large number of pupils who subscribed to what we might describe roughly as National Front ideas. Perhaps surprisingly, she identified an equally large number of pupils who supported principles of racial justice. But while the former had a vocabulary, a terminology and a framework for action, those pupils with some commitment to notions of fair treatment for all people in Britain's multi-ethnic society, were at a disadvantage with respect to translating their rather vague ideas into a clearly articulated position.

This is a shocking reflection on schooling and family up-bringing in this country. If questions of discipline and behaviour are to be properly addressed, educationists will need to ask themselves what it is about our traditional practices that makes it easier to adopt negative attitudes than positive ones. Why indeed is it at an adult level that people who protest their law-abiding nature, feel free to opt out from the demands of the Race Relations Act 1976 (and usually the Sex Discrimination Act 1975 as well)?

The Commission for Racial Equality (CRE) has published a Code of Practice for the elimination of racial discrimination in education (CRE, 1990). It deals clearly and concisely with the concepts of direct and indirect racial discrimination and refers to individual complaints supported by the Commission and to the outcome of formal investigations carried out by the Commission. The latter are presented in greater detail in a collection of case studies (CRE, 1991a). Between them they clarify what authorities and institutions are required to do if they are going to provide a non-discriminatory education aimed at genuine equality of opportunity.

The Commission's *Learning in Terror* is a report of a survey of racial harassment in schools and colleges in England, Scotland and Wales (CRE, 1988a). It includes model policies and guidelines for authorities and institutions as well as a legal opinion about the liabilities of LEAs and institutions in the event of failure to undertake preventive or remedial measures in relation to incidents of racial harassment which may be brought to their attention.

The Elton Report (DES, 1989) recommends that 'headteachers and staff should be alert to signs of bullying and racial harassment; deal firmly with all such behaviour; and take action based on clear rules which are backed by appropriate sanctions and systems to protect and support victims'. As far as the pupils are concerned, it recommends that they 'should tell staff about serious cases of bullying and racial harassment of which they are aware'.

There is a problem here, however, in persuading people to implement these recommendations. Young people generally do not report their experiences because of their disillusionment with their teachers who, on the one hand, may prove indifferent to their reports or, on the other, may prove so ineffective that the victim may be subjected to further victimization by the assailant.

Reports of name-calling and racial abuse are often met by the teachers' rejoinder that 'Sticks and stones may break my bones but names will never hurt me'. Pupils who report acts of bullying or racial harassment are sometimes told 'It's a big bad world out there, and the sooner you get used to it, the better'. It is incomprehensible that one should be expected to tolerate any form of mistreatment in the first place. And why should one expect a learning institution to mimic aspects of the outside world that are clearly unacceptable and which may indeed be subject to legal consequences?

The Swann Committee Report (DES, 1985) very clearly draws the distinction between so-called everyday name-calling and racial abuse, and describes the damage that is caused by directing abuse not only against individuals but against their families, their communities and their ethnic groups.

The Report also includes the results of its survey of largely white schools in six local education authorities. It paints a distressing picture of ignorance and racial bigotry.

What is clear from all this is that in the period of almost four years between the publication of the Swann and Elton Reports there has been little fundamental or widespread change. Policy development, while exciting in some cases, has been extremely limited. Again some interesting and imaginative local initiatives, a few funded by Education Support Grants from the DES, have failed to make a general, lasting impact.

Why is it that interest in Swann seems to have waned so quickly? Is it likely that the Elton recommendations directed at combatting racial harassment will also fail to be implemented and thus leave yet another hole in the fabric of mutual understanding and respect that should characterize the discipline and order expected in all educational institutions in Britain's multi-ethnic society?

What kind of discipline is it that ignores the important issues of racial understanding and respect as well as non-discriminatory, equal opportunities provision and treatment throughout the educational institution? There is the alarming prospect that, despite the implementation of all the various reports' recommendations, black young people in particular will continue to experience racial harassment and discrimination.

Technical changes en route from authoritarian to democratic systems of discipline in educational institutions will not necessarily change the life-chances of young people visible by the colour of their skin and consequently subject to the effects of prejudice and stereotyping both individually and institutionally. On the other hand, an open, participatory, democratic system of discipline must perforce be more likely than the imposed, closed, authoritarian system to ventilate issues like racial justice, for example, and thus inspire some changes. But if we take the model of the British democratic state, we may be more inclined to feel that racial harassment and discrimination will persist for as long as we fail to adopt determined anti-racist strategies characterized by a time-related set of goals and objectives.

Both Swann and Elton recommend the increased recruitment of teachers from ethnic minority groups. On the one hand, they will provide the pupils with good role models, and, on the other hand, they will be able, from their particular background of experience, to facilitate better 'race' relations. However, the Macdonald Inquiry into the Burnage High School tragedy did not find that such an aspiration was fulfilled: black teachers were harassed and humiliated by white pupils and colleagues, and racial conflict was widespread. In 1986 the CRE published a report of a survey of black teacher employment in eight LEAs and of black student enrolment in all teacher education institutions (CRE, 1988b). It revealed an ageing black workforce and an apparently declining pool of available black students for teacher education courses. Research by Iram Siraj-Blatchford (1990) has revealed why young black people have been reluctant to enrol on such courses as a result of their own experiences and what they have witnessed as the treatment of black teachers.

One is aware of similar recruitment initiatives undertaken by the police and similar disappointments in expanding the black sector of the workforce. The exposure of indiscipline there in relation to the treatment of colleagues and members of the public might well provide a lesson to educational institutions: unless there is a profound change in ethos and unless recruitment is based first of all on the principle of justice, black staff will continue to be subject to tokenism and mistreatment and thus never fulfil their potential as valued contributors to agreed authority, discipline and order and the creation of congenial conditions for teaching and learning. The absence of black staff operating confidently in adequate numbers and in positions of equal authority must be taken as a symptom of institutional malfunction and disorder and a threat to effective teaching and learning.

Similarly, the absence of persons from ethnic minority groups from boards of governors at school and college level, and the failure of local and central government to ensure that bodies established by them reflect the multi-ethnic nature of British society, indicate a breakdown in discipline that must seep down to the pupil and student level and affect their individual and collective relationship with the learning community. This must in turn influence standards both of behaviour and academic achievement. Progress towards agreed and shared goals of excellence is impeded as a result.

But the black presence is not of itself enough to combat the racially discriminatory effects of institutional and structural inertia. Take for example the English as a Second Language Units in the Metropolitan Borough of Calderdale, West Yorkshire, which were the subject of a formal investigation by the CRE (1986). It was found that the language screening arrangements applied largely to Asian children of whom some 80 per cent spent between one and two years in the language units where the more restricted curriculum put them at a disadvantage when they were returned to the mainstream schools. The investigation concluded that the arrangements amounted to indirect discrimination.

The units were well staffed and funded. The teachers were dedicated to their jobs. Some were so well disposed towards the children in their care that they delayed their return to the mainstream because of their desire to protect them from harassment and discrimination that might be encountered there. This is an important lesson to learn about racism: racially discriminatory effects can result from an exercise in good-will just as much as with malice aforethought!

The children were happy, cooperative and well behaved. The staff were cheerful and hard-working. Standards of order and discipline were high. But with all that, the children were being discriminated against and disadvantaged in terms of their life and career prospects. This illustrates the need for policy-makers, governors and practitioners to examine all aspects of their educational organization to ensure that there is no obstacle at all to universal equality of opportunity.

Training in anti-racist strategies is therefore necessary for every level of the education service so that the subtle, complex workings of racism can be properly understood and eliminated. Who would have thought, for example, that an institution of higher education like St Georges Hospital Medical School could ever be discriminating against applicants on racial (and gender) grounds? And yet this is what the CRE's formal investigation found (CRE, 1988c). The School's computer program was used to sort out applicants and decide who would be called for interview. While female applicants were given an adverse loading of 5 per cent, black applicants faced a handicap of 35 per cent. It is estimated that between 1982 and 1988 over 60 applicants a year were discriminated against on racial grounds.

These were people who had excellent qualifications, sixth formers who were highly recommended by the heads of their institutions for their hard work, their sound motivation and their good behaviour. *These young people were generally models of self-discipline eagerly ready to conform to the rules and expectations of their schools and the institutions where they sought admission.* And even when some of them had strong feelings that something was wrong when they were not called for interview, and even when they were advised that they had grounds for complaint under the Race Relations Act, still they exercised patience and restraint. While there is an element of self-interest in the way that one accepts a particular kind of disciplinary code, systems can also impose an acceptance of their workings through the intimidation of 'clients' with thoughts of consequences or even reprisals for 'rocking the boat' by asserting one's right.

The St Georges system also enjoyed the added aura of high technology, and that always suggests consistency and objectivity in appraising candidates according to clear criteria. Except for one thing, all these claims were true, of course. And that thing was racism, and had it not been for the persistence of two members of the staff who were devoted to racial justice, the racist loading of the computer program might have taken much longer to expose. These two doctors started with a fundamental question about the qualities needed by a good doctor if s/he was to be a source of genuine individual and community well-being. They looked at patterns thrown up by statistics: why were there so few black (and women) students? Shouldn't the institution have an equal opportunities policy? Was there something wrong with the selection process?

This is never an easy role to adopt. One may be regarded as a trouble-maker, an eccentric or even disloyal. What they were in fact doing – questioning, criticizing, exposing unpalatable truths, asserting their rights as professionals and the rights of others to be treated fairly – was what the institution itself should have been doing, especially since there were a handful of people who knew that the computer program was loaded against black people.

Unfortunately, there is a traditional view of discipline in Britain which is concerned with producing obedient subjects rather than responsible citizens. The former just do their jobs and help thereby to maintain the status quo while the latter will express their criticisms of working conditions and the effectiveness of the service to the public. Where the organization itself has no built-in system of evaluation and no means of monitoring progress in implementing a policy of equal opportunities covering employment and service delivery, the 'whistle-blowers' face harassment and victimization, of course.

In the case of St Georges, there was also another factor that hindered the process of self-examination: that was the fact that compared with most of the other medical schools in London, it had quite a good record on the admission of black students (and women). While this might lead to complacency or even resisting charges of racial discrimination in the admissions practices, it seems also to have led to the feeling that there might be problems if more black students (and women) were admitted.

The idea of an optimum number and upper limit of black enrolment was first manifested in DES Circular 7/65, 'The Education of Immigrants', (DES, 1965) which advocated the dispersal of immigrant pupils by 'bussing' where they constituted 30 per cent of a school population. What this ministerial edict did of course was to combine a kind of sentimental liberalism with a sense of racial realism: 'They are here. We must accommodate, even welcome them. But too many of them in the same institution will cause problems for themselves, for the white pupils and for their teachers.' The numbers game has not disappeared of course. Black people know how it is played out in parliament, at ports of entry and in overseas British embassies. It should be remembered that there is a life outside the institution to which the internal systems of order and discipline need to be related. Otherwise while there may well be a superficial acceptance and conformity, the pupils are unlikely to be inspired by or deeply engaged with their institutions. The result will be alienation, disillusionment and an increasing lack of respect for what purports to be authority.

Educational institutions can all too easily become isolated from their communities. While they may provide manual employment for local people, in inner-city institutions in particular, teachers are unlikely to live locally. While there may be good reason for this, it is also very often the case that these teachers have little to do with the local community either after school hours or at weekends. And while the institution may concern itself with national and global issues at morning worship or even in personal and social education, there is often a block to examining community issues affecting the young people in their care – issues such as unemployment, housing, poverty, the environment and public facilities as well as the vital issue of relations between the police and young people. There is a feeling that such issues are politically sensitive and therefore to be avoided at all costs.

Education is conceived as taking place in neutral spaces where the real everyday experiences of young people will prove a distraction to the task of schooling them. In such circumstances it is little wonder that the curriculum, the organization and the system of discipline generally receive no more than a perfunctory tribute from the young people who are obliged to attend school. Where teachers are not seen as sharing the real everyday experiences of their pupils or even being interested in what is actually happening to them, then schools and what they have to offer will be largely a matter of indifference to the pupils, at best a period to be borne with a kind of gentle tolerance and at worst a time of confrontation and conflict.

And more often than not the young people are right: nothing changes in any fundamental sense for them, for their families, for the community as a whole or in relation to that vague concept of the *future* so often used by teachers to exhort and challenge them to greater efforts.

For black pupils and their families that *future* is seen to be nothing more than a persistent extension of their past experiences of harassment and discrimination. This is why educational development and innovation of all kinds must be conceived and implemented from an anti-racist perspective. Questions need to be asked about the historical roots of racism. What is it that sustains the ideas and practices of white supremacy? What is it in the experiences of white young people that makes them mirror the views of adults with whom they come into contact at home, in schools, in the media, in government and elsewhere? Why have they come to regard whites as superior and blacks in particular as inferior, and how have these views managed to suppurate into individual attitudes and institutional practices in such a way that black people, people from ethnic minorities, people seen as different, people distinguished in particular by the colour of their skin are excluded from the full range of opportunities to which they should be entitled in a country that claims to be democratic and pluralist?

The proof is there for all to see if they wish. The facts of racial harassment and racial discrimination are well documented. There are detailed records of racial abuse and racial violence in schools and colleges, on the streets, on the football terraces, on housing estates and in the workplace. There are similar records of all kinds of racial discrimination in all walks of life in Britain – in employment, housing, health and social services, policing and criminal justice, education and so on. There are clear well-argued accounts of the growth of racist ideas and attitudes and of racist practices, procedures and structures along with strong practical recommendations about ways of resisting, countering and dismantling them.

But change does not take place because there is a complex web of individual and institutional factors that resist it. People are products of their conditioning who find it difficult to believe that they could be part of an unjust regime. There is the inertia of custom and tradition that carries an institution forward from one day to the next with very little opportunity for fundamental change although superficial innovations may be introduced. Educational institutions, while they may be able to exercise some degree of autonomy, are nevertheless the result of political and economic intentions. The denial of access to black children or their mistreatment with respect to allocation to teaching groups and their exclusion from class and school may find some justification on the part of those in authority in that it happens to white pupils as well, and that is bound up with the class divisions in British society that reproduce themselves in schools and colleges. There is a whole range of variables that makes it difficult to pinpoint racial discrimination – or sexual or class discrimination for that matter. Underachievement may be explained to enquiring or protesting parents of black children by recourse to the argument of infinite regression that can go back to the womb and even beyond to past generations: poor 16-plus prospects or performance must be the result of previous lack of effort, the wrong option choices, allocation to lower streams or sets based on attainment levels when transferring to secondary school, misbehaviour or absenteeism, sudden or traumatic changes in domestic and family circumstances such as divorce or separation and so on.

But no matter how sophisticated the arguments about underachievement and the variable factors involved, the fact remains that female, working-class and black pupils will generally come out at the bottom of the pile. It will be no consolation to their parents to hear that when consideration is given to all the obstacles barring their academic progress, their overall achievement is really as good as white male middle-class pupils gaining significant numbers of ordinary and advanced level examination passes! Similarly, taking all factors into account, their behaviour is not all that bad either despite the fact that they have to be punished more often and even more severely than their peers. Lurking in the background are the stereotypes of black children: Afro-Caribbean pupils are argumentative and even militant, especially when compared with their docile Asian peers; they lack discipline especially in their one-parent families; their parents beat them and want them severely chastized at school; it is therefore difficult to reason with them.

The Elton Report outlines the steps that might be taken in securing cooperation between the home and the school in order to develop the highest standards of discipline. One of the recommendations is 'that schools should ensure that written communications to parents are in language easily understood by them and that, where significant numbers of parents use first languages other than English, communications are available in these languages as well as in English'. Also recommended are a welcoming environment for parents, respect for their views, home-school liaison arrangements, positive comments by the school about their children's work and behaviour, the early involvement of parents when disciplinary problems arise, effective induction arrangements for the parents of new pupils and the proper notification to them of significant changes in school organization.

But there is a lot more to effective home-school partnership than a Welcome sign at the school gates and multilingual communication with parents. Partnership implies a sharing of power, a willingness to be guided by the views of parents and their children and a readiness to incorporate their suggestions and even their objections into the programme of preventive or remedial measures. Indeed, what will be gained by a multilingual communication policy if community languages are regarded as a matter of convenience rather than unique skills worthy of the same respect as all the other languages including English? What may appear to be an enlightened policy may merely be the means of impressing the status and importance of the school so much more quickly upon the parents and their children and thus inhibiting the development of the partnership.

When partnership is interpreted as unanimity, it can lead to the exclusion of the dissenters. What it should mean is the kind of community where all can be integrated on their own terms in the first place – the non-conformists and the eccentrics whose criticisms need to be heard and responded to if the community is to learn to live according to the principles of freedom, justice and equality. Ignorance, prejudice and bigotry also need to be brought out into the open but that can only happen when the community as a whole, and especially those employed to run it, are ready to adopt and declare a determined, confident and articulate anti-racist position. In such circumstances, discipline and order will be seen as a vigorous challenge to the oppressive and divisive authoritarian systems that perpetuate racism (and sexism and class discrimination).

In *Racial Equality in Education* edited by Barry Troyna (1987) there is an essay by Bob Carter and Jenny Williams entitled 'Attacking Racism in Education' which offers an interesting and thought-provoking critique of the anti-racist positions adopted by the Swann Report and the Racism Awareness Training programmes based on the work of Judith Katz (1978). It deals also with the problems of statistical interpretation, as in the case of the CRE's formal investigation into the suspensions policy of the Birmingham Local Education Authority (see above). The authority responded to the investigation report's criticisms by streamlining the procedures and centralizing decisions about suspensions as though that was in itself a guarantee that officers and elected councillors would be incapable of making such mistakes. (As stated above, the Education (No. 2) Act 1986 defines, controls and nationally centralizes the procedures, and still black parents complain that their children are being discriminated against.) Carter and Williams offer a good practical definition of racism and the complex network of relationships that need to be considered in embarking on a strategy aimed at dismantling it. They are concerned with the 'standard' inequalities in the education system where incremental changes in the treatment of those who have been experiencing discrimination 'will not alter the life chances of the majority of pupils'. They identify two kinds of strategy aimed at change: one, the central initiatives of local education authorities to tackle racial discrimination and inequality, and the other, the production of whole-school policies as a result of opening up the power structure within the school as well as in relation to the outside communities.

Again they advocate careful analysis of their efficacy in achieving anti-racist goals, and they quote Dummett (1985) who recommends a 'series of practical steps, moving towards clearly defined aims each time and taken after careful thought and observation' instead of vague exhortations and long-term policies dependent on complete or overwhelming consensus.

DES Circular 16/89 requires all LEAs and grant-maintained schools to submit data on the ethnicity, language and religion of pupils entering school at ages 5 and 11. Properly collected and carefully analysed, such data could supply interesting information about the capacity of institutions and authorities to provide equality in access, treatment and outcome.

Supplemented by the data collected on teachers and students in Further and Higher Education, which are also a statutory requirement, their regular monitoring would allow policy-makers, providers and practitioners to see whether their systems were actually discriminating on racial grounds in the child's or the young person's educational career. One would be encouraged to see the elements at work in influencing institutional decisions at crucial points in and between infant, primary, secondary, further and higher education.

But there is an inherent conflict in what we are trying to do: we are demanding an anti-racist stance from people who, through no fault of their own, because they are products of their conditioning, occupy various positions on the continuum of racism. Unless they make the connection between themselves and racism, nothing will change, of course. It is that sudden and sometimes electrifying recognition of their contribution to racist practices that leads to the transformation of personal relationships, classroom organization and institutional structures.

The institution's analysis of its own performance in relation to young people from the different ethnic groups is often an immediate and effective means of inspiring such changes. The Commission for

Racial Equality recently undertook a pilot study at a secondary school in the north of England (with the full cooperation of the staff and the local authority) into the arrangements for allocating pupils to teaching groups, determining subject option choices and allocation to courses as well as deciding on entry for examinations at fifth form level (CRE, 1992b). The school was in the fortunate position of maintaining detailed records on its pupils. It was also concerned to ensure that it offered genuine equality of opportunity. Nevertheless the pilot study revealed patterns of discrimination in the treatment of its Asian pupils that might not have come to light had it not been for the careful collection and analysis of ethnic data. In the light of such an analysis, a programme of remedial action has been undertaken. That programme's effectiveness will be revealed by a regular annual analysis of the ethnic data and a monitoring of progress towards the equal opportunity goals.

When pupils (and their parents and teachers) witness such commitment, it inspires feelings of community solidarity which are fundamental in developing patterns of conduct based on self-discipline, mutual respect and cooperation.

In a group of schools in a large township in a south of England county, Education Support Grant funds have been used to look at problems of bullying and racial harassment (ESG, 1991). While there have been no overnight miracles, there has been a transformation among pupils hitherto regarded as the victim group in those schools where the project has led to staff taking the problem seriously and encouraging pupils to report incidents on the assurance that something would be done about it. On the other hand, in one of the schools covered by the project, while there is the superficial impression of order under a rather authoritarian regime, pupil morale especially among black pupils remains low because they are aware that the staff refuse to take the issue seriously. In such cases pupils are forced to conclude that the school rules are for the convenience of the institution and the staff rather than for the welfare of the pupils. In such circumstances it is difficult for young people to identify with what should really be a community but which in reality remains nothing more than an institution which they are obliged to attend.

Unless the school reflects and respects the presence of black people in the world as well as in the surrounding community, there will be separation, division and conflict. The school will not therefore be able to generate the fullest kind of corporate energy and thus fulfil the potential of all its pupils individually and together. Where the content of courses and the books and other materials used in teaching them, where staffing and other arrangements for governing and servicing schools, and where outreach to parents, families and communities exclude, marginalize or disparage people visible by the colour of their skin, the system of discipline may well exact a degree of orderly conduct but it will not inspire young people to want to involve themselves in the life of their school over and above their role as compulsory attenders for a large portion of their lives.

Where harassment and discrimination on racial grounds are allowed to persist and no effort is made to address the issue of racism as the root cause of harassment and discrimination, then the quality of life for all the pupils must be adversely affected. Take for example a school in an English southern county where the antipathy to pupils from the travelling communities is so strong that the local authority officer in charge of traveller education will direct travellers' children to a school rather further away than send them to the nearby one where they will experience harassment and discrimination from staff and pupils alike. While this may seem to be a benevolent solution, it fails to address the root cause, and it may well be an unlawful act under the Race Relations Act 1976 (ACERT, 1989).

What kind of learning community is this? What values are being absorbed by the children? What kind of attitudes are they developing? What kind of problems are being stored up for them as future adults, parents and citizens in a democratic, plural society? Indeed, if they cannot welcome the apparent stranger, what skills are they likely to develop in pushing back the horizons of their own minds in order to learn new, exciting and unfamiliar things? Their sense of exclusivity and their rejection of others already point to an extremely limited learning environment. The school in question was said to be disciplined and orderly but that is a description that we have heard about racist, indeed genocidal, regimes elsewhere!

Thus when we talk about discipline we mean a pattern of relationships and opportunities encouraging the development of confident, self-respecting, truly tolerant, hospitable, magnanimous, curious, questing, committed and dependable human beings able to live in and value Britain's diverse society.

The task of teachers must be to enable them to understand that society and its divisions and conflicts while pointing them towards the realization of equality, freedom and justice for all. With such an understanding, it should then be possible for teachers, parents, governors and especially pupils to work out a detailed policy with clear, precise goals capable of early evaluation and regular monitoring to ensure the effective combatting of racism as one of the factors inhibiting genuine equality of opportunity.

Like the curriculum, the organization of teaching groups, examination entry and performance, library and classroom resources, and involvement in extra-curricular activities, the institution's Code of Discipline and Statement of Rules need also to be evaluated and monitored in terms of their contribution to equality of opportunity. To what extent are ethnic minority groups represented in the School Council and Prefect Body, and how do their discussions and activities incorporate non-dicriminatory, equal opportunity considerations? Are rewards and sanctions fairly distributed throughout the school community? And is the effect to develop a safe, encouraging, courteous, considerate and cooperative community in which all young people can feel free and relaxed enough to be themselves? In short, is it clear that, as part of the struggle for real equality, the school's system of discipline is also firmly rooted in a determined anti-racist strategy?

References

ACERT (Advisory Council for the Education of Romanys and Travellers) (1989) Annual General Meeting. Report of a delegate.

Berkshire County Research and Intelligence Unit (BCRI) (1989) *The Performance of Children from Different Ethnic Groups*, 1986/7.

Commission for Racial Equality (CRE) (1985) Report of a Formal Investigation into the Birmingham LEA – Referral and Suspension of Pupils, London: CRE.

Commission for Racial Equality (CRE) (1986) Teaching English as a Second Language. Report of a Formal Investigation in Calderdale Local Education Authority, London: CRE.

Commission for Racial Equality (CRE) (1988a) *Learning in Terror: A Survey of Racial Harassment in Schools and Colleges in England, Scotland and Wales*, London: CRE.

Commission for Racial Equality (CRE) (1988b) *Ethnic Minority School Teachers: A Survey in Eight Local Education Authorities*, London: CRE.

Commission for Racial Equality (CRE) (1988c) Medical School Admissions. Report of a Formal Investigation into St Georges Hospital Medical School, London: CRE.

Commission for Racial Equality (CRE) (1990) *Code of Practice for the Elimination of Racial Discrimination in Education*, London: CRE.

Commission for Racial Equality (CRE) (1991) *Lessons of the Law. A Casebook of Racial Discrimination in Education*, London: CRE.

Commission for Racial Equality (CRE) (1992) *Set to Fail*, London: CRE.

Department of Education and Science (DES) (1965) DES Circular 7/65 *The Education of Immigrants*, London: HMSO.

Department of Education and Science (DES) (1985) Education for All: the Report of the Committee of Inquiry into the Education of Children from Ethnic Minority Groups, Cmnd 9543, London: HMSO

Department of Education and Science (DES) (1989) Discipline in Schools. Report of the Committee of Enquiry chaired by Lord Elton, London: HMSO.

ESG (1991) Action Research Project into Racial Harassment in Schools in a Rural County Town. Restricted circulation on a confidential basis.

Dummett, A. (1985) *In the Shadows of Understanding: Institutional Racism*, Links 21, London Third World First 7–13.

Katz, J. (1978) *White Awareness: A Handbook of Anti-Racism Training*, University of Oklahoma Press.

Kelly, E. (1989) In *Murder in the Playground*, Longsight Press, ch. 26.

Mortimore, P., Sammons, P., Stoll, L., Lewis, D. and Ecob, R. (1988) *School Matters: The Junior Years*, Ch. 7, p. 155. Wells, Somerset: Open Books.

Siraj-Blatchford, I. (1990) 'Positive discrimination: the under achievement of initial teacher education', in *Multicultural Teaching*, Trentham Books.

Troyna, B. (ed.) (1987) *Racial Inequality in Education*, London: Tavistock.

Wright, C. (1985) 'School Processes: an ethnographic study', in Eggleston et al. Educational and Vocational Experiences of 15–18 Year-Old Young People of Ethnic Minority Groups. A report to the Department of Education and Science, University of Warwick.

Wright, C. (1992) *An Ethnographic Study of A Selected Number of Nursery and Primary Schools*, London: Commission for Racial Equality (CRE). Unpublished. Available on a confidential basis.

CHAPTER 5

Home experience and the classroom discipline problems that can arise when needed skills are lacking

MICHAEL J.A. HOWE

Introduction: failure leads to discontent

By and large, efforts to understand and ameliorate classroom discipline problems start with the reasonable assumption that the causes of such problems are primarily social, behavioural and emotional rather than cognitive or intellectual. Without wishing to argue with that view, I shall attempt to demonstrate in this chapter that the absence of cognitive skills that are needed for success as a classroom learner forms one important cause of discipline problems in the school classroom. The discipline problems that have these origins occur largely because children who lack such skills are prone to experience frustrations and feelings of failure. These lead to actions and behaviours which tend to disrupt the classroom and diminish its effectiveness as an environment for children's learning.

Like many people, I have sometimes attended adult instructional courses of one kind or another. In most cases the courses have been ones that were intended to help me gain abilities that I thought would be useful to me, such as foreign languages, statistics, or computer programming. I have to admit that most of my experiences of such adult learning courses have been rather negative: more often than not I have failed to learn very much, and on a number of occasions I have chosen to drop out of a course of instruction before it ended.

Young children at school are in much the same position as adults attending courses of instruction, but with one important difference. The difference is that children, unlike adult learners, do not have the option of dropping out of an educational course that they feel is not going well for them. They have no choice but to remain in the classroom. But in their minds they often do drop out, and they stop concentrating. Of course, having to sit still and silent in a school classroom when your mind is not on the teaching and learning activities that are going on is a frustrating and boring experience. Understandably, children look for ways to escape the boredom. Daydreaming is one way. Chatting to your neighbour is another. Other, more exciting possibilities are making paper aeroplanes, getting into a fight, and making faces while the teacher's back is turned. Most readers who can recall their school days will doubtless be able to think of other possibilities.

Unfortunately, if you happen to be a child at school most of these activities are frowned upon by the authorities. Teachers have a term for them: 'discipline problems'. Such problem behaviours take numerous forms, but, from the teacher's point of view these activities are almost always seen as being undesirable because they tend to reduce the effectiveness of the classroom as a place in which learning takes place. These pupil activities typically involve noise or some other kind of disruption in the school classroom. As a result, even those teachers who are generally tolerant of interruptions and committed to encouraging relatively unconstrained self-expression on the part of pupils find that it is hard to maintain a good environment for learning. Even the most liberal and pupil-centred teachers require a degree of peace and quiet in their classrooms, and freedom from noise disruptions.

So teachers find it necessary to prevent or discourage the kinds of pupil activities that are seen as discipline problems. How is that achieved? The obvious strategy is to identify the causes of the disruptive activities, and then, if that proves possible, attempt to eliminate those causes. Of course, a moment's reflection makes it clear that the causes of the various children's activities that are seen as creating discipline problems are numerous and diverse. Consequently, there is no single best approach either to understanding the problems or to solving them.

As I implied earlier, in this chapter I shall concentrate on those classroom problems that have their roots in the absence of the skills and abilities which a child needs to have in order to succeed as a learner at school. One particular source of potential discipline problems is the failure of the child's early environment to equip the individual with basic skills that a child needs in order to be able to take advantage of the learning experiences that are provided at school. As it happens this particular source of difficulties directly or indirectly accounts for rather a large proportion of the classroom discipline problems that teachers encounter and remark upon.

Why do some children not concentrate on the learning activities that are taking place in the classroom? When and why does their attention begin to wander? One way in which I can begin to answer these questions is to cast my mind back again to my own experiences as a classroom learner, and try asking myself why *I* found it hard to concentrate on some of the adult education courses I was attending. There were a number of different reasons. Sometimes the teacher referred to words or concepts that I failed to understand. On other occasions the teacher introduced unfamiliar ideas at a rate that was too fast for me to keep up. At times I found it difficult to attend for long periods of time to new or difficult items of information. In short, a major cause of the difficulties I was experiencing was that I lacked skills, abilities, knowledge or attributes that I needed to have in order to understand and learn from the teaching that was being provided.

Many of the classroom frustrations that children experience are similar or identical to these ones. For young children, of course, the difficulties they experience in the classroom are compounded by their immaturity, their need for adult attention, and the many anxieties and fears to which children are especially prone. Nevertheless, many of the reasons that cause children to behave in the ways that present teachers with discipline problems stem from varieties of unpreparedness that are not too unlike the ones that produce the kinds of frustrations that an adult learner may experience.

By the time they arrive at school for the first time, all children will be highly experienced learners in some respects and will have notched up some substantial learned achievement. All the same, children vary considerably in the extent to which their lives before school have made them ready for the particular kinds of learning that are crucial in the school classroom. School makes demands upon the young learner that are different from those experienced in the child's own home.

For a number of different reasons, a child who is unprepared for classroom learning will experience failures and frustrations that may lead to behaviours that cause discipline and management problems for the teacher.

First, a lack of the *listening skills* which a child needs in order to learn at school, especially in relation to gaining the vital ability of reading, may lead to problems being experienced.

Second, there are a number of negative outcomes of the absence of needed *attending skills*.

Third, there are various negative consequences for the child of not having acquired the capacity to make use of certain simple *learning strategies*, such as rehearsing information the student is trying to learn.

Fourth, a child may suffer from the consequences of lacking various attributes that contribute to the beginnings of independence, autonomy and *self-control* in a young learner. To compound the problems that arise, the failures that a child experiences accentuate the problems. A child may acquire a *fear of failure*, and an outcome of this is to direct the individual's attention even further away from classroom tasks.

Problems that arise from a lack of vital skills

There is considerable evidence that the likelihood of a child making normal progress towards learning to read at school will be reduced if certain basic skills have not been gained before the beginning of formal instruction. As we have seen, a child who is not making reasonable progress in the classroom is likely to be a frustrated, bored, and unhappy child, and one who will find it difficult to concentrate on classroom learning activities. The ways in which such a child is likely to react are all too likely to be ones which will cause discipline problems for the teacher.

One basic skill that any child must possess in order to be successful as a classroom learner, especially in connection with learning to read, takes the form of the ability to hear spoken language accurately. It is necessary to hear the small sound units that make up words, and to be able to discriminate between different sounds. Since failure to learn to read has damaging consequences for the child, it is clear that the lack of this basic skill will seriously disadvantage a child in ways that may lead to the failures and frustrations that underly many discipline problems in the school classroom.

The particular listening skills that are especially crucial for learning to read involve the ability to be aware of, and discriminate between *phonemes*, the smallest sound units of language. Any child who cannot perceive phonemes accurately and cannot discriminate between two different phonemes (such as the *b* in *bad* and the *d* in *dad*) will find it difficult, if not impossible, to gain the ability to read (Bryant and Bradley, 1985; Coles, 1987).

In one investigation aimed at exploring the role of listening skills in reading and assessing the outcome of deficient listening abilities, Bradley and Bryant (1983) asked 4 and 5 year olds to listen to lists of three words. The lists were constructed so that each word but one contained a phoneme in common. The child's task was to say which was the odd word. The researchers discovered that the children's performance level at this task was a good predictor of the same children's achievements at reading and spelling four years later. This finding establishes that there is a connection of some kind between phonologicial skills in early childhood and subsequent progress at learning to read.

The next step in the project was to discover whether or not the differences between children in their phonological listening skills are a cause of variability in children's reading achievements. To investigate this, Bradley and Bryant started by selecting 65 children who did poorly at the phoneme discrimination task. These children would have been regarded as being 'at risk', so far as later success at reading was concerned.

The children were divided into four groups. Children in the first two groups received training in categorizing language sounds. Each child was seen for twenty ten-minute sessions per year, for two years. Clearly, the training that was needed was not particularly time-consuming or intensive: it took just over three hours in all. Children in the first group were taught to discriminate between phoneme sounds, Group Two children were given the same instruction but were also taught to associate letter sounds with actual letters. The children in Group Three were taught to discriminate between categories, but their training did not include discriminating between sounds, and Group Four received no instruction at all.

All the children were tested again when they reached the age of 8 years. By this time Group Four, who had not been given any special training, were lagging a year behind the normal standard of achievement at reading. Their progress at spelling was two whole years behind the average. Group Three, who had received training at making discriminations, but ones that did not involve phonemes, were also below average at both the reading and spelling tests. In contrast, the children in each of the groups who had been given training at discriminating between phonemes did much better. The Group One children were slightly below average at reading, and worse at spelling, but the children who had been in Group Two, and who had been trained to discriminate between phonemes and to make associations between sounds and letters were successfully reading at the level that was expected for children of their age.

The research I have described is just one of a number of studies that have demonstrated how a lack of basic skills can impede classroom learning, leading to the failures and the frustrations that underlie the kinds of behaviours by children which create discipline problems for the classroom teacher. Other studies have provided additional evidence that preschool instruction in basic skills involving letters, sounds and phonemes can lead to big improvements in a child's progress in reading at school and can considerably reduce the likelihood of a child experiencing difficulties in learning to read. For instance, it has been found that training your children to blend sounds together and to break words down into their constituent sounds leads to increased progress at early reading (Goldstein, 1976).

A number of the frustrations experienced by young children at school as a result of their failure to make good progress stem (at least in part) from failures on the part of teachers to appreciate that the child is beginning school lacking certain fundamental skills that form essential prerequisites for school learning. Typically, these are skills that many children *do* acquire before they enter school, as an outcome of learning experiences at home. For instance, a child whose parents read to her fairly regularly, or play games involving rhymes or poems, will almost certainly gain the phoneme descrimination skills mentioned above, without any deliberate intention to teach the skills being required. But a child whose parents do not read to her, and who has little experience of listening to stories, verses or prose narratives, may arrive at school without certain key skills that are necessary. If the classroom teacher wrongly assumes that all children have acquired all the prerequisite skills they require in order to profit from the instruction provided in the classroom, the resulting lack of progress by those children who have failed to acquire those skills before beginning school will be an inevitable cause of frustration for a child and, very possibly, a cause of discipline problems for the child's teacher.

Problems caused by inability to attend or concentrate

The ability to pay attention to the teacher is a crucial prerequisite for classroom learning, but the presence of that ability cannot be taken for granted in all young children. School makes many demands upon the young learner that are different from those experienced in life at home. One important difference is that whilst language is undoubtedly important in the home as a medium of communication, in school it is often necessary to rely exclusively on language alone. In the child's home, the mother who teaches her child in a one-to-one situation is able to supplement language with various kinds of non-verbal communication such as facial expressions and gestures. She can demonstrate things to her child and show her how to do things. In school, by contrast, language alone often has to do things which in the home are partly achieved by non-verbal aids of communication. In order to communicate information to a large number of children, to give instructions to them, it may be necessary for the teacher to rely almost exclusively on language as such. So in the school, unlike the home, a child who has not mastered the ability to attend carefully to the human voice, in the absence of other aids to communication, will regularly fail to receive informative communications that are vital if the child is to be a successful school learner.

Also, at school, unlike home, the child will often be expected to make a deliberate effort to learn things, or to remember information for its own sake, in the absence of any practical reason that is immediately clear to the child. At home, activities that have the express purpose of learning or recalling something are rather unusual. So although a preschool child may have learned numerous skills at home, she may be not at all familiar with some of the phrases that are common in classrooms, such as 'Now try to learn this' or 'I'd like you to remember what I'm going to tell you'. A child who begins school may be totally unprepared for this kind of deliberate, intentional learning, situation.

So the ability to attend to classroom instruction is not something that can be taken for granted in a young child. And a young child's failure to do so should not be taken to indicate that the child has chosen not to attend: it is just as likely to be a matter of that child lacking the necessary skills for being an attentive classroom learner. The teacher may need to give some children a considerable amount of help and support in order for them to gain the habit of regularly attending.

Children's attending behaviours such as listening carefully and concentrating on classroom tasks are clearly related to achievement

(Good and Beckerman, 1978), and low-achievers are less successful than high-achievers at focusing on the tasks they are doing. Moreover, when so-called 'fast' and 'slow' learners are compared, it turns out that the fast learners spend much more of their time actually concentrating on their assignments (in one study as much as twice the time) than the slow learners. This finding suggests that much of the difference between children in what they achieve as classroom learners is not caused by any inherent differences in children's abilities but by differences in the extent to which different children have acquired the capacity to attend to and concentrate on classroom tasks. If that is true, it is no wonder that children who are ill-equipped for attending tend to fail to learn, and to be prone to the resulting frustrations that make it likely that they will provide discipline problems for the teacher. It is interesting to note that Japanese schools, which have been so conspicuously successful in recent years, make considerably more provision than schools in the West for encouraging children to attend and concentrate in the classroom. Japanese education places,

an extremely high priority on careful structuring of novice students' introduction to learning situations. Typically, the period of transition from initial application to fully accepted beginning student is considerably protracted, encompassing several months or more. During this period the new student undergoes systematic training in the basic attitudes and cognitive support skills fundamental to the medium to be learned. (Peak, 1986, pp. 113–14)

The need for learning strategies

Compared with the learning that takes place in a child's own home, school learning tasks are typically less 'natural', more abstract, more closely tied to language and knowledge, more complex, and more highly organized in the sense of building upon knowledge and skills that have previously been acquired. For instance, in learning arithmetic, the child will have to gain a sequence of different skills that depend on existing skills and form an essential base for more advanced skills that are yet to be acquired.

As well as requiring a deliberate effort to learn on the child's part, the additional demands of school learning produce a situation in which it is desirable, and sometimes essential, for the learner to be able to make use of various methods, techniques, and strategies that aid learning, especially when what is to be learned takes the form of knowledge or information rather than practical skills. Here again, children differ in the extent to which their home environments have prepared them for the special demands of school learning. So far as success at school is concerned, some children's home environments are less than optimal not because the home is 'unstimulating' or the parents uncaring or uninterested in their child's education, or because the total amount of learning that the children achieve is below average, but simply because the *match* between home and school in the forms and contexts of learning, and the circumstances in which it occurs is rather poor. That is, some home environments do not provide as good a grounding for school learning as others, not because the child fails to learn but because she has rather few opportunities to be exposed to the kinds of situations and demands that prepare one for the particular kinds of learning situations that will be encountered at school.

Various methods, techniques, and learning strategies contribute to success in the classroom. Take rehearsal for example. The activity of rehearsing, which involves a learner deliberately repeating information to him or herself in order to commit it to memory is a widely used strategy that can facilitate learning and remembering in many of the everyday tasks that are confronted by a child at school. Some children learn how to rehearse, and acquire the habit of doing so, before they begin school, as a consequence of learning experiences at home. Other children are taught to rehearse by their classroom teachers. But many other young children, for one reason or another, never get into the habit of rehearsing, and they lose out as classroom learners, simply because of their failure to make use of a strategy that could often be helpful to them.

Of all the deliberate strategies used by children at school in order to aid the acquisition of knowledge and skills, rehearsal is the most widespread. By the time they have been attending school for two or three years, the majority of children have gained the habit of rehearsing when it is helpful to do so. However, rehearsing is a learned strategy: it is a skill which does have to be learned and which a substantial number of children fail to acquire.

As it happens, most children who do not spontaneously rehearse when they are confronted with classroom learning tasks can fairly easily be taught to do so, and when they do their efforts to learn and remember new information are more successful. In one study (Flavell et al., 1966) the researchers found that most 10 year olds but only a minority of 5 year olds spontaneously rehearsed when they were told to look at pictures of a number of common objects and try to remember them. At each age, those children who did rehearse correctly recalled substantially more of the objects than those children who did not rehearse. Later, the children who had not rehearsed were given instruction in a simple rehearsal method. (They were told to whisper the names of the objects they were looking at until the time when they were instructed to begin recalling.) These children were able to follow the rehearsal instructions with little difficulty, and when they did rehearse, their level of performance at the recall task rose to the level of the children who did rehearse spontaneously. So the strategy of rehearsing, which is widely applicable, appears to be not only very helpful but also easy to acquire, although it is not quite so easy to gain the habit of rehearsing regularly whenever it is useful to do so. An implication is that by identifying children who do not rehearse and encouraging them to do so, a teacher can help to prevent those children experiencing some frustrations and failures in the classroom, and thereby reduce the problem behaviours that such children often resort to.

Self-control and success in the classroom

Children and adults who experience repeated failures become unhappy and lose confidence. Eventually they become distressed and inactive, and they experience feelings of hopelessness (Covington, 1986; Covington and Omelich, 1981). These authors conducted an experiment which investigated the effects of repeatedly failing. The participants, who were college students, soon began to reduce their estimates of their own ability, they became less happy and more shameful, and with more and more failures they became increasingly distressed.

It is hardly surprising that children who fail to make progress in the classroom, perhaps because they lack some of the basic prerequisite skills I have already discussed, become disenchanted with school learning and uncooperative. They 'switch off', and end up presenting their teachers with various kinds of discipline problems. It is not hard to understand why such children cease to concentrate on classroom tasks. By doing so, a child avoids the shame-evoking implications of failing at a task that has been seriously attempted, and being made to feel stupid and lacking in ability. For such a child, a good way to avoid feeling stupid and a failure is to stop even trying to succeed.

How can this self-defeating cycle of events be avoided, and with it the discipline problems that failure and the fear of it can produce? The findings of a number of investigations point to effective strategies for the teacher. Research has shown that, for a child, the extent to which she is able to be in control of various aspects of life is important, and the extent to which she *feels* in control is particularly crucial. If a pupil believes that succeeding at school depends upon her own actions she will be much more likely to attend to school tasks and concentrate upon her work than if she believes that sucess depends upon external factors that are outside her control. A child who feels that she is in control will also be more likely than another child to take an active approach to learning, and make use of strategies such as rehearsing, which, as we have already seen, further increase the individual's chances of being successful.

A child's feelings about self-control are correlated with school achievement, with high achievement being associated with the perception of control as being internal, rather than external to the child. Classroom experiments have demonstrated that altering children's perceptions of control can have very positive outcomes. For example, in one experiment (Matheny and Edwards, 1974) teachers were instructed to give the children greater responsibility for controlling and organizing their own learning activities. It was found that not only did this change lead to very large improvements in the children's achievements, but that the largest positive effects occurred in those classrooms in which the teacher had been most successful in following the instructions to give more control to the children. In another study it was found that even when the choice of classroom tasks remained with the teacher, simply allowing the children to make decisions for themselves about the timing of their study activities led to higher achievements, and also produced (according to reports by the children) increased feelings of being in control. In short, the evidence suggests that some of the problems associated with failure and the resulting frustration and hopelessness are reduced when steps are taken to help pupils have more control over their learning activities.

Conclusion

In this chapter I have suggested that a significant proportion of the discipline problems teachers confront in their classroom have their roots in the failure of some children to make progress as school learners. Children who fail in the classroom are often bored, frustrated and unhappy. They react to failing by ceasing to concentrate on classroom tasks and behaving in various ways which are likely to present problems for their classroom teacher.

Generally speaking, children fail not because they are stupid or lack sufficient intelligence to do well, but for a number of other reasons. One frequent cause is that a child is simply not prepared for the kinds of learning challenges that are first encountered when beginning school. To succeed at school learning tasks it is necessary not simply to be able to learn, but to be capable of learning in circumstances which, for some children, are totally different from the kinds of learning situations they have met in their own homes. Many children, although their home learning environments may have been both stimulating and caring, are unprepared for school because the demands of the school classroom are too different from the demands of home. That is particularly the case for children whose home and family lives are ones in which little emphasis is placed on books and literacy or on the extensive use of language to convey complex thoughts and ideas. For such children, being confronted with classroom tasks which require them to concentrate for long periods of time, to make a deliberate effort to remember information, to follow complicated instructions, to deal with materials that are abstract and solve problems that have no obvious or immediate practical value, may present overwhelming problems. The result is that these children fail to make good progress, and react in the negative ways that are associated with failure.

How can we eliminate these causes of discipline problems? The short answer is that if the causes lie in children's failing, we should make failure impossible. Of course, that is more easily said than done: preventing all experiences of failure may be simply impossible. But a number of steps that we can take provide moves in that direction. For example, first, something can be achieved by simply alerting teachers to the fact that some of their pupils may be less well prepared for classroom learning than others, and may be failing because they do not possess certain elementary but essential skills. Second, teachers might be encouraged to do more to help children acquire some of the basic attributes that are drawn upon by the successful classroom learner. These include certain key abilities such as the listening skills that, as I noted earlier in the chapter, a child must have in order to be able to learn to read. The needed attributes also include the learned ability to introduce strategies that facilitate classroom learning, such as rehearsing. Yet another necessity, as we have seen, is that the child is able to have some control over her learning activities, and to be able to see herself as being at least to some extent in control.

References

Bradley, I. and Bryant, P.E. (1983) 'Categorizing sounds and learning to read in preschoolers', *Journal of Educational Psychology*, 68: 680–88.

Bryant, P. and Bradley, L. (1985) *Children's Reading Problems: Psychology and Education*, Oxford: Blackwell.

Coles, G. (1987) *The Learning Mystique*, New York: Fawcett Ballantine.

Covington, M.V. (1986) 'Strategic thinking and the fear of failure', in J.W. Segal, S.F. Chipman and R. Glaser (eds) *Thinking and Learning Skills Volume One: Relating Instruction to Research*, Hillsdale, NJ: Erlbaum.

Covington, M.V. and Omelich, C.L. (1981) 'As failures mount: affective and cognitive consequences of ability demotion in the classroom', *Journal of Educational Psychology*, 92: 149–54.

Flavell, J.H., Beach, D.R. and Chinsky, J.M. (1966) 'Spontaneous verbal rehearsal in a memory task as a function of age', *Child Development*, 37: 324–40.

Goldstein, D.M. (1976) 'Cognitive-linguistic functioning and learning to read in preschoolers', *Journal of Educational Psychology*, 68: 680–88.

Good, T.L., and Beckerman, T. (1978) 'An examination of teacher's effects on high, middle and low aptitude students' performance on a standardized achievement test', *American Educational Research Journal*, 15: 477–82.

Matheny, K. and Edwards, C. (1974) 'Academic improvement through an experimental classroom management system', *Journal of School Psychology*, 12, 222–32.

Peak, L. (1986) 'Training learning skills and attitudes in Japanese early educational settings', in W. Fowler (ed.) *Early Experience and the Development of Competence. New Directions in Child Development. No. 32*, San Francisco: Jossey Bass.

CHAPTER 6

Social reasons for bad behaviour

CLIVE R. HOLLIN

In this chapter the focus is on the way in which we seek to understand bad behaviour. Two basic positions, that which focuses on the individual and that which focuses on the environment, will be outlined and contrasted. The proposition will be advanced that the preferred type of explanation will directly influence the way in which efforts are directed to change bad behaviour. In this light, examples of different approaches to changing behaviour will be discussed. However, it is important at the outset to clarify the meaning of the term 'bad behaviour' in the context of school discipline. A number of researchers have addressed this question and it is therefore to their work that we turn first.

What is bad behaviour?

A number of terms are synonymous with bad behaviour; the following selection has been culled from several texts and papers on the topic of school discipline – *disorderly behaviour*, *conduct disorder*, *disruptive behaviour*, *delinquency*, *misbehaviour*, *deviant behaviour*, and *maladaptive behaviour*. All of these are familiar terms, but what exactly do they mean? A number of studies have attempted to specify the types of behaviour that might be classified under one of the above terms. Wickman (1974a) carried out a survey (in American schools) asking teachers to submit a list of behaviour problems that they had encountered during their professional careers. The teachers provided a list containing no fewer than 428 items, although when duplications were eliminated this figure was reduced to a final list of 185 separate items of undesirable behaviour. Wickman then assembled these various behaviours into seven different groups: a summary is given in Table 6.1.

This is an extensive list, but do the teachers see all these behaviours as equally problematic? To answer this question, Wickman (1974b) carried out a second piece of work in which teachers were asked to rate the seriousness of the types of behaviour shown in Table 6.1. While, as will be discussed presently, there were differences among teachers, Wickman summarized the seriousness ratings as shown in Table 6.2.

In concluding, Wickman makes the observation that the teachers'

Table 6.1 **Groups of bad behaviours**

GROUP 1: *Variations of general standards of morality and integrity*
  Stealing
  Dishonesty (e.g. lying, cheating)
  Immorality (e.g. bad physical habits, unclean thoughts)
  Profanity (e.g. swearing)
  Smoking
  Unlawfulness

GROUP 2: *Transgressions against authority*
  Disobedience
  Disrespect
  Defiance
  Impertinence
  Refusal to follow instructions and commands

GROUP 3: *Violations of general school regulations*
  Truancy
  Lateness
  Irregular attendance
  Taking school property home
  Vandalism

GROUP 4: *Violations of classroom rules*
  Disorderliness (e.g. unnecessary noise, not complying with routines)
  Restlessness
  Interruptions
  Too social
  Whispering

GROUP 5: *Violations of school work requirements*
  Inattention and lack of concentration
  Lack of interest and indifference
  Carelessness (e.g. unreliability, lack of pride in work)
  Laziness (e.g. lack of effort, procrastination)

GROUP 6: *Difficulties with other children*
  Annoying other children (e.g. fighting, bullying)
  Telling tales
  Disregards of the rights of other children
  Getting other children into trouble
  Interfering with the work of other children

GROUP 7: *Undesirable personality traits*
  Negativisms (e.g. stubborn, sulky)
  Unacceptable social manners (e.g. impudence, rude and impolite)
  Self-indulgencies (e.g. selfish, unsupporting)
  Arrogance (e.g. overbearing, boastful)
  Diffidence (e.g. bashful, too timid)
  Evasions (e.g. insincere, thoughtless)
  Interference (e.g. destructiveness, curiosity)
  Lack of emotional control (e.g. temper, crying)
  Undesirable mental states (e.g. dissatisfied, resentful)
  Unclean habits and personal appearance
  Lack of pride in self

Source: after Wickman, 1974a.

*Table 6.2   **Teachers' views on the seriousness of bad behaviour***

Stealing, Untruthfulness, Cheating, Sex problems, Disobedience, Impertinence, Defiance, Temper outbursts, Impudence, Rudeness, Truancy

More serious than:
Disorderly in class, Inattentiveness, Lack of interest in work, Carelessness, Laziness, Unreliability

More serious than:
Domineering, Attracting attention, Sullenness, Interrupting, Meddlesomeness

More serious than:
Shyness, Unsocialness, Sensitivity, Fearfulness, Suspiciousness, Imaginative lying, Dreaminess

Source: after Wickman, 1974b.

view of the seriousness of the bad behaviour is in direct relation to the impact the behaviour of the pupils has on them both as people *and* as teachers. In other words: 'The problems which transgress the teachers' moral sensitivities and authority or which frustrate their immediate teaching purposes are regarded as relatively more serious than problems which affect for the most part only the welfare of the individual child' (Wickman, 1974b, p. 37).

Findings from similar British research have been discussed by Tattum (1982). With the emphasis on violent behaviour, as shown in Table 6.3, Tattum notes the conclusions of a national survey in maintained primary, middle, and secondary schools in England and Wales.

It is clear from the above that the term *bad behaviour* – or, indeed, substitute the term of your choice – covers a multitude of sins. It is also clear that, to a greater or lesser extent, such behaviours are problematic on a number of fronts: they are problematic because they provoke and offend members of the teaching profession; they are problematic because they are detrimental to the educational progress

*Table 6.3   **Violent and disruptive behaviour in schools in England and Wales***

Physical attacks on other children
Disruptive behaviour
Truancy
Verbal abuse towards teachers
Vandalism
Extortion
Breaking and entering school property
Gang violence
Attacks on teachers and other adults
Racial violence

Source: after Tattum, 1982.

of the 'bad child'; they are problematic because such behaviours and associated educational failures may well have untoward effects later in the child's life; they are problematic because they may hinder and disrupt the educational and social progress of the 'good children' who share a classroom with the 'bad children'. In short, bad behaviours of the type discussed above are a threat to good discipline and require effective management. However, in order to formulate effective management strategies we need to be clear about the causes of these bad behaviours – just where do they come from? There is a large research literature on the types of behaviour detailed in Table 6.1 – generally referred to as *conduct disorders* (Herbert, 1987) – which allows some statements to be made on the topic of aetiology. The studies of the aetiology of bad behaviour fall into two broad schools: the first takes the child as the focus of attention, the second concentrates on the social context in which the child's behaviour takes place. My brief in this chapter is to consider the latter, but for the sake of contrast it is necessary to discuss briefly the former.

Focus on the child

Genetic and biological accounts

The view that behavioural disorders can be accounted for in terms of physiological functioning, in essence by biological reductionism, is a very ancient idea. However, contemporary research has begun to investigate in depth the role of physiological factors in behaviour generally and disorderly behaviour in particular. In considering this issue it is helpful to distinguish between two types of genetic effect: a *pathological* effect, in which a particular genetic configuration causes, for want of a better term, some malfunction in development; and a *variation* effect which gives rise to differences in the 'normal' population. For example, it seems probable that pathalogical genes play a role in some organic disorders as well as in some of the major psychoses (e.g. schizophrenia). Similarly, chromosomal variations can result in congenital abnormalities. However, with regard to behaviours of the type shown in Table 6.1, there is little, if any, evidence to suggest that they can be accounted for by either a pathological or a varietal genetic effect. Most certainly in the absence of known pathological genetic effects, the notion of a genetic basis to 'bad behaviour' remains hypothetical at the present time. Having said that, it is important to be aware of the research findings that suggest the possibility of a genetic component in extreme antisocial and criminal behaviour (e.g. Rowe and Osgood, 1984).

As genes function through complex biochemical systems – involving enzymes, hormones, neurotransmitters and so on – another strand of research has looked at the role of such factors in problem behaviour.

Some studies have suggested that variations in biochemical function-ing correlate with pathological conditions such as autism (e.g. Young, et al., 1982), while others have explored similar areas for conduct disorders (e.g. Rogenes, et al., 1982) and for delinquency (e.g. Trasler, 1987). It is, however, a moot point whether certain patterns of biochemical functioning indicate a broader picture of brain disorder of some type as yet unknown; or are a specific marker for a particular behavioural pattern; or are a variation of normal functioning. Indeed, any biochemical theorizing is hazardous given both the research difficulties and the problem of distinguishing correlational and causal relationships between biological functioning and behaviour. Another problem, as Rowe and Osgood (1984) have observed, is that in much social science there is a suspicion of explanations which rely upon or incorporate genetic explanations for behaviour. However, it is of course *un*scientific to ignore evidence in any relevant sphere; to be interested in behaviour and neglect brain–behaviour relationships is short-sighted in the extreme. It seems highly likely that present and future research in psychopharmacology will contribute to our under-standing of behaviour, both good and bad.

Psychological accounts

There are as many psychological accounts of bad behaviour as there are theories in psychology. Each theory has its own particular thrust, its own style of research, and points of contact and opposition with other psychological theories. In an admittedly Procrustean manner, distinctions can be made between psychodynamic theories, cognitive theories, developmental theories, learning and behavioural theories, and personality theories. It is impossible here even to begin to summarize the contribution made by theorists working within each of these traditions to our understanding of bad behaviour: however, to make a point, consider briefly the ideas of theorists such as Bowlby, Piaget, Kohlberg, and Eysenck.

The role of parental attachment

Following a tradition that can be traced back to Freud and beyond, Bowlby (1953, 1971) laid great stress on the role of maternal care in the child's first years of life as a precursor of his or her future mental health. Bowlby argued that in many cases the cause of bad behaviours – exemplified by an 'affectionless character' marked by superficial relationships, an uncaring attitude towards other people, delinquency, poor concentration, and so on – stems from a failure to form a stable attachment with a mother-figure during very early childhood. Any disruption of the bonding between child and mother-figure is seen as impairing the child's emotional and personal development, leading to later bad behaviour. The cause of the bad behaviour can, therefore, be traced to two sources: the quality of parenting that the child experiences, and the child's own psychological functioning. Bowlby's views have, of course, instigated a lively debate, particularly around the role and importance of attachment and bonding (Rutter, 1981; Sluckin, et al., 1983).

Morals, cognition, and personality

Another psychological approach, synonymous with names such as Jean Piaget, Jerome Bruner, and Lawrence Kohlberg, focuses not so much on parental attachment as on the child's cognitive and moral development. The thrust of this theoretical approach is on the way the child perceives, understands, and constructs their world. Thus, for Piaget, the child actively attempts to make sense of his or her environment and so adapt to their surroundings: simply, this process of adaptation is guided and directed by the child's cognitive structures, or *schemas*, of their environment. As children mature through distinct developmental stages, so their cognitive structures become more and more complex. The children's behaviour is directed by their cognitive map of the world and so it follows that the information from which the map is drawn is crucially important. If the child is faced with an inconsistent or incoherent social world, or one lacking in stimulation, then the child's schema will become more and more idiosyncratic. Thus bad behaviour is the result of a lack of congruence in the cognitive structures of those involved: the teacher has one way of seeing and understanding the world, the child a different way: the differences in their behaviour as guided by their respective schema gives rise to problems. Kohlberg, like Piaget, argues that moral reasoning develops in a sequential fashion as the child attains maturity. In the initial stages moral reasoning is concrete in orientation, being concerned with deferring to authority, avoiding punishment, and satisfying one's own needs and wishes. However, with maturity comes a growing sense of social responsibility and an acknowledgement of the rights of others in society. In this view the relationship between the process of moral reasoning and the content of one's moral code needs to be separated: it is perfectly possible to be able to argue eloquently about moral issues, yet hold a hedonistic set of moral values. Yet further, the relationship between morality and behaviour is not always predictable: a number of well-known experiments in psychology have shown that people will behave in ways that they believe to be wrong (Asch, 1956; Milgram, 1963).

While moral reasoning is one aspect of cognition, a cognitive account of bad behaviour would necessarily be extensive, covering areas such as intellectual functioning, self-concept, social cognition, attributional style and so on: interested readers are referred to texts by Quay and Werry (1986), Quay (1987) and, with an emphasis on delinquency, by Ross and Fabiano (1985). However, the point to be made here is that this type of explanation for bad behaviour places the cause of the behaviour on some complex system *within* the child. Some theoretical accounts seek to incorporate more than one type of internal system. Hans Eysenck (1970) has formulated a theory that suggests that through genetic endowment some individuals are born with central and autonomic nervous systems which affect their ability to learn from, or more properly to *condition to*, environmental stimuli. Conditionability, in turn, sets patterns of behaviour that define the individual's *personality*. The thrust of Eysenck's theory, as far as antisocial behaviour is concerned, is that children learn to control bad behaviour through the development of a 'conscience': this conscience, Eysenck maintains, is a set of conditioned emotional responses to environmental events associated with (i.e. conditioned to) antisocial behaviour. For example, the misbehaving child is reprimanded by an adult, the fear and pain this brings is associated with the antisocial act, thereby making the behaviour less likely to recur in the future – and so the process of socialization is underway. The speed and efficiency of the individual's socialization, according to Eysenck, are related to that person's personality. Eysenck has defined two personality dimensions – *extraversion/introversion* and *neuroticism/stability* – crucial to the development of a conscience. The theory predicts that certain personality characteristics – specifically high extraversion and high neuroticism – are related to less efficient conditionability: individuals who display these specific personality traits are predicted to be less socialized and more likely to be antisocial (Eysenck and Gudjonsson, 1989). There is some empirical evidence in support of this theoretical account (see Hollin, 1989, for a review). The important point to note with Eysenck's theory is that while it has an emphasis on the person, it includes environmental events as playing a role in the process of socialization.

Note the role of environmental influences on behaviour is also to be found in Michael Argyle's account of socially skilled behaviour. This then brings us to explanations that focus on social factors in accounting for an individual's behaviour.

Focus on social accounts

Social skills

Like most other creatures, humans are social animals. The smooth functioning of our world depends on our ability as a species to communicate effectively with each other. We need to be able to inform other people of our wishes and intentions, and we must be receptive to similar messages from other people. In order to communicate effectively humans have evolved a complex *verbal* language, including both the spoken and written word. However, like most other animals, humans have also developed a highly sophisticated communication system that relies on *non-verbal* language.

Argyle (1983) describes the many facets of non-verbal communication, including bodily contact, the use of gesture and posture, facial expression, eye contact, and manipulation of appearance through clothing and cosmetics. While there are many subtleties to both verbal and non-verbal communication, there are two points to note. First, each person should be able to use their communication skills in a coordinated manner, so that their eye contact, posture, gesture, speech and so on, mesh in a smooth, uniform style to maximize their chances of successfully communicating their feelings and intentions. Second, with an emphasis on the social aspects of social skills, the passage of communication between two people should ebb and flow in a synchronized manner: like two skilled tennis players, those involved in communication should, according to the rules of the game, move both to make their shot and then to anticipate the return signalled by their opponent's movements. Thus the 'micro' behaviours of verbal and non-verbal communication combine to form complex amalgams of 'macro' behaviour – social skills such as holding a conversation and being assertive – that are required to communicate with other people. This shared level of communication then allows us to achieve social goals such as having friends, being an effective teacher, maintaining a long-term relationship, or being a parent.

Argyle suggests that the socially skilled person, in a given social situation, calls on three distinct aspects of social functioning. *Social perception* skills allow us to 'decode' the signals from the other person: for example, we can recognize when someone is happy, sad, concerned, or angry from their verbal and non-verbal behaviour. Thus a socially perceptive person is aware of which messages to look for and attend to, and understands the shared meaning of those messages. The next step in the sequence Argyle terms *translation*: here the person is faced with the task of translating their perception into action. The social communications from the world around us must be evaluated according to the rules of the situation in order to decide on an appropriate response. In essence, this is social problem solving: we must consider the options we can take, evaluate their likely consequences, and select the best course of action. The final part of Argyle's scheme demands that we have the *response* skills to put our selected course of action into operation. The socially skilled person must have command over their own verbal and non-verbal performance in order to behave in (as they judge it) an appropriate manner. Of course, not every social situation we meet requires careful scrutiny and evaluation; we encounter some situations so often that our actions become habitual and do not need careful planning. Indeed, if we had to think our way through every situation as though we were meeting it for the first time life would be very slow. The socially skilled person can quickly negotiate most situations without too much strain, it is when we find ourselves in unfamiliar or complex situations that we tend to find interaction difficult and stressful.

As this is a social account of behaviour it must take into account social factors and, of course, the main social influence is the behaviour of other people. Argyle suggests that the responses we make will have an effect on our social world in that others will perceive our actions, make their decisions, and in turn respond to us. The socially skilled person will be able to perceive this *feedback* on their response so as to understand the effect of their behaviour on the other person, judge the effectiveness of their actions, and translate this new information into a new response. Thus Argyle proposes a dynamic interaction between the individual and his or her social world: our behaviour is constantly changing and shifting as the people and the situation change, while people and situations change as a consequence of our behaviour. Understanding of the complexities of the processes involved in social skills is continually advancing; Argyle (1986) offers a concise summary of recent research.

When it comes to using explanations of this type to account for bad behaviour the immediate question is whether the social skills of children who display bad behaviour are any different from those of good children.

Social skills and bad behaviour

Discovering the nature of the relationship between social skills and bad behaviour is a difficult task. One of my own long-standing research interests lies in the relationship between delinquency and social skills (Henderson and Hollin, 1983, 1986; Hollin, 1990a), and a brief discussion of this area illustrates some of the general issues involved.

Beginning with social perception, there is evidence to suggest that, compared to non-delinquents, aggressive young people search for and take notice of fewer social cues from their environment (Slaby and Guerra, 1988); that they are more likely to interpret the actions of other children in a hostile fashion, mistakenly attributing aggressive intent to the actions of others (Stefanek et al., 1987); and that they are more likely to make mistakes in recognition of non-verbal cues such as facial expression (McCown et al., 1986). With regard to translation skills, again studies have pointed to a limited social problem solving ability in both delinquents (Freedman et al., 1978) and aggressive children and adolescents (Spivack et al., 1976). This limited social problem solving extends to the ability to generate only a limited range of potential courses of action; the tendency to produce antisocial response alternatives; and to select the antisocial option as their preferred course of action (Dodge and Crick, 1990). In addition, this limited social problem solving ability is accompanied by the view that antisocial behaviour is acceptable, legitimate conduct (Slaby and

Guerra, 1988). Finally, there is some evidence to suggest that, on average, delinquents display less competent social response skills than non-delinquents (Spence, 1981).

This body of research evidence convincingly demonstrates that some (but not all) aggressive and delinquent children and adolescents have social skills difficulties. However, the issue then arises of the nature of the relationship between social competence and bad behaviour: is the bad behaviour caused by the limited social ability, or is the delinquent behaviour and the limited social ability merely correlated, both being the product of some other causative agent? While the research evidence is limited, it seems unlikely that there is a simple cause and effect relationship between social skills ability and delinquency: social competence does not appear to be related to any significant degree with either type or frequency of delinquent behaviour (Hunter and Kelley, 1986). Thus, while it would be foolish to dismiss the idea that an explanation for delinquency must *consider* the role of social skills, it would be equally foolish to suggest that an explanation for delinquency lies solely in the child's level of social competence. This statement applies, to a greater or lesser extent, to all bad behaviour: it is generally the case that human behaviour is too complex for simple explanations.

If it is too simple to account for bad behaviours in terms of moral development, or biological functioning, or social competence, then what is needed? There are two avenues of approach: the first is to construct complex models based on causative interrelationships between biological factors, intelligence, cognitive functioning, moral development and so on; the second is to move to the environment in the search for the causes of bad behaviour.

Social process and social structure

In sociology texts the distinction is often made between social processes and social structures: theories that emphasize the former take the view that behaviour is best explained in terms of the interactions between people and societal processes; the latter style of theorizing, on the other hand, is concerned with the effects on the individual of the strata that exist within society. Both of these social approaches have the advantage over purely psychological theories in that they seek to elaborate on what many psychological approaches simply refer to as 'the environment'. (Conversely, they can often be criticized for neglecting the role of factors such as biological and psychological functioning.) Thus social process theories are, for example, concerned with the role of family relationships, peer group relations, and the process of education in explaining behaviour; while social structure theories may be concerned with social class, political and economic struggle between groups within society, and the unequal distribution of wealth and power within society. Explanations based on social process and social structure theories have, of course, been advanced to account for many human actions. For the present purpose a number of areas have been selected to illustrate the explanatory force of social process and social structure accounts of bad behaviour.

The family

Looking first to family influences, it has been established beyond reasonable doubt that the family can play a crucial role in the aetiology of bad behaviour (Loeber and Stouthamer-Loeber, 1986; West, 1982). The important predictors of juvenile conduct problems uncovered by a vast amount of research include factors such as poor, harsh or erratic discipline, parental conflict, poor supervision of the child, and parental attitudes and actions that condone the child's bad behaviour. Thus parents who are antipathetic or even hostile to social processes such as education and maintaining social and legal boundaries are unlikely to transmit values conducive to the child's engaging in those social processes. The erratic rewards and punishments delivered by the parents make it unlikely that the child will be strongly motivated towards academic achievement. This is hardly revolutionary: it is long established that there are strong relationships between parents' feelings about school and intellectual attainment, and their feelings about and participation in their child's educational progress (e.g. Christopher, 1967). Thus, accepting the force of these arguments, bad behaviour can be seen to have its roots in the quality – *not* the number of parents – of parenting as evinced by erratic discipline, parental disharmony, and the modelling and approval of bad behaviour.

Peer group

If the family can be a source of modelling and reinforcement for bad behaviour, then the same can equally be said for the role of the peer group. Of course, family and peer group can overlap: Farrington and West (1990) found that the delinquent acts committed by young males with brothers of a similar age were, indeed, most likely to be carried out with their brother. It is clear that, particularly for children under 10 years of age, most antisocial acts are carried out in small groups of two or three young people. Thus acts of bad behaviour, particularly those that involve some status offence, can convincingly be portrayed as *social* acts, performed in the company of a like-minded peer group and with social payoffs such as approval and improved peer group status. However, these social payoffs for bad behaviour cannot be assumed to extend to the classroom: a number of studies (e.g. Reid, 1984) have shown that persistent absentees have few friends at school and tend to be unpopular among their peers. Thus some young people may be accepted and popular within a delinquent counter-culture, yet be rejected by and unpopular among social, conforming children and adolescents.

Peer group values are another important consideration when seeking to explain the behaviour of individual members of the group. Such values may, for example, be manifest in the sex roles found in different adolescent subcultures. In some groups of young people academic effort and performance are seen as feminine, therefore boys who do well educationally run the risk of being outlawed from their male peers: the peer group values run counter to any motivation to succeed academically. Conversely, in other adolescent groups educational achievement is considered a masculine pursuit. Thus young women who wish to study hard to follow a career that demands further education may find their femininity called into question. As with the outlawed males, these peer group influences may pull young women away from educational goals, creating a fear of success: this fear may push them towards achieving social approval for the rejection of academic targets and compliance with group norms which favour bad behaviour (Weinreich-Haste, 1978).

The school

As well as family and peer influences, the school itself can also be an important factor in understanding bad behaviour. This can be seen, for example, in some of the research findings on persistent absenteeism. A number of studies have shown that children and adolescents who spend long periods away from school believe that their teachers are condescending to them and their work (e.g. Reid, 1985). Wickman (1974a) wryly comments that there can be little doubt about the type of discipline maintained by the teacher who frowned upon the following as examples of bad behaviour: the child whispering when s/he should be working, not putting pens down when told to, raising hands when standing, asking to leave the room when not necessary, and talking aloud in the library. This catalogue introduces an important variable into the equation – the behaviour of the teacher.

If the child's bad behaviour can be thought of as social behaviour, so the teacher's actions in the classroom can be considered in the same way. The teacher's social perception, decision-making, conception of social rules, understanding of the child's behaviour, and social skills interacts with those same elements of their pupils' behaviour. Where there is concordance between teacher and pupil then, like the two skilled tennis players maintaining the flow of their game, successful and mutually reinforcing social exchanges can take place. On the other hand, if one player is playing according to the rules of lawn tennis but the other is playing squash, then the result is at best chaos, and at the worst open conflict. It is important to emphasize that this level of analysis does not invoke explanations in terms of psychopathology – in either teacher or pupil! – but suggests instead that both sets of behaviour are rational and understandable within the social context of each individual. It is only when the individuals are forced together that problems arise: the bad behaviour is only 'bad' when other people have the power to be able to deliver that verdict. This type of explanation is, of course, exactly that which falls within the frame of reference of labelling theory. Becker (1963) crystallizes the argument:

Social groups create deviance by making rules whose infractions constitute deviance, and by applying those rules to particular people and labeling them as outsiders. From this point of view, deviance is not a quality of the act a person commits, but rather a consequence of the application by others of rules and sanctions to an 'offender'. The deviant is one to whom the label has successfully been applied; deviant behavior is behavior that people so label (p. 9).

Once the label has been conferred there is, in Erikson's (1962) terminology, a 'formal confrontation' between the deviant and representatives of the community. This confrontation serves the function of assigning the person a special role which redefines his or her standing in the community and labels them as 'bad' or as 'maladjusted', or whatever label the current, socially acceptable, jargon confers. For example, as Berg, Brown, and Hullin (1988) have documented, the failure to attend school can result in confrontation between children and agencies of the state, culminating in court appearances, referral to truancy projects, and the re-defining of the young person as a 'truant'.

In terms of the immediate educational setting, it is clear from the work of Michael Rutter and his colleagues that different schools have different characteristics which, in turn, promote different rates of bad behaviour. In their study of inner-city secondary schools in London, Rutter et al. (1979) found a range of organizational factors related to the schools and their operation that were correlated with pupil conduct. These factors included the degree of emphasis placed on academic matters, the school's system of reward and punishment, the pupils' participation and responsibility for school activities, and the stability of teaching and peer groups within the school. This organizational aspect suggests that it is not enough to end the analysis of bad behaviour at the point of interaction between the child or adolescent and his or her immediate environment. The analysis must be pushed further, posing the issue of the structural forces acting on parents and teachers and, to a greater or lesser degree, influencing their actions and ultimately the quality of their interactions with the young people entrusted to their care.

Economics and politics

In his telling analysis of the social aspects of truancy and absenteeism, Reid (1985) offers a summary of what is known about these two

Table 6.4   **Home and social backgrounds of truants and school absentees**

1. Families at the lower end of the social scale; fathers typically in semi-skilled or unskilled work.
2. Families in which parental (both paternal and maternal) unemployment or erratic employment is the norm.
3. Families on low incomes.
4. Families living in overcrowded conditions.
5. Families living in poor standard housing.
6. Poor material conditions within the home.
7. Families where the children are supplied with free school meals.
8. Families where the parents are passive victims of a dreadful environment and unsure of their constitutional rights.

Source: after Reid, 1985.

particular forms of bad behaviour. From Reid's long list of the home and social backgrounds of truants and school absentees, the selection given in Table 6.4 offers a small insight into the lives of the parents of children who exhibit these forms of bad behaviour. As Reid's findings bear a marked similarity to those known to be associated with delinquent behaviour (e.g. West, 1982), it seems likely that the conditions noted in Table 6.4 are consistent with a range of bad behaviours.

If conditions of the type outlined in Table 6.4 are considered in conjunction with what has already been outlined about the role of the family in promoting bad behaviour, then a position is reached in which such pupils: 'Do not normally receive proper parental encouragement and support at home, emanate from backgrounds where books or learning are valued or find themselves provided with the financial back-up necessary to clothe and equip them properly for their education' (Reid, 1985, p. 53).

It is clearly not satisfactory that the proverbial buck stops at the parents: is it a coincidence that the parents who have badly behaved children are predominantly from the lower social classes, have low financial income, live in areas of poor housing, and are likely to be unemployed? Indeed, is it likely that the schools which serve the children of these disadvantaged families will be of the highest educational standards? Of course, none of this is coincidental and to understand why not everyone within a given society enjoys the same standard of living we must look to theories of social structure. There are many approaches to this task, which by definition must entail a political and economic analysis of society. This level of analysis reaches beyond the educational system, it must consider the place of education within the greater social structure; and ask what, in a sociological sense, the educational system is attempting to achieve. It is perhaps the educational 'countertheorists' who come closest to the spirit of this level of analysis in advancing, for example, the views that traditional approaches to the education of disturbed children have been dehumanizing, exclusive, labelling, and serve the ends of political exploitation (see Macmillan and Kavale, 1986).

One of the problems with this much broader level of analysis is that it demands a different way of thinking, using different theoretical constructs, than most professionals in the 'people business' – such as teachers, psychologists, psychiatrists – are used to employing. When faced with a difficult child, most of us are trained to focus on that child's behaviour with perhaps some regard to the immediate environmental forces. What we are less familiar with is a structural analysis in which we understand that child's behaviour as a reflection of his or her place within a given political and economic system. A personal anecdote will perhaps make my point.

Mid-way through the time I spent writing this chapter I attended a conference in a small city in the south-east of England. As the conference stretched over a number of days, two colleagues (coincidentally both teachers) and myself took an afternoon off to explore the city. It was one of those very cold but beautifully clear January days, and the cathedral was quite splendid in the sharp sunlight. As we wandered around the outside of the cathedral we found ourselves in the grounds of a very famous independent school. Like the cathedral it too was a sight to behold: ancient yellow stone buildings, lawns, school notices about open days and sports events pinned to dark brown studded doors, the quad, the book-lined rooms glimpsed through leaded windows. In a tourist frame of mind, I meandered happily. Talking between themselves, I overheard one of my colleagues remark to the other that this was rather different to a comprehensive school in Birmingham in which they had both taught. Surrounded by the evidence, I realized just how absolutely true this must be: the educational experience of the young people at that school is surely so different to that of their counterparts in Birmingham as to defy comparison. Why should such diversity exist within the same educational system (if, indeed, one accepts that they are part of the same system)? What role do such schools play, by their very existence, in the broader social structure in this country? What part in society are the products of these schools being groomed to play?

Managing bad behaviour

Focus on the child

As noted earlier, bad behaviour in school is not to anyone's advantage and therefore must be managed. Whether implicit or explicit, the management techniques employed will depend on the way in which the bad behaviour is understood; that is, either by focusing on the child, or by focusing on the environment, or both. Considering first the child as the focus for attention, the distinction can be made between two approaches to understanding the child's behaviour. The first, in essence, holds the child responsible for his or her behaviour: thus the child might be said to be *choosing* to play truancy, or *deliberately* being aggressive, or *wilfully* being disobedient in class. This type of explanation demands that the child is held to account for their actions and, if he or she freely chooses to break the rules, then sanctions must be brought to bear. These sanctions can take many forms ranging from detention, to corporal punishment, and to suspension and expulsion. This level of management is based on the notion of *deterrence*, of which there are two forms. *General deterrence* refers to the inhibiting effect of the sanctions on other members of the population: thus if the school population is aware that the penalty for truancy is detention, then that awareness should deter pupils from playing truancy. *Special deterrence* refers to the effects of the sanctions on the individual who experiences them personally: for example, the apprehended truant who spends his or her evenings in detention should come to see that the punishment outweighs the crime and, when future opportunities arise, will desist from truancy.

The problems with deterrence arise when sanctions fail to work. Once a school is committed to a policy of deterrence and that policy fails to be effective, then the only alternative that is consistent with the policy is to increase the severity of the sanctions. In other words, if pupils calculate that the payoffs for truancy are worth the risks of detention, then the system has to be modified so that the penalty outweighs the payoffs. Instead of detention for truancy, the equation is changed so that now truancy leads to expulsion and appearances in the juvenile court. However, the real crisis for this type of policy comes when even the most punitive sanctions fail either to lower the truancy rates, that is there is a failure of general deterrence; or fail to stop the individual truant from future acts of truancy, that is a failure of special deterrence. One way out of this dilemma is to widen the range of responsibility: so that while the pupil is held to be acting wilfully in disobeying the rules, the net of culpability is widened to include the pupil's parents or guardians and sanctions are implemented to punish them as well as their child.

There are two pressing issues with this type of explanation. First, is it correct that the child or adolescent (and their parents) acts from wilful intention when behaving badly? Second, while policies that exclude the child from school may solve the school's immediate problems, does this simply displace the problem to another sector of society – namely the social and legal services – rather than offering any long-standing solution that will be to the benefit of all concerned?

An alternative way of conceptualizing bad behaviour is to take a *determinist* stance: to see the bad behaviour as a product of some causal agent – biological, psychological, social, or a combination thereof – over which the individual has little or no control. While these causal agents vary from theory to theory, they all hold a common philosophy with regard to policies for managing bad behaviour – to intervene and offer a remedy for the cause of the ailment. The type of remedy depends, of course, on the factors perceived as giving rise to the bad behaviour.

Biological intervention

In the early stages of this chapter it was suggested that physiological factors may play a causal role in the aetiology and maintenance of some bad behaviours. If this is accepted, then it follows that some form of psychopharmacological intervention is called for to remedy the biological dysfunction and hence 'cure' the bad behaviour. There are many types of drugs – such as stimulants, antidepressants, sedatives, anticonvulsants, and neuroleptics – that can be used in this way. While the use of drugs is common in the treatment of major clinical disturbances, for example childhood psychosis and depression, they are also used with children and adolescents displaying conduct disorders such as aggressive behaviour and outbursts of rage. However, it should be noted that Gittelman and Kanner (1986) conclude their overview of this area with the suggestion that, in the main, 'There is no well-established pharmacotherapy of conduct disorders' (p. 474). None the less, it would seem probable that this is an area likely to receive increasingly greater attention as the research base relating to the biological basis of behaviour continues to grow.

Psychological intervention

There are as many, if not more, forms of psychological intervention as there are theories of psychology. Even the most brief glance through the literature suggests that nearly all have been tried with bad behaviour. The one thread that runs through most of these interventions is that they are based primarily on working with the child. Kazdin (1987) notes four styles of intervention widely used in this area: these are *individual psychotherapy*, *group psychotherapy*, *behaviour therapy*, and *problem-solving skills training*. Of course, each of these broad classes includes a plethora of different approaches: individual psychotherapy, for example, might include psychodynamic therapies, play therapy, non-directive psychotherapy, and so on. There are many accounts and reviews of each of these areas and, for those who wish to read further on these topics, a number of sources are noted: Kovacs and Paulauskas (1986) and Monahan (1989) provide overviews of the traditional psychotherapies; Ruggles and LeBlanc (1982) and Sabatino et al. (1983) discuss the behavioural management of discipline and classroom procedures; cognitive-behavioural theory and its applications, including traditional behaviour therapies and cognitive-behavioural therapies such as problem-solving skills training, moral education, and anger management, are discussed in texts by Hollin (1990b) and by Hughes and Hall (1989).

Moving towards a social explanation, although to some extent retaining a focus on the individual, interventions have been devised which focus on social skills: the technique of *social skills training* has been applied widely (Hollin and Trower, 1986a,b), with some emphasis on children (Matson and Ollendick, 1988). Social skills training can also address broader social issues associated with bad behaviour. *Peer group* interaction can be a target for social skills training and Furnham (1986) documents its successful use with a range of adolescent problems including disruption and isolation and withdrawal. Finally, the current trend is towards *multimodal programmes* that incorporate elements from different approaches, although usually from within the same broad theoretical school. For example, Glick and Goldstein (1987) devised a system termed *Aggression Replacement Training* that involves social skills training, problem solving training, anger control training, and moral education directed at the amelioration of aggressive and violent behaviour.

Focus on social factors

Family therapy

As discussed previously, it is undoubtedly the case that the family plays some role in bad behaviour. It follows therefore that some interventions have been pitched at the level of family change. There are many approaches to family therapy, however two approaches that are receiving particular attention at present are *parent management training* (PMT) and *functional family therapy* (FFT).

The aims of PMT are to change, through training, the style with which parents interact with their children. While originally designed for use with parents of young children, PMT has become popular in family work with older children. Simply, PMT concerns having the parents observe their child's behaviour; set targets for change with the child; and maintain a reinforcement system for achieving the required changes. Social problem-solving and skills training can be built into PMT as required. Such interventions have been used with even the most problematic behaviours (e.g. Serna, et al., 1986): although it appears that parents who have few positive social contacts outside the home with friends and relatives are less likely to be successful with PMT.

The basis of FFT is that any behaviour within a family system, including bad behaviour, serves some functional purpose for that family. This purpose may be one of maintaining some level of personal intimacy, or providing a means by which some level of frustration or anger can be relieved (Alexander and Parsons, 1982).

While there are some similarities between FFT and PMT, in FFT the focus is much sharper with respect to the style and quality of interactions between family members. The goals of the intervention are to increase the level and quality of communication between family members, to increase constructive problem-solving and negotiation, and to increase reciprocal reinforcement. The technique of *contingency contracting* is much used in FFT: this involves a written, negotiated statement that specifies the responsibilities of each family member for other members of the families, together with a clear listing of the rewards and penalties for performance in light of that agreed in the contract. While popular, successful FFT demands a high level of therapist skill in negotiating and facilitating communication within the family.

Schools and teachers

If, as intimated at the beginning of this chapter using the quote from Wickman, bad behaviour is behaviour that offends the teacher's moral sensitivity or frustrates immediate teaching goals, then perhaps the solution lies in changing the nature of the interaction between teacher and pupil. In this light, the Teacher–Child Interaction Project reported by Berger, Yule, and Wigley (1987) is of interest in that it attempted to 'foster positive teacher–child interaction as a means of reducing the mutual difficulties experienced by teachers and a proportion of children in their classes' (Berger et al., 1987, p. 90). The evaluation of the project revealed that there were some changes in the pupils' behaviour and that the teachers reported changes such as an increased liking for the particular children.

Other methods of managing bad behaviour concern styles of classroom management, the development of pastoral care, and the provision of special facilities for 'problem children' (Docking, 1980; Tattum, 1982). The use of on-site units to manage problem behaviour appears to be popular and, while able to claim some successes, this strategy is also capable of creating problems. A recent doctoral thesis by one of my post-graduate students (Sherriff, 1990) reported that on-site units can be beneficial in increasing student learning. However, Sherriff also found that on-site units run the risk of being a convenient 'dustbin' for problem children, alienating both the unit teachers and pupils from mainstream school – thereby labelling the pupils and disillusioning the unit's teachers.

Finally, there is the proposition of progress through radical changes in social, economic, and political structure. While perhaps changes of this type might have the most far-reaching effects, they are also likely to be the most difficult type of changes to implement as they run far beyond the individual pupil and, indeed, the educational system. It would be wrong to say that it is impossible to bring about such changes, although to bring about change at political and social levels demands skills of a very different nature to those possessed by the majority of teachers and psychologists.

Conclusion

As hinted at in this chapter, and explored elsewhere in this book, there are many ways of accounting for bad behaviour. I have attempted here to make the point that understanding such behaviour demands an analysis not just of the 'bad child', but an appreciation of the social context in which the behaviour takes place. Further, I have suggested that such a social analysis can be made at many levels beginning with the child's social skills, to the social judgements of those with whom the child interacts, moving then to peer group and family influences, and finally to the very fabric of the society of which child, family, school and all are members. Taking the view that analysis should precede intervention, I put the case that the type of procedures used to manage bad behaviour will depend on the level of analysis chosen. It is important to add that not everything is possible: much as we may want to change matters at a broad social level, we may have to settle for a narrower focus. It does not a jot of harm, however, to be aware of the broader context in which all behaviour takes place.

References

Alexander, J.F. and Parsons, B.V. (1982) *Functional Family Therapy*, Monterey, CA: Brooks/Cole.

Argyle, M. (1983) *The Psychology of Interpersonal Behaviour* 4th edn., Harmondsworth, Middlesex: Penguin.

Argyle, M. (1986) 'Social skills and the analysis of situations and conversations', in C.R. Hollin and P. Trower (eds) *Handbook of Social Skills Training, Vol. 2: Clinical Applications and New Directions*, Oxford: Pergamon, pp. 185–216.

Asch, S. (1956) 'Studies of the independence and submission to group pressure: a minority of one against a unanimous majority', *Psychological Monographs*, 70: 416–688.

Becker, H.S. (1963) *Outsiders: Studies in the Sociology of Deviance*, New York: Free Press.

Berg, I., Brown, I. and Hullin, R. (1988) *Off School, In Court: an Experimental and Psychiatric Investigation of Severe School Attendance Problems*, New York: Springer-Verlag.

Berger, M., Yule, W. and Wigley, V. (1987)'The Teacher–Child Interaction Project (TCIP): Implementing behavioural programmes with troublesome individual children in the primary school', in K. Wheldall (ed.) *The Behaviourist in the Classroom*, London: Allen and Unwin, pp. 90–111.

Bowlby, J. (1953) *Child Care and the Growth of Love*, Harmondsworth, Middlesex: Penguin.

Bowlby, J. (1971) *Attachment and Loss, Vol. 1: Attachment*, Harmondsworth, Middlesex: Penguin.

Christopher, S. (1967) 'Parental relationships and value orientation as factors in academic achievement', *Personnel and Guidance Journal*, 45: 921–5.

Docking, J.W. (1980) *Control and Discipline in Schools: Perspectives and Approaches*, London: Harper and Row.

Dodge, K.A. and Crick, N.R. (1990) 'Social information-processing bases of aggressive behavior in children', *Personality and Social Psychology Bulletin*, 16: 8–22.

Erikson, K.T. (1962) 'Notes on the sociology of deviance', *Social Problems*, 9: 307–14.

Eysenck, H.J. (1970) *The Structure of Human Personality* 3rd edn., London: Methuen.

Eysenck, H.J., and Gudjonsson, G.H. (1989) *The Causes and Cures of Criminality*, New York: Plenum.

Farrington, D.P. and West, D.J. (1990) 'The Cambridge study in delinquent development: a long-term follow-up of 411 London males', in H.J. Kerner and G. Kaiser (eds) *Criminality: Personality, Behaviour, Life History*, New York: Springer-Verlag, pp. 115–38.

Freedman, B.J., Rosenthal, L., Donahoe, C.P., Schlundt, D.G. and McFall, R.M. (1978) 'A social-behavioral analysis of skills deficits in delinquent and non-delinquent adolescent boys', *Journal of Consulting and Clinical Psychology*, 46: 1448–62.

Furnham, A. (1986) 'Social skills training with adolescents and young adults', in C.R. Hollin and P. Trower (eds) *Handbook of Social Skills Training, Vol. 1: Applications Across the Life Span*, Oxford: Pergamon, pp. 33–57.

Gittelman, R. and Kanner, A. (1986) 'Psychopharmacotherapy', in H.C. Quay and J.S. Werry (eds) *Psychopathological Disorders of Childhood*, 3rd edn. New York: Wiley, pp. 455–94.

Glick, B. and Goldstein, A.P. (1987) 'Aggression replacement training', *Journal of Counselling and Development*, 65: 356–67.

Henderson, M. and Hollin, C.R. (1983) 'A critical review of social skills training with young offenders', *Criminal Justice and Behavior*, 10, 316–41.

Henderson, M. and Hollin, C.R. (1986) 'Social skills training and delinquency', in C.R. Hollin and P. Trower (eds) *Handbook of Social Skills Training, Vol. 1: Applications Across the Life Span*, Oxford: Pergamon, pp. 79–101.

Herbert, M. (1987) *Conduct Disorders of Childhood and Adolescence*, 2nd edn, Chichester: Wiley.

Hollin, C.R. (1989) *Psychology and Crime: An Introduction to Criminological Psychology*, London: Routledge.

Hollin, C.R. (1990a) 'Social skills training with delinquents: a look at the evidence and some recommendations for practice', *British Journal of Social Work*, 20: 483–93.

Hollin, C.R. (1990b) *Cognitive-Behavioral Interventions with Young Offenders*, Elmsford, NY: Pergamon.

Hollin, C.R. and Trower, P. (eds) (1986a) *Handbook of Social Skills Training, Vol. 1: Applications Across the Life Span*, Oxford: Pergamon.

Hollin, C.R. and Trower, P. (eds) (1986b) *Handbook of Social Skills Training, Vol. 2: Clinical Applications and New Directions*, Oxford: Pergamon Press.

Hughes, J.N. and Hall, R.J. (eds) (1989) *Cognitive Behavioral Psychology in the Schools: A Comprehensive Handbook*, New York: Guildford Press.

Hunter, N. and Kelley, C.K. (1986) 'Examination of the validity of the Adolescent Problem Inventory among incarcerated delinquent adolescents', *Journal of Consulting and Clinical Psychology*, 54: 301–302.

Kazdin, A.E. (1987) 'Treatment of antisocial behaviour in children: Current status and future directions', *Psychological Bulletin*, 102: 187–203.

Kovacs, M. and Paulauskas, S. (1986) 'The traditional psychotherapies', in H.C. Quay and J.S. Werry (eds) *Psychopathological Disorders of Childhood*, 3rd edn. New York: Wiley, pp. 496–552.

Loeber, R. and Stouthamer-Loeber, M. (1986) 'Family factors as correlates and predictors of juvenile conduct problems and delinquency', in M. Tonry and N. Morris (eds) *Crime and Justice: an Annual Review of Research, Vol. 7*, Chicago: University of Chicago Press, pp. 129–49.

Macmillan, D.L. and Kavale, K.A. (1986) 'Educational intervention', in H.C. Quay and J.S. Werry (eds) *Psychopathological Disorders of Childhood*, 3rd edn, New York: Wiley pp. 583–621.

Matson, J.L. and Ollendick, T.H. (1988) *Enhancing Children's Social Skills: Assessment and Training*, Elmsford, NY: Pergamon.

McCown, W., Johnson, J. and Austin, S. (1986) 'Inability of delinquents to recognize facial affects', *Journal of Social Behavior and Personality*, 1: 489–96.

Milgram, S. (1963) 'Behavioral study of obedience', *Journal of Abnormal and Social Psychology*, 67: 371–8.

Monahan, R.T. (1989) 'Individual and group psychotherapy', in R.D. Lyman, S. Prentice-Dunn and S. Gabel (eds) *Residential Inpatient Treatment of Children and Adolescents*, New York: Plenum, pp. 191–205.

Quay, H.C. (ed.). (1987) *Handbook of Juvenile Delinquency*, New York: Wiley.

Quay, H.C. and Werry, J.S. (eds) (1986) *Psychopathological Disorders of Childhood*, 3rd edn, New York: Wiley.

Reid, K.(1984) 'Some social, psychological and educational aspects related to persistent school absenteeism', *Research in Education*, 31: 63–82.

Reid, K. (1985) *Truancy and School Absenteeism*, London: Hodder and Stoughton.

Rogenes, G.A., Hernandez, J.M., Macedo, C.A. and Mitchell, E.L. (1982). 'Biochemical differences in children with conduct disorder socialized and undersocialized', *American Journal of Psychiatry*, 139: 307–11.

Ross, R.R. and Fabiano, E.A. (1985) *Time to Think: a Cognitive Model of Delinquency Prevention and Offender Rehabilitation*, Johnson City, TN: Institute of Social Sciences and Arts.

Rowe, D.C. and Osgood, D.W. (1984) 'Heredity and sociological theories of delinquency: a reconsideration', *American Sociological Review*, 49: 526–540.

Ruggles, T.R. and LeBlanc, J.M. (1982) 'Behavior analysis procedures in classroom teaching', in A.S. Bellack, M. Hersen, and A.E. Kazdin (eds) *International Handbook of Behavior Modification and Therapy*, New York: Plenum, pp. 959–96.

Rutter, M. (1981) *Maternal Deprivation Reassessed*, 2nd edn. Harmondsworth, Middlesex: Penguin Books.

Rutter, M., Maughan, B., Mortimore, P., Ouston, J. and Smith, A. (1979) *Fifteen Thousand Hours: Secondary Schools and Their Effects on Children*, London: Open Books.

Sabatino, D.A., Sabatino, A.C. and Mann, L. (1983) *Discipline and Behav-*

ioral Management: a Handbook of Tactics, Strategies, and Programs, Rockvill, MD: Aspen Systems Corporation.

Serna, L.A., Schumaker, J.B., Hazel, J.S. and Sheldon, J.B. (1986) 'Teaching reciprocal social skills to delinquents and their parents', *Journal of Clinical Child Psychology*, 15: 64–77.

Sherriff, I.H. (1990) *A Multi-Disciplinary Approach to the Management of Non-School Attendance*. Unpublished doctoral thesis, University of Leicester, Leicester.

Slaby, R.G. and Guerra, N.G. (1988) 'Cognitive mediators of aggression in adolescent offenders: 1. Assessment', *Developmental Psychology*, 24: 580–88.

Sluckin, W., Herbert, M. and Sluckin, A. (1983) *Maternal Bonding*, Oxford: Blackwell.

Spence, S.H. (1981) 'Differences in social skills performance between institutionalized juvenile male offenders and a comparable group of boys without offence records', *British Journal of Clinical Psychology*, 20: 163–71.

Spivack, G., Platt, J.J. and Shure, M.B. (1976) *The Problem-Solving Approach to Adjustment: A Guide to Research and Intervention*, San Francisco, CA: Jossey-Bass.

Stefanek, M.E., Ollendick, T.H., Baldock, W.P., Francis, G. and Yaeger, N.J. (1987) 'Self-statements in aggressive, withdrawn, and popular children', *Cognitive Research and Therapy*, 11: 229–39.

Tattum, D.P. (1982) *Disruptive Pupils in Schools and Units*, New York: Wiley.

Trasler,G. (1987) 'Biogenetic factors', in H.C. Quay (ed.) *Handbook of Juvenile Delinquency*, New York: Wiley, pp. 184–215.

West, D.J. (1982) *Delinquency: Its Roots, Careers and Prospects*, London: Heinemann.

Weinreich-Haste, H. (1978) 'Sex differences in "fear of success" among British students', *British Journal of Social and Clinical Psychology*, 17: 37–42.

Wickman, E.K. (1974a) 'Teachers' list of undesirable forms of behaviour', in P. Williams (ed.) *Behaviour Problems in School*, London: University of London Press, pp. 6–15.

Wickman, E.K. (1974b), 'Teachers' reactions to behavior problems of children', in P. Williams (ed.) *Behaviour Problems in School*, London: University of London Press, pp. 16–38.

Young, J.G., Cavanagh, M.E., Anderson, G.M., Shaywitz, A. and Cohen, D.J. (1982) 'Clinical neurochemistry of autism and associated disorders', *Journal of Autism and Developmental Disorders*, 12: 177–86.

PART TWO

Assessment

CHAPTER 7

The psychiatric examination of children with behaviour problems

PHILIP BARKER

Children's behaviours, and their behaviour problems, are very much context dependent. The psychiatric assessment of a child therefore involves a study not only of the child, but also of the child's social environment – especially home and school but also the wider context in which child, family and school exist. It is usually necessary to conduct several interviews to achieve this. While at least one individual interview with the child being assessed is essential, conclusions reached on the basis of that interview alone are likely to be at best limited and perhaps even incorrect.

Children with behaviour problems, more than some others, tend to be defensive. They may have little subjective sense of distress. Although the problem behaviours may be of great concern to those caring for or attempting to educate them, they themselves may be unconcerned; or they may even be getting vicarious satisfaction from their behaviour and the responses of others to it.

Background considerations

It is helpful, before carrying out any medical examination, to have some idea what one is looking for. So why do children develop behaviour disorders? In brief, we may say that such children have not been successfully trained to behave in a socially acceptable manner. The process of social development has somehow gone wrong. We usually find that we are dealing with a long-standing failure of socialization (Shamsie, 1981), rather than with a disorder afflicting a child who has hitherto been developing normally. In many cases the roots of the problem can be traced back to the first years, or even months, of life.

Children are not born with inherent drives towards socially acceptable behaviour; on the contrary, the standards of social behaviour that are acceptable in any society have to be learned. When we are faced with a child with a behaviour problem, we must therefore ask, 'Why has this child failed to learn and practise the accepted and generally desired norms of behaviour?' Finding the answer is seldom simple. Only rarely is it possible to identify one specific causative factor. Indeed behaviour disorders, like most child psychiatric disorders, are multifactorial in origin. We must look for a variety of possible factors, all of which must be thoroughly explored in the course of a comprehensive psychiatric assessment. These are:

1 Factors in the child
2 The interplay between child and parents
3 Factors in the family
4 Factors in the wider social environment, including, but not confined to, the school environment.

Factors in the child

Under this heading, we must consider the child's genetic make-up, biological status, emotional state and cognitive functioning. To come to a proper understanding of the child's current medical and emotional condition and social functioning, we need to know the child's developmental, medical and social history. How much of this information we can obtain from the child will depend on the child's age, memory, and general level of cognitive functioning. Also, some children are more forthcoming in providing information than others; and some, whether consciously or unconsciously, try to deceive us.

While much information may be obtained from older children and adolescents, it is essential also to obtain supplementary and confirmatory information on their developmental, medical and social history from independent sources, especially – but not necessarily exclusively – the parents.

The question of whether the child has been subject to abuse must also be considered. During the last two to three decades, increasing attention has been paid to the physical, sexual and emotional abuse of children, and the consequences of abuse. Not only has the prevalence of abuse, in its various forms, been shown to be much greater than most people had supposed, but its ill effects have also been recognized as being more widespread. Among these, behaviour problems are prominent. If a child is acting out in an antisocial way, and there is no obvious reason for this, the possibility should always be entertained that the child has been, or is currently being, abused in one way or another.

Children who are abused *physically* are most likely to act out by displaying physical aggression towards others. This may be both because the use of physical aggression has been modelled for them by their abusers, and also because of the feelings of anger, or rage, they are experiencing as a result of their abuse.

Sexually abused children's problem behaviours often include sexual acting out. They may display such sexualized behaviours as attempting to fondle others, exposing themselves, masturbating in public, using obscene gestures and making sexualized remarks to peers and adults.

Emotional abuse is a less clearly defined phenomenon. Its essence is the 'putting down' or degrading of children by constant criticism, blaming and devaluation by deeds or words or both. In the place of the affirmation and encouragement children require for healthy emotional development, their failings and shortcomings, real or imagined, are stressed, rather than their achievements, strengths and assets. Such children tend to show evidence of low self-esteem, which is often associated with behavioural difficulties. Children who consider themselves 'bad' are likely to act accordingly. The behaviourally disturbed child's self-esteem is thus something of which the psychiatrist will wish to get a sense during the assessment. Evidence of any form of past or current abuse will also be sought.

The vulnerability of children to adverse environments and dysfunctional rearing varies greatly. The reasons for this are not entirely clear, but some children – perhaps 20 per cent – seem to be able to survive whole combinations of risk factors and become socially well-adjusted individuals. On the other hand, some children seem specially at risk. As we will see, temperamental factors play a part. So also may other genetically determined personality features. Other important factors are intelligence level and the intactness of the central nervous system. The lower a child's level of assessed intelligence, the greater the chance that the child will show psychiatric problems, the commonest of which are behaviour disorders. Neurological damage or disorder has similar correlations. In the Isle of Wight epidemiological study children with evidence of brain damage were found to show a prevalence of psychiatric problems five times greater than in the general child population and three times as great as that in children with chronic physical handicaps not involving the brain (Rutter, et al., 1970).

The interplay between parents and child

Although factors in the child are important in determining how that child develops and what methods of child rearing will be most effective, the importance of the family environment in nurturing children and helping them realize their potential can hardly be overemphasized. Moreover, the family environment is generally more susceptible to change than are temperamental and biological factors in the child. It seems that a child's genetic makeup, temperamental characteristics, and neurological condition place certain limits upon what the final result may be. But how far development approaches the possible limits depends on the child's rearing experiences.

An important factor is the 'fit' between the temperamental characteristics of the parents and those of the child. Chess and Thomas (1984) have described various combinations of temperamental traits which children may display. To one of these combinations they gave the label 'difficult'.

'Difficult' children show:

irregularity in biological functions, negative withdrawal responses to new stimuli, non-adaptability or slow adaptability to change, and intense mood expressions which are frequently negative. These children show irregular sleep and feeding schedules, slow acceptance of new foods, prolonged adjustment periods to new routines, people, or situations, and relatively frequent loud periods of crying. Laughter, also, is characteristically loud. Frustration typically produces a violent tantrum. (Chess and Thomas, 1984, p. 43)

In their New York Longitudinal Study, these authors found that 10 per cent of their sample of children studied from early infancy fell into this category.

Children with 'difficult' temperaments are clearly prime candidates for the development of behaviour problems in later life – and it may not be very much later. Yet such an outcome is not inevitable. Whether it occurs depends in part on the 'goodness of fit' between the temperaments of child and parents (Chess and Thomas, 1984). Some parents handle these 'difficult' children calmly and firmly, and at the same time – despite the frustrations these children tend to cause – kindly and lovingly. In such cases the likelihood is that the child will learn acceptable social behaviour and will not develop serious behaviour problems. Other parents find these children exceedingly hard to rear. Rather than remaining calm and firm they may fluctuate between being firm and 'giving up', at times imposing – often impulsively – 'punishments' which may be quite draconian, while on other occasions giving in to their child in response to feelings of frustration or defeat.

The goodness of fit of the respective temperaments is not the only factor which determines the interplay between parents (and others responsible for rearing children) and child. The knowledge and beliefs of the parents are important. Mental or emotional illness in the parents may also adversely affect their parenting. Depression in a parent is commonly associated with behaviour problems in the child(ren). Other powerful determining factors are the childhood experiences of the parents. Our own upbringing greatly affects the way we rear our children. Indeed, the way we each were brought up by our parents is our main, if unconscious, model of how children are to be reared.

Factors in the family

The factors in the family the psychiatrist must consider go a long way beyond the question of the goodness of fit between the temperaments of those concerned. The *way the family system functions* is a matter of great importance. In every family, there is an allocation of roles to each member. This is seldom if ever formally, or even consciously, decided. Roles develop over time. Some children fall, or are in some way guided or pressured, into the role of 'good child', 'sick child', 'scapegoat' or 'parental child' – to give but four examples among many. This role allocation is but one facet of family systems functioning (for further discussion, see *Basic Family Therapy*, Barker, 1992).

How far should the psychiatric assessment of a child include a comprehensive assessment also of the family system? A categorical answer to this question is not possible. It is safe to say, however, that the better one understands how a child's family functions, the better one's understanding of the child and his or her behaviour is likely to be. In practice, much depends on the time available, the nature and severity of the problem behaviours, and the interests and skills of the examiner.

Because children's behaviour is so much context dependent it follows that their behavioural problems may be manifest in certain situations and not in others; or they may be more marked and serious in some situations than in others. This has been shown to be the case. In the epidemiological study carried out in the Isle of Wight (Rutter et al., 1970), for example, a majority of those found to be disturbed at home were not so considered in school, and *vice versa*. This might suggest that if behaviour problems are confined to situations other than at home, an in-depth study of the family and home system may not be as necessary as in those cases in which the problems are manifest within the family context. Even in these cases, however, a careful assessment of the functioning of the family system may be worthwhile, if only because it may help define the conditions that are necessary for the child's behaviour to be acceptable.

In summary, it is safe to say that the family and how it functions can never with impunity be ignored, and the more that is known about it, the better. A further point is that the active involvement and cooperation of the family, especially the parents, is usually essential for a satisfactory resolution of behaviour problems in children – wherever the problems are manifest.

The wider social environment

For most children, the school environment is the next most important situation after the home. Teachers and other school staff frequently seek psychiatric consultations regarding the management of difficult children. This is no doubt because they perceive a need to handle these children differently in order to lessen or resolve their behaviour problems.

It must also be pointed out that classroom and wider school systems can be dysfunctional. The importance of the social environment in schools was well shown by the research reported in the book *Fifteen Thousand Hours* (Rutter et al., 1979) and summarized by Rutter (1980). The progress, both behavioural and academic, of children moving from primary to secondary schools was assessed. After making allowance for the children's prior progress and adjustment, which had been assessed, it was found that certain factors in the environments of the secondary schools were significantly related to the progress of their pupils.

Clinical experience also suggests that the 'goodness of fit' between the child and the school may be important. It is not unusual to find that an apparently severe behaviour problem disappears when a child changes school. Unfortunately, the converse sometimes happens, a behaviour problem appearing *de novo* when a child moves from one school to another. The importance of the school environment was no doubt also a factor in the thinking behind the preparation of this book. Clearly, we must look carefully at the characteristics of the school system in which our behaviourally disturbed child is placed.

Finally, we must look at the wider social system in which the behaviourally disturbed child lives. We must consider the cultural expectations of the community of which the child is a part; the child's peer group; and the characteristics of the neighbourbood. On the whole these factors become of greater importance the older the child gets.

In some urban areas, especially impoverished inner city districts, there are strong social pressures encouraging antisocial behaviours. In some North American cities, for example, children below the age of criminal responsibility are used for such tasks as stealing and transporting or selling drugs. The 'Artful Dodger' is with us still! In Canada, the federal Young Offenders Act, which applies to young people between the ages of 12 and 18, provides for relatively mild penalties for offences for which adults would be liable to much heavier punishment. It is therefore not uncommon for young people to be made use of by older criminal elements for drug-related and other criminal activities.

Rapport

Most interactions between human beings are greatly facilitated if there is good rapport between those concerned. Every successful salesman knows this and the establishment and maintenance of rapport is an essential part of the work of the mental health professional. When we are dealing with disturbed children, good rapport is a basic requirement. Without it, we will make little or no progress in either assessment or treatment.

Rapport is easier to experience than to describe. When we are in rapport with someone we experience feelings of trust, acceptance and empathy. But it is more a non-verbal, feeling state than a cognitive one. It is promoted by using the same voice tones, manner of speaking, body postures, movements and vocabulary as the person with whom we wish to establish rapport. The objective is a feeling of 'oneness'. Observing the non-verbal feedback the person is offering and adjusting one's behaviour accordingly is important. How to establish rapport is discussed at greater length in *Clinical Interviews With Children and Adolescents* (Barker, 1990).

The interviews

The psychiatric assessment is achieved by means of a series of interviews. These will always include at least one interview with the child concerned, and one with the parents – or other care-givers if the child is not living with the parents. In addition, an interview with the whole family group is useful in providing information about how the family system is structured and functions; and it may be helpful to interview others concerned, for example teachers, social workers or the care staff in institutions in which the child may be, or may have been, resident.

Whom should the psychiatrist interview first? This is not always an easy question to answer. There is much to be said for interviewing the child first. If the parents, for example, have been interviewed first, many children assume – often rightly – that unfavourable reports about them have already been made to the interviewer. This is especially likely with children who are brought because of behaviour problems. It may lead them to approach the psychiatrist with negative expectations. They may expect to be criticized, blamed or lectured – as many of them have been previously. 'He's been told what a bad kid I am,' the child may think, 'So he's going to give me a hard time. But I can handle that.' 'Handling that' may then consist of adopting an uncooperative attitude and declining to answer questions frankly.

The main disadvantage of interviewing the child first is that the psychiatrist may have little prior knowledge of the nature of the problems for which the child has been referred. It is helpful to have a clear idea of the problem areas which are of particular concern to those bringing the child, so that the relevant issues can be addressed. It is not really possible to carry out a 'generic' psychiatric interview. Moreover, there are usually time constraints which make it important to put the time that is available to the best possible use. My own practice is to start, whenever possible, with a meeting with the whole family.

The family interivew

During the meeting with the whole family group, I focus initially on the membership, structure and functioning of the family system, rather than on the problem behaviours of the identified patient. I also encourage discussion of the *changes* the family members desire to see, rather than of the problem behaviours themselves. In a sense, asking about desired changes is not much different from asking about problems. But it sets the problems in a more positive perspective. It carries the messages, first, that change is possible, second, that change is what the interview is designed to lead to and, third, that the family as a whole may have a part to play in bringing about the changes desired. It might be argued that a psychiatric assessment is not a therapeutic endeavour, but there is little point in carrying out an assessment if it is not to be a first step in a change process – unless it reveals that no change is required.

Even though I structure the family interview as above, it often happens that many negative statements are made by other family members about the 'problem' child. This is not surprising, since the family has usually come because of the child's problems. Being present, however, the child at least knows what has been said, and what allegations and accusations have been made concerning him or her. Moreover, I make a point of asking all present to comment on what others say. It is a truism that any situation or behaviour is open to being viewed in more than one way. It is important to take note not only of what the parents have to say but also of the views of the other family members.

A useful line of questions takes the form, 'How do *you* see it?' Or, 'Is that how *you* understand things to be?' Or, 'Do you agree with what [so-and-so] says?' Such questions may be addressed to all the family members present in turn. Asking questions which carry the implication that more than one view of a situation is possible often leads to a variety of different opinions being expressed. A factor which commonly emerges in the families of many behaviourally disturbed children is disagreement between the parents, often on child management issues or disciplinary techniques, but also on other issues. This is all valuable diagnostic information.

The family interview may also yield important information about the family's relationship with the 'outside' world. Sometimes highly negative views are expressed, by the parents as well as by the children, about the school the identified patient attends. The behaviour problems may be attributed to faults in the school staff, an unsympathetic teacher or an incompetent school principal. While on occasion there proves to be some substance to such complaints, they raise some other considerations. Are the parents' attitudes related to their own childhood experiences at school? Or is the child's problem behaviour at some level, perhaps an unconscious one, an acting out of the parents' attitudes towards authority figures? It is certainly true to say that negative and hostile attitudes by parents towards schools and their staffs are a recipe for disaster – the disaster usually consisting of behavioural deviation and academic underachievement by the child(ren) concerned.

It is not possible here to describe in detail the process of family interviewing. Approaches to this are discussed in *Basic Family Therapy* (Barker, 1992) and in other textbooks of family therapy. Among the areas in which information should be obtained are the following. (These are derived from the McMaster Model of Family Functioning (Epstein et al., 1978) and the Process Model of Family Functioning (Steinhauer et al., 1984).)

1. *The general level of instrumental and affective functioning in the family*

When considering *instrumental* functioning we take note of the extent to which the family appears to be meeting the basic needs of its members for such things as food, clothing, shelter, medical attention, education and a physically safe and secure place in which to live.

Affective functioning is concerned with meeting the emotional and psychological needs of the family's members. These include providing an emotionally warm, affirming and secure evironment for all members but, when we are dealing with children's problems, especially for the children in the family. Is there mutual love and support within the family group? When members are upset or under emotional stress is there comfort and supportive counsel available within the family system?

2. *The amount and quality of the communication, both verbal and non-verbal, within the family*

There are several ways in which communication may be deficient. It may be insufficient, indirect or masked. It is sometimes quite striking to discover, during family assessment interviews, how little family members know about each others' feelings, points of view or wishes, or even about their day-to-day activities. In many dysfunctional families, communication is indirect, member A communicating his or her messages to member B by telling member C, in the expectation that the latter will pass on the information. This is generally not a good way to proceed, since there is no guarantee that the information will be passed on either at all, or without alteration.

Another phenomenon commonly observed in dysfunctional families is the giving of non-verbal messages that conflict with the verbal ones being given at the same time. Facial expressions, tone of voice, gestures and body postures may all belie parents' expressions of love or even acceptance of their children.

3. *Family members' roles*

Reference has already been made to some of the roles children may play in family systems. While it is not possible to set out an 'ideal' or 'normal' set of roles for family members, we can say that all the functions that need to be carried out should be assigned. Moreover, the assignments should be appropriate. Thus the role of 'parental' child – in which a child is given the task of caring for either a parent or a sibling – is seldom appropriate. Generally speaking, the parents should be working together in an harmonious relationship, caring for the children and meeting each others' and the children's instrumental and emotional needs. The role of 'family scapegoat' is one that many children with behaviour problems are found to play.

4. *The affective involvement of the family members*

Families may fall anywhere on a continuum whose extremes are 'enmeshment' and 'disengagement' (Minuchin, 1974). In disengaged families substantial changes in the emotional state or behaviour of one member produce little reaction in the other family members. In enmeshed families the repercussions in other members are excessive. Minuchin (1974) suggests that, while it is not possible to define a normal range, extremes of either enmeshment or disengagement increase the likelihood that the family will have problems. Child-rearing is likely to be more effective if the parents are neither too emotionally 'distant' from their children, nor emotionally overinvolved with them. Overinvolvement – that is, enmeshment – results in an inadequately defined boundary between parents and children, with a confused hierarchy and uncertainty about who is supposed to be looking after, and setting limits for whom.

5. *The system of control in the family*

Every family – indeed every social group of any sort – needs some mechanism whereby control is exercised over its members. Without an effective control system there will not be a coherent functioning system but a state of chaos. In families, the control process is not a simple one. There need to be many checks and balances, and multiple feedback loops. In one way or another every family member is exerting some form and degree of control over every other.

At first consideration, it might be thought that when a baby is born into a family, the parents are in charge and have fairly complete control over what happens to their child. In reality, this is far from the truth. Infants control much of the behaviour of their parents by such means as crying, smiling, laughing, and feeding or refusing to feed. Only gradually, as the child develops through the preschool years, are the parents able to establish a system whereby they take a degree of control over the behaviour of their offspring. Some fail to do so properly, and thus may develop the roots of a serious behaviour problem later in childhood.

The control systems in a family may be, in any degree, flexible, rigid or inconsistent. Generally, a flexible system is most likely to yield the best results.

6. The family's values and norms

These are important factors determining, among many other things, what is expected of the children and what forms of encouragement, rewards or punishments are acceptable.

Interviewing the child

This section will emphasize the special points which need to be considered when a child with behaviour problems is interviewed as part of a psychiatric assessment. The assessment process is basically the same whatever the presenting problem (for a description see *Basic Child Psychiatry*, Barker, 1988, and other textbooks on child psychiatry). The objectives are to observe the child's behaviour, emotional reactions and relationship to the examiner and to discover as much as possible about the child's inner world. This is achieved by some combination of conversation and play.

Here again, the importance of rapport must be stressed. Children rarely come for psychiatric assessment of their own accord, and in many instances they are not complaining of any particular problem. So the approach one might make to an adult patient coming for help – that is, asking what the problem is, or how the patient would like things to change – is not appropriate. While rapport is important with all patients, with those who are aware of a problem and are seeking change it may be developed as the presenting problems are explored. Indeed if the psychiatrist lets half or more of the initial interview pass without bringing up the matter of why the patient has come, concentrating instead on rapport building, this may lead the patient to wonder what is going on.

Quite the reverse tends to be the case when one is assessing a behaviourally disturbed child. Unless the child brings up the subject of the presenting behaviour problems, it is usually best left until towards the end of the interview. Even if the child does quickly bring the problems up it may be wise to respond by saying something like, 'I know that there are these problems with your behaviour at school, but I would first like to get to know you a bit and learn about your family, friends and interests. We can get round to the problems a little later.' This approach helps define the psychiatrist as someone interested in the child as a person, rather than as an authority figure concerned primarily with the presenting behaviours.

The latter point is important because, in order to carry out a good psychiatric examination it is the child as a person that we most need to come to know. This is what leads us to an understanding of the presenting symptoms.

Attempting to get full accounts from children of their misdeeds is generally of little help. It may indeed set back the process of assessment by causing children to identify those interviewing them with others who have been questioning and lecturing them. This information is usually readily available from others. It is generally unproductive to ask children why they have been stealing, hitting others, disrupting their school classes or running away. Most children, even if they wish to answer such questions, have difficulty understanding the processes which have led to their behaviour. As we saw in an earlier section, the causes of their behaviour are usually multiple, complex and long-standing. It is the function of the psychiatrist to figure them out. The disturbed child can seldom do this job for us. (In this respect children with behaviour disorders differ from some other categories of psychiatric patient. For example, when we are assessing those who may be psychotic a detailed study of the presenting symptoms may be essential to accurate diagnosis.)

How then should the psychiatrist proceed? To a certain extent this depends on the age of the child. Younger children often prefer to play, older ones to talk, though there are exceptions to this generalization. Children who have not yet reached puberty are best seen in a playroom equipped with a variety of toys and play, drawing, painting and modelling equipment. Some of the less inhibited children will rush excitedly into the room and immediately start playing. They provide their own answer to the question of what they want to do. When this does not happen, I tell the child that the various play materials are available and invite him or her to choose to play with them or to talk for a while. I usually frame the invitation in terms of, 'What would you like to do first?' – implying that by the end of the interview we will have engaged in both play and conversation.

Younger children often tell us more through their play or painting or drawing than through their talk. Yet it is remarkable how much young, even preschool, children can sometimes communicate verbally. But however the interview starts, there are certain points I try to cover in conversation. I try to get the child talking about his or her family, friends, interests, hobbies, fears, worries, ambitions in life and school experiences. The child's fantasy life is explored, partly through the medium of play and partly by asking questions such as, 'If you could wish for any three things to happen, and whatever you wished would, by magic, come true, what would your wishes be?' And, 'If you were shipwrecked on an uninhabited island, with plenty to eat and drink but nobody else there, who would you most want to have with you?' The child can then be asked to name a second person, then a third.

Other questions that may yield revealing answers include asking about the worst thing, and the best thing that could ever happen to the child. Children may be asked about the dreams they have at night and about daydreams.

It is important to ask whether the child has ever experienced feelings of depression, or the desire to commit suicide, and also to discover whether such feelings are currently present. Enquiries about the use of medical or 'street' drugs and alcohol are also in order, even in children who have not yet left primary school.

The question of possible physical, sexual or emotional abuse should also be explored, but it is important not to ask leading questions. One may start with enquiries along the lines of, 'Has anyone ever hurt you in any way?' or, 'Has anyone ever touched you in a way you did not like?' If affirmative answers to such questions are given, they may be followed up by asking what happened and when. Questioning may then address the matters of who did whatever is reported and how often. At all stages it is important not to put words into the child's mouth.

Discovering whether there has been emotional abuse can be difficult, not least because – while very real – such abuse is hard to define. When does legitimate criticism become emotional abuse? The answer may be, when it is persistent and excessive and it becomes the predominant content of what is said to the child; also when it takes the place of affirming statements and acknowledgement of the child's strengths, assets and achievements. But what is 'persistent' and what is 'excessive?' In clinical practice answering such questions is less important than discovering what has been happening and assessing how far it has been, or is, playing a part in the aetiology of the child's problem behaviour.

Many children communicate information with less defensiveness through play or artistic productions. I always invite, indeed encourage, children to draw or paint. As a basic minimum I ask each child to draw (or paint) his or her family and then to do a picture of his or her choice. The content of children's play can also be revealing. Some children who will acknowledge verbally the existence of no strife or problems in the family will play out scenes in which adults shout, argue or engage in physical fights, or children are called insulting and demeaning names and perhaps physically beaten. Children with behaviour problems often play out their aggressive feelings and fantasies in the sand tray or doll's house, or with animal, soldier or other figures.

The following is a summary of the areas in which information should be sought during the interview with the child:

1. general appearance
2. motor function
3. speech and language skills
4. content of talk and thought
5. intellectual function, as estimated during the clinical interview. This may need to be explored further by testing
6. the child's mood and emotional state
7. the child's attitude towards other family members
8. the child's attitudes to school
9. fantasy life as revealed during the interview

10. sleep patterns and problems
11. the child's view of the reported behaviour problems and of the referral and assessment procedure
12. the child's view of any previous placements away from home
13. indications of social adjustment and information about the child's peer group and its activities
14. other problems that come to light during the interview
15. the nature and content of the child's play
16. the child's self-image as revealed during the interview
17. any indications that the child may have been abused.

Children's behaviour should always be described as objectively as possible. A good account of how to do this is provided by Savicki and Brown (1981, ch. 15). A more detailed account of the observations that should be made on the child is to be found in *Basic Child Psychiatry* (Barker, 1988, ch. 3).

The interview with the parents

This should fill in any gaps in the information that has been obtained from the family and child interviews. It should also cover the parents' own histories, especially their childhood experiences and backgrounds. The parents should be invited to mention anything which they felt unable to bring up while the child or children were present. If the psychiatrist suspects the presence of psychiatric disorder in a parent, or of alcoholism or drug abuse, these issues may now be explored. If a genogram has not been constructed, this should now be done.

Other interviews

Depending on the nature of the case, it may be helpful – with the informed consent of the family – to interview others with knowledge of the child and/or family. These may include teachers and other school staff, other involved professionals (for example, psychologists, social workers, and the child care workers). In certain cases other relatives – grandparents, uncles, aunts and others – may have useful additional information.

The formulation

When all the above information has been obtained it is put together in a *diagnostic formulation*. This sets out, in narrative form, the psychiatrist's understanding of the case and of the various factors that have combined to cause the presenting problems. The formulation is much more than a listing of causative factors. It should state the relative importance each is considered to have, and also how the various factors are seen as having combined to cause the presenting problems. It should also lead logically to a treatment plan.

The diagnosis

When the diagnostic process is complete it is customary for the psychiatrist to assign the disorder from which the child is suffering to a category. The two main diagnostic systems currently in use are the ninth edition (soon to be succeeded by the tenth) of the *International Classification of Diseases (ICD-9)* (World Health Organisation, 1977), and the revised third edition of the American Psychiatric Association's *Diagnostic and Statistical Manual of Mental Disorders (DSM-III)* (American Psychiatric Association, 1987). Such categorization is of value when it is desired to compare findings from different centres, and for other research purposes, but it is less useful than the formulation as a guide to treatment.

References

American Psychiatric Association (1987) *Diagnostic and Statistical Manual of Mental Disorders (DSM-III-R)*, 3rd edn, revised, Washington, DC: APA.

Barker, P. (1992) *Basic Family Therapy*, 3rd edn, Oxford: Blackwell.

Barker, P. (1988) *Basic Child Psychiatry*, 5th edn, Oxford: Blackwell; Chicago: Yearbook.

Barker, P. (1990) *Clinical Interviews with Children and Adolescents*, New York: Norton.

Chess, S. and Thomas, A. (1984) *Origins and Evolution of Behaviour Disorders from Infancy to Early Adult Life*, New York: Brunner/Mazel.

Epstein, N.B., Bishop, D.S. and Levin, S. (1978) 'The McMaster model of family functioning', *Journal of Marital and Family Therapy*, 4: 19–31.

Minuchin, S. (1974) *Families and Family Therapy*, Cambridge, Mass.: Harvard University Press.

Rutter, M. (1980) 'School influences on children's behaviour and development', *Pediatrics*, 65: 208–220.

Rutter, M., Grahaam, P. and Yule, W. (1970) *A Neuropsychiatric Study in Childhood*, London: Heinemann.

Rutter, M., Maughan, N., Mortimore, P. and Ouston, J. (1979) *Fifteen Thousand Hours*, London: Open Books.

Rutter, M., Tizard, J. and Whitmore, K. (1970) *Education, Health and Behaviour*, London: Longman.

Savicki, V. and Brown, R. (1981) *Working with Troubled Children*, New York: Human Sciences Press.

Shamsie, S.J. (1981) 'Antisocial adolescents: our treatments do not work – where do we go from here?' *Canadian Journal of Psychiatry*, 26: 357–64.

Steinhauer, P.D., Santa-Barbara, J. and Skinner, H. (1984) 'The process model of family functioning', *Canadian Journal of Psychiatry*, 29: 77–88.

World Health Organisation (1977) *International Classification of Diseases*, 1975 revision, Geneva: WHO.

CHAPTER 8

The psychological assessment of behavioural difficulties

ROBERT POVEY

Maths teacher:	That boy's definitely disturbed – in fact, he's a nut case!
Art teacher:	Who?
Maths teacher:	Dobson. He's rude, defiant and disruptive. A real pain in the bum.
Art teacher:	You mean John Dobson in 4D?
Maths teacher:	Yes, Dopey Dobson. Who else?
Art teacher:	But he's a lovely boy! I've never found him any trouble in Art.

This staff room conversation identifies one of the central dilemmas in assessing behavioural disturbance in schoolchildren, namely how far the observed behaviour of a particular pupil represents a genuine personal problem resulting from the psychological make-up of that pupil and how far it is situationally determined.[1] As Hargreaves puts it in the context of whole class behaviour: 'given that the conduct of the same class varies enormously with different teachers any explanation which rests exclusively at the pupil level must be deficient'.[2]

In assessing the psychological significance of behavioural disturbance, therefore, we have to accept that any form of assessment will be coloured to some extent by the perception (and behaviour) of the assessor and by the context in which the behaviour takes place. Thus Dobson could be a gifted and enthusiastic artist whose work is encouraged by a sympathetic Art teacher but he might also be a weak and unwilling mathematician whose efforts are frequently ridiculed by a sarcastic Maths teacher. To explain the discrepancy in Dobson's behaviour in Art as compared with Maths lessons it is necessary to examine the whole teaching environment including the interrelationships between the personalities, abilities, attitudes and classroom behaviours of the teachers and pupils involved. The observed behaviour cannot be explained satisfactorily by examining the pupil's behaviour in isolation from the physical and social context in which it takes place.

Similarly, in order for any individual assessment procedure to be interpreted meaningfully *it must be supplemented by information relating to the total context within which the particular behaviour takes place*. This principle is of overriding importance and should be taken as the essential framework within which the ensuing discussion of assessment procedures is presented.

The nature of the problem

There is considerable confusion over the use of such terms as 'disruptive', 'disturbed', 'maladjusted', 'emotional and behavioural difficulties'.[3] Not everybody would accept Galloway's cynical view that whether a child is labelled disruptive or maladjusted 'has nothing to do with educational, psychological or medical assessment . . . [but with] the type of provision available locally'.[4] Nevertheless, there is almost certainly more than a grain of 'administrative truth' in the claim, and a type of 'Parkinson's Law' undoubtedly does operate at times, the 'incidence' of special needs pupils tending to increase to fill the number of special school places available![5] Recent evidence also suggests that such an effect may be most likely to operate in relation to the sort of pupils commonly referred to these days as 'EBD' children (i.e. those considered to have emotional and behaviour difficulties).[6] In this chapter, however, I shall follow the Warnock[7] view that it is the nature of the problem relating to each *individual* child rather than to *categories* of children which is important. I shall, therefore, make no sharp distinction between categories of behavioural difficulties, but I shall consider ways of assessing their *seriousness* from both the pupil's and teacher's viewpoint.

Behavioural problems in school are often said to become serious when they interfere with the teaching process.[8] Yet, paradoxically, the most attention-demanding pupils with the greatest nuisance value to the teacher are often the *least* seriously disturbed *psychologically*. As I have written elsewhere[9] 'The nuisance value of the offending behaviour should not be used as a criterion of its seriousness from a psychological viewpoint. The quiet, withdrawn child may often be much more seriously disturbed than the boisterous, attention-demanding child.' But how is the teacher to know whether the child needs help, the teacher needs help (or both need help!); or whether the problem lies in the nature of the curriculum or the classroom or school organization?

In many situations some headway can be made by using common-sense approaches to the problem behaviour. In the first instance, for example, emphasis might be placed on the systematic observation and recording of the behaviour which is causing concern, noting its intensity and frequency in comparison with the behaviour of peer group pupils. This could then be coupled with a close examination of the teaching and classroom management techniques being employed in the contexts in which the behaviour takes place.[10-13] Where the behavioural difficulties are related to poor classroom or school management these can be rectified by the development of more effective teaching techniques and management skills, as described in this book and elsewhere.[14-21] Where the difficulties are related to the development of inappropriate habits on the part of the pupil (such as excessive 'off-task' behaviour, 'out-of-seat wanderings', 'calling out') these may be susceptible to modification by behavioural approaches such as those described in BATPACK[22]. Indeed, according to the findings of a survey carried out for the Elton Report[23] and by a similar survey by Houghton et al.[24] the most common irritants to teachers are behaviours such as 'talking out of turn', 'hindering other pupils', 'making unnecessary noise' and 'calculated idleness or work avoidance'. In contrast to the suggestions in more 'high profile' reports[25] produced by the teachers' unions, episodes involving physical violence tended to be placed very low in the rank order of problem behaviours.[26]

In order to remedy these sorts of irritating classroom behaviours the initial advice might well be 'teacher heal thyself' since some of the problems can be self-inflicted! A vicious circle can be seen to operate in many classrooms. The stressed teacher, for example, will inadvertently reinforce 'difficult' behaviour by paying undue attention to the petty misbehaviour of attention-seeking children rather than to their less frequent (but from a management point of view often more crucial) episodes of 'good' behaviour. This then leads to an increase in the attention-seeking behaviour and to further teacher stress! It can be argued, therefore, that faulty classroom management techniques, together with inappropriate curricula,[27] are responsible for many of the teacher's problems and in such situations there may be little necessity for further assessments of the pupils themselves.

What the teacher has to decide, however, is what sort of problem is being presented and what type of remedy should be sought; or, to put it in the words of the Elton Report, what distinguishes between 'ordinary' bad behaviour and disturbed behaviour.[28] The Report accepts that this is often a difficult distinction to make but argues that 'the distinction has to be made'. One of the problems with the Report, however, is that it is singularly lacking in advice about how to make the distinction, partly perhaps because the Committee lacked representation from the educational psychology profession, a point which Burden[29] makes with some force. The only advice it offers to teachers is that children with emotional and behavioural difficulties tend to present problems earlier in their school careers than other types of children, that they show difficulties regardless of the teaching group in which they happen to be placed and exhibit problems which are more severe than those exhibited by other 'non-disturbed' pupils. This advice has value but it would have been more valuable if some reference had also been made to ways in which the teacher could gain some indication as to the nature and severity of the problem by the use of criterion and norm-referenced measures.

Criterion and norm-referenced assessments

Criterion-referenced assessments provide information on the basis of predetermined criteria without reference to normative standards of performance or behaviour. Norm-referenced assessments, on the other hand, provide a norm or standard against which to compare pupil behaviours.[30] In some educational circles it has become fashionable to deride norm-referenced assessments as 'old hat' and unhelpful since they do not offer specific curricular prescriptions for the teacher. If assessment is not curriculum-led it cannot be respectable and anything which offers a normative perspective is totally outside the pale! It is true that criterion-based assessments are generally of more value to the teacher than norm-referenced approaches in providing ideas for curricular programmes. In the context of identifying and managing behaviour problems criterion-related checklists can also be of great value in helping to select behavioural targets for individual pupils or groups of pupils and to evaluate progress towards specific objectives. But some kind of normative reference can also be important in giving support to teachers' judgements about the seriousness of the behavioural (or cognitive) difficulties of pupils at particular ages and stages of development and to aid decisions about possible referral to supporting professionals such as the Educational Psychologist.

The remainder of this chapter is devoted to a discussion of two checklist measures offering both criterion and norm-referenced information which a teacher can use in helping to establish the degree of severity of behavioural difficulties. I have also included a section on sociometric techniques as a counterbalance to the scant treatment they tend to receive in current texts on the management of behaviour problems. Finally, a case study is provided to illustrate the use of the measures in a classroom setting.

The Bristol Social Adjustment Guides (BSAG)

The BSAGs[31] were devised as an aid to the detection and diagnosis of behavioural disturbances in children aged 5 to 16 years and they have been used in a variety of settings from longitudinal 'cohort' studies[32,33], to exploratory studies of juvenile aggression[34] and use in support service settings[35]. There are three separate forms of the BSAG: *The Child in School, The Child in Residential Care* and *The Child in the Family*. Each has been compiled in a similar manner but *The Child in School* is the guide which has been most widely used and is the one selected for consideration in this chapter.

The 1970 revision of the BSAG, incorporated in the most recent editions of the Manual, differs in certain respects from the earlier 1956 edition[36]. In particular, the use of an over-all, 'global' BSAG score is now discouraged, as also is the practice of assigning pupils to the categories of *maladjusted, unsettled* or *stable*. These categories will, however, be found in the reports of several research studies which used the 1956 edition[37]. Several of these studies are summarized in the Manual to the 1974 edition.

The present version concentrates on the identification of two main scales: *Under-reaction (Unract)* and *Over-reaction (Ovract)*. These diagnostic categories are based on the patterns of pupil behaviour reported by the teacher completing the form. Thus the Guides consist of a collection of short statements about a child's behaviour in relation to a number of situations (e.g. interaction with the teacher, school work, games and play, attitude to other children). For each situation the teacher is asked to underline the phrases which apply to the child. In the section on *Interaction with the teacher*, for example, the first set of phrases concerns 'Greeting the teacher' and the teacher has to underline one of the following phrases: *Waits to be noticed/hails teacher loudly/greets normally/can be surly/never thinks of greeting/is too unaware of other people to greet/not noticed*. Most of the phrases in the Guide can be considered to be broadly criterion-referenced in nature and have been selected 'from the range of expressions which teachers would use professionally in describing the behaviour of a child . . . (and) the teacher is not asked to make any interpretation, but to report factually what can be observed'.[38]

Although the majority of statements can be viewed as essentially 'non-interpretive' this cannot be taken as an entirely consistent rule, however, as can be seen from at least one of the phrases in the first section. Thus the phrase *never thinks of greeting* is probably meant to be read as *never greets* (i.e. a statement of behaviour which can be observed). If interpreted literally, however, it is not a statement which can be underlined as an 'observed response' of a 'non-interpretive' kind. It requires the teacher to *infer* an intention (or lack of intention) on the part of the pupil and clearly this is not a feasible proposition without a good deal of further probing on the part of the teacher and honest reflection on the part of the pupil who is being interrogated! When the Guide has been completed a transparent template is placed over the sheet and items indicative of under/over-reaction and of certain syndromes are scored on a diagnostic form.

Test-retest reliability over one year for data relating to total score is reported in the Manual to be a respectable 0.80. Modified Alpha coefficients for Unract and Ovract scores are also reported as 0.83 and 0.91 respectively. Validity data are also offered both in a criterion-related sense (comparing pupil profiles against several independent criteria such as ratings by teachers and houseparents) and also in relation to construct validity which is presented in two ways. In the first place attempts are made to provide justification for the constructs employed and, secondly, these constructs are examined in relation to a number of hypotheses, especially the multiple impairment hypothesis[39]. Clear evidence in support of this hypothesis is advanced by the presentation of data which show, for example, that boys and girls with four or five morbid conditions show between two and four times more under-reacting and over-reacting maladjustment than healthy children.

For a test which has been the subject of so much revision, in particular the major study by Stott et al.[40], and the 1980 study by McDermott[41] substantiating the factorial validity of the Unract/Ovract dichotomy, there are some surprising anomalies and omissions in the current Manual. For example, the diagnostic form has changed slightly over the revisions and this sometimes makes it difficult to interpret the normative data. The norms are frequently an amalgamation of data from age groups ranging from 5 to 15 and this obscures possible differences between the profiles of children at different age levels. More detailed tables for different age groups would increase the value of the normative data provided in the Manual. Similarly, there does not appear to have been any major study examining the degree of inter-rater agreement which might be expected between different teachers using the Guides in relation to the same pupils. Pringle[42] first drew attention to this omission in 1965! Fortunately, she also made reference to some evidence provided from a study carried out by the NFER on this issue. Pairs of teachers completed the 1956 version of the Guides independently for some 88 children. Correlations between *maladjusted* scores were 0.76 and between *unsettled* scores 0.78. It would make sense for future editions of the Manual to include details of this study and to provide further evidence from more recent studies using the 1970 (or preferably a more up-to-date) revision.

In situations where teachers are viewing pupils from similar vantage points, therefore, and interpreting behaviour in a similar manner, the degree of agreement between profiles may well be very close. But the inherent problems concerning the subjectivity of teachers' obser-vations caution against regarding any diagnostic profile as a precise, objective measure of social adjustment. In general, however, the Guides do provide a useful tool for the teacher if used with sensitivity and discretion on the part of the teacher or psychologist – and the discrepancies between teachers' profiles can sometimes provide a valuable basis for staff room or case conference discussion.

The Children's Behaviour Questionnaire

The CBQ[43] (see Appendix 1 at the end of this chapter) is another measure of behavioural adjustment which has been used extensively in research studies from large-scale surveys[44] to investigations into the relationship between pupils' behaviour and blood levels[45]. It is a questionnaire for completion by teachers and it was first used in a major research context in the survey into the education, health and behaviour of 9 to 12 year-old children living on the Isle of Wight[46].

This survey also included a version of the questionnaire for completion by parents.

The teachers' questionnaire consists of 26 statements concerning a child's behaviour and the teacher has to indicate whether the statement *Certainly applies* (2 points) *Applies somewhat* (1 point) or *Doesn't apply* (0 points). Again the questionnaire has criterion-referenced features in that the behaviours are generally specified with a reasonable degree of precision. It also offers normative data and it is suggested that a score of nine or more can be taken to indicate some evidence of 'problem' behaviour in 9 to 12 year-old pupils. This score was chosen because in the Isle of Wight survey it selected 72–88 per cent of boys and 50–70 per cent of girls attending Child Guidance Clinics compared with only 9–11 per cent of boys and 3–5 per cent of girls gaining this score in the general population. The questionnaire has also been shown to discriminate between different types of psychiatric disorder, in particular between neurotic and antisocial behaviours.[47] A neurotic sub-score can be obtained by adding the scores obtained on items 7,10,17 and 23; and an antisocial sub-score by adding the scores on items, 4,5,15,19,20 and 26.

In constructing the test the reliability of the questionnaire was assessed by the test-retest method. Four teachers rated the same 80 7 year-old children (40 boys and 40 girls) on two occasions separated by an interval of two months.[48] The reliability coefficient produced in this exercise (on children somewhat younger than those involved in the Isle of Wight survey) was 0.89. This is a very respectable figure and one might surmise that an even higher figure would be obtained with older children. For inter-rater agreement (comparing the ratings given by different teachers independently in relation to the same children) a coefficient of 0.72 is reported, the age range also being younger than that used in the Isle of Wight survey. Four teachers rated 70 children (35 girls and 35 boys) in the last term of the infant school and four other teachers rated the same children two to three months later in the children's first term in the junior school. Again, it might be argued that this coefficient is probably an underestimate since the difference in time scale and setting is likely to have lowered the degree of correlation between the ratings.

The criterion-related validity of the questionnaire was assessed by comparing the scores of children attending Child Guidance Clinics with children not attending and by comparing the designation of children as 'neurotic' or 'anti-social' on the basis of questionnaire sub-scores with psychiatric diagnosis on the basis of intensive investigation. A good degree of comparability emerged from both approaches.

As with the BSAG, however, the degree of subjectivity involved in the completion of such rating scales is quite considerable and I have experienced situations in which weak teachers with 30 or so quite unexceptional children in their class have recorded scores of 9+ for the great majority of their pupils! Thus the variety and range of experience of individual teachers is clearly of relevance in any judgements of pupils' behaviour in the classroom.[49] There is also evidence that questionnaires, if used on their own as the sole criterion of maladjustment will provide rather dubious estimates of incidence[50] and that different instruments will not always select the same pupils to be allocated to the *maladjusted* category.[51] The McMichael study[52], in fact, compared the use of the BSAG and the CBQ by teachers with 198 boys between the ages of 4 years 9 months and 5 years 9 months at the time of initial completion (ten weeks after the beginning of the pupils' first term at school). The questionnaire was also given to the same children (less transfers and absentees) at the end of the first year at school and at the end of the second year. The level of agreement between the questionnaires as to which boys should be regarded as *stable* increased with age (63 per cent on the first occasion, 65 per cent on the second and 74 per cent on the third) but even on the last occasion there was still disagreement about whether the pupils should be regarded as *stable* or *unstable* in over a quarter of the cases.

If we translate this sort of information into a diagnostic setting it is clear that we are likely to find a number of *false positives* (children who are finally diagnosed as 'stable' – say by psychiatric interview – who were incorrectly judged to be maladjusted on one or other of the questionnaires) and also *false negatives* (children who *are* maladjusted but are not identified on the questionnaires). The involvement of sensitive teacher judgements according to circumstances is clearly, therefore, of immense importance in the interpretation of questionnaire scores. With the availability of such sensitive teacher judgement, however, the questionnaire can be very helpful in confirming or identifying areas of concern about pupil behaviour and in providing reassurance that a request for external help, for example, from local support services is an appropriate course of action.

Sociometric techniques

Sociometric techniques were first suggested by Moreno[53] and more recent accounts can be found in texts such as Gronlund[54], Evans[55], Northway and Weld[56] and Thomas[57]. They attempt to measure informal friendship (or association) patterns by asking individuals to nominate those group members with whom they would like to associate for particular activities. They are a very simple tool for teachers or group leaders to use in examining the social relationships within a group and have been widely used in both informal teacher-based settings and in larger research programmes[58-61]. There are a number of ways of obtaining sociometric data including the use of ratings and the adoption of a *guess who?* approach[62]. In its simplest form, however, pupils will be asked to make a choice about which other pupils they wish to associate with in relation to a particular criterion (e.g. for working on practical mathematics). This presents the tester with a *choice/criterion* decision which is often resolved into a *three choice/three criteria* arrangement. This represents, perhaps, the best compromise between the variety of combinations of choices and criteria which could be employed. Pupils are asked to choose three pupils with whom they would like to associate in relation to three different activities. It is argued that this arrangement gives a sufficiently wide range of choices and situations to allow individuals with different skills and interests to be accommodated in the pattern of choices whilst at the same time being sufficiently circumscribed to prevent the introduction of problems of repetition or indiscriminate selection.[63] An example of a 3 × 3 format would be where the children are asked to give the names of the first, second and third choices in respect to the following questions:

1. Who are the three children you would most like to sit next to in maths?
2. Who are the three children you would most like to play with in the playground?
3. Who are the three children in your class you would most like to invite home to tea?

It is also possible to use negative criteria (e.g. Who would you *not* want to sit next to?) but there are certain points which should be considered before adopting such an approach. In the first place, although the information obtained in this way may be useful in highlighting negative feelings it often does not add substantially to the information provided from the use of positive criteria. On the other hand, by asking children consciously to *reject* other children we may be creating or increasing tension between individuals or subgroups and, in some circumstances, the self-esteem of individual pupils may be severely dented. In general, therefore, researchers in Britain have tended to avoid negative criteria.

There is no magic about a 3 × 3 format, of course, although it is very frequently found in research studies. Two British studies of inter-ethnic friendship patterns in British primary schools illustrate the variety of approaches well. Thus Rowley[64] used a 3 × 3 format with similar questions to the three above (without the 'maths' and 'tea' elements) whereas Davey and Mullin[65] used the same three situations but with only two choices.

Some testers[66] also argue for the use of five choices with older children and it is clear that the number of situations should be determined by the particular purpose for which the test is devised. It is also especially important that the situations selected as criteria should be meaningful for the children, that the individuals involved should be given a clear rationale for their involvement in the test and that there is some form of follow-up to the exercise. The presentation to the pupils of a meaningful context (e.g. the need to re-arrange classroom seating for practical maths) in which the test is related to a specific outcome (the post-test re-arrangement of seating) will make for much greater 'face validity' than a test which is given without adequate explanation and without follow-up.

Having obtained the choices (or ratings or *guess who?* responses if these formats are used) then a method of presenting the data has to be decided upon. There are a number of methods available but the most usual approach is to construct either a *sociogram* or a *sociomatrix*. (An example of each is provided in the case study below.)

Sociogram

A *sociogram* (see Figure 8.1) attempts to show the pattern of relationships within a group in diagrammatic form, often using circles to denote the individuals and arrows to indicate the direction of choice. An individual who attracts the most choices is described as a *star*, and, at the opposite extreme, a pupil who is neither given nor receives any choices is an *isolate*. A pupil who offers choices but is not chosen by any other pupil is known as a *neglectee*.

Sociomatrix

The same information can be displayed in the form of a *sociomatrix* (see Figure 8.2) which can cope more readily than the sociogram with large amounts of data.

Reliability and validity of sociometric techniques

As far as the reliability of sociometric techniques is concerned the main concern is with the *stability* of the measure and there is evidence that stability in a 'repeated testing' context increases with the age of the subjects[67]. It is also clear that, in general, methods involving the use of rating scales (e.g. where each pupil rates every other pupil in the class for *social acceptability* from 1 = *very best friend* to 4 = *don't know very well*) offer better reliability estimates than *nomination* methods[68]. This is clearly because a pupil's acceptability score is based on the mean of a large number of ratings which remain constant from one test to the next as compared with the variability which is inherent in the *nomination* method. In a research study involving 495 nine and ten year-old children Oden and Asher[69], for example, report significant test-retest reliability coefficients of 0.82 and 0.84 on a rating scale method ($p<0.01$ in both cases). Reliability coefficients in excess of 0.80 are also reported by Northway[70] in a longitudinal study involving children in the infant age range, the sociometric status of the girls in the sample being more stable, in general, than that of the boys at this age.

The question of the validity of sociometric tests is not often referred to in the literature but it is important to remember that the choices are only *hypothetical* selections. Their validity is determined by the extent to which such *paper* choices match up with *realistic* choices made in the criterion setting, and in one of the few discussions of criterion-related validity in relation to sociometric tests Cronbach[71] reports coefficients of around 0.80.

In general, therefore, sociometric techniques seem to have satisfactory reliability and validity for use in classroom settings and they offer teachers a valuable and inexpensive aid in their attempts to understand the social relationships within their class or school.

Case study

Peter is 9 years 6 months old and in his third year at a junior school. He has an older brother in the second year at secondary school. The home background is very unstable. There has been a history of parental rows often leading to either the father or mother temporarily leaving home. The father (who died of a heart attack just after Peter had started Junior school) also sometimes reacted with physical violence towards both his wife and children, especially Peter. Parental supervision has always been very lax and Peter is often left at home on his own or under his brother's supervision. His physical health is satisfactory and he is good at PE but his academic progress has been slow, especially in reading. At infant school his teachers reported that he tended to be aggressive with other children. After transfer to the junior school he became increasingly aggressive and disruptive, although in a report on Peter's second year his teacher reported that he had settled down and made reasonable progress. During his third year with a new teacher and further unsettling episodes at home Peter's behaviour began to deteriorate.

His new class teacher, in her first year as a qualified teacher, found Peter and the three boys he tended to associate with, extremely difficult to manage; and his previous teacher from the second year also experienced a deterioration in Peter's behaviour during the special maths lessons he took with this third year class. Following discussions with the second year teacher his new teacher decided to keep an 'incident record' in relation to Peter's behaviour. Apart, however, from an increase in disruptive behaviour during an oral follow-up to a schools' history television programme there did not appear to be any particular pattern to the episodes. Both the head and Peter's second year teacher offered advice about management techniques, especially in relation to the sequencing of oral and written work and in the use of oral questioning techniques. These resulted in an improvement in behaviour during a drawing/writing (rather than oral) follow-up to the television programme and some general improvement to over-all class management. But Peter's behaviour still gave rise to concern and the headteacher asked Peter's teacher to complete the BSAG and Rutter's Children's Behaviour Question-naire. She had come across these check lists on her in-service MA course and welcomed the opportunity of trying them out in school. (They would also conveniently provide the basis for a future course work assignment!) Knowing from experience how dependent these measures are upon the perspective of individual teachers the head also asked Peter's second year teacher to complete the form.

The scores for Peter on the CBQ were class teacher 21 and second year teacher 15, each with a high antisocial sub-score. On the Bristol Social Adjustment Guides Peter emerged, as expected, as a high scorer on the *Ovract scale* (class teacher, 30 and second year teacher 25). Both scores placed Peter within the highest 2 per cent and 'severely maladjusted' range. On the *Unract Scale* he scored 1 and 2, respectively, placing him at the 70th and 52nd percentiles and at the 'stable' end of the continuum. The head felt that these ratings tended to confirm the feeling of the staff that Peter's behaviour was suf-ficiently generalized (i.e. not simply reactive to an inexperienced teacher) and 'serious' to merit further advice from the educational psychologist and allied support services.

The head discussed the problem with the Educational Psychologist who asked, as a preliminary to his visit if the class teacher could carry out a sociometric study with her class. For the sociometric study the teacher was asked to use three contexts:

1. Who would you like to work with in project work? (The project on 'Space' took place on three afternoons a week and involved pupils working in self-chosen groups for different aspects of the topic.)
2. Who would you like to play with in the games period?
3. Who would you like to invite home for tea?

The sociometric data confirmed the position which could be readily observed in class, namely that Peter belonged to a small 'clique' of four boys (see sociogram and sociomatrix (8.1 and 8.2 below) for first context in which Peter is pupil 'P'.). The second sociogram showed Peter to be more integrated, and popular in the 'games' context but the third sociogram reverted to the predominance of the clique. The first sociogram shown below (girls A–H; boys I–T) clearly identifies two strong sub-groupings in the class, one of girls (ABCD) and the other of boys (PQRT). There is a clear 'star', S and a 'neglectee', N. (There could be no 'isolates' in this particular exercise since each pupil was required to give three choices.)

The educational psychologist visited the school to observe Peter's behaviour in class in the context of the project work supervised by his class teacher. He was also able to discuss the results of the Bristol Social Adjustment Guide, CBQ and sociometric data with the rele-

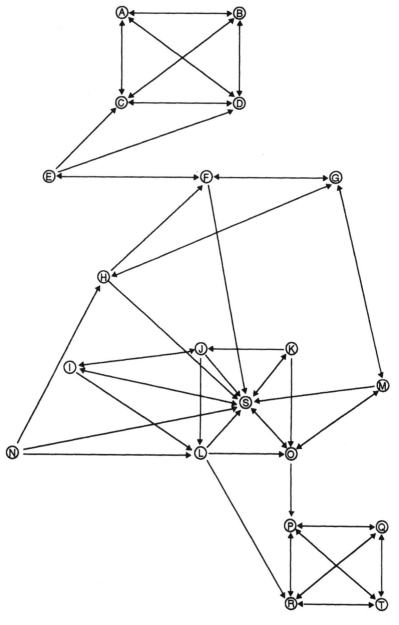

Fig 8.1

vant staff and head. The psychologist drew the class teacher's attention to the fact that her difficulties in controlling the class during the project periods were exacerbated to some extent by the seating

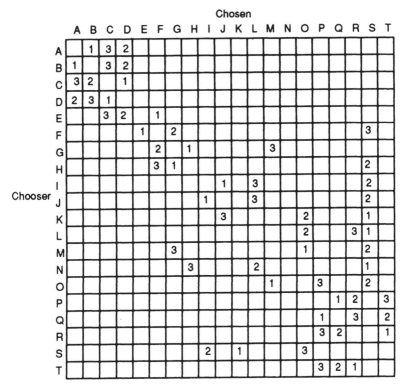

Chooser \ Chosen	A	B	C	D	E	F	G	H	I	J	K	L	M	N	O	P	Q	R	S	T
A		1	3	2																
B	1		3	2																
C	3	2		1																
D	2	3	1																	
E			3	2		1														
F					1		2												3	
G							2		1				3							
H							3	1											2	
I									1		3								2	
J								1			3								2	
K									3						2				1	
L															2			3	1	
M							3								1				2	
N								3				2							1	
O													1			3			2	
P																	1	2		3
Q																1		3		2
R																3	2			1
S							2		1						3					
T																3	2	1		

Fig 8.2

arrangements in which the boy's group of P, Q, R and T tended to work together, partly on the 'Space' project but more often on their own disruptive projects! It was suggested that she might use the results of the sociometric exercise (and to tell the class that she was using their choices) to re-group the pupils on some occasions. Since O (a relatively well-behaved and responsible pupil) had given Peter as one of his three choices this provided the teacher with an opportunity to introduce Peter to a 'new' relationship (and set of relationships, since O has inter-links with S and M, and through them a number of other chain links). The attention of the teacher was also drawn to N who appeared to be very much a fringe member of the class social structure, a feature hitherto unnoticed in everyday observations. Again, it was suggested that with attention to the composition of working groups this boy might be helped to become a little more integrated into the social group. The class teacher was also asked to try to pin-point a little more precisely exactly which of Peter's behaviours were causing her concern, to note their frequency of occurrence and the context in which they occurred. This would then form the baseline from which to measure future progress. (Coulby and Harper's Checklist[72] was suggested as a useful reference list to use for this purpose. The list is shown in Appendix 2 at the end of this chapter.) The educational psychologist also identified the main lines of approach which he would advise – especially to be on the look out for Peter's 'good' behaviours and to give these immediate positive reinforcement. One of the support team would help with these tasks and in working out suitable approaches.

Since Peter's academic progress was also causing some concern the psychologist planned to see him individually later on (when he had also arranged to see his mother). He would assess him on the British Ability Scales and look closely at the nature of his reading difficulties. Since Peter's profile on the BSAG also indicated some 'depressive' features the psychologist also indicated that he would administer the Battle inventory[73,74] to provide a measure of self-esteem. Again, he intended to use this as a base-line for measuring improvement in Peter's adjustment.[75,76]

The case study is unfinished since the diagnosis and intervention is still proceeding. I hope, however, that it does give a flavour of the type of use to which psychological measures can be put in approaching the problem of behaviour difficulties in the classroom. It might be argued, of course, that many of the teacher's and psychologist's actions could have been taken without recourse to such measures and it is certainly possible that an experienced teacher would have prevented the behaviour difficulties reaching such an intractable stage. In the present context, however, the assessments have provided a greater degree of insight into the nature of the difficulties than was provided by general classroom observation alone and they have established a useful base-line from which to evaluate future progress. It seems reasonable to conclude, therefore, that such measures, if used with sensitivity and good judgement, can offer a valuable aid to the assessment and amelioration of behavioural difficulties in the classroom.

Notes and references

1. See P. Kline (1983) *Personality: Measurement and theory*, London: Hutchinson, pp. 107–111.
2. D.H. Hargreaves, K.H. Hestor and J.M. Mellor (1975) *Deviance in Classrooms*, London: Routledge and Kegan Paul, p.37.
3. See C. Kyriacou (1986) *Effective teaching in schools*, Oxford: Blackwell, ch. 8.
4. D. Galloway, T. Ball, D. Blomfield and R. Seyd (1982) *Schools and Disruptive Pupils*, London: Longman, pp. 98–9.
5. See T. Booth (1981) 'Demystifying integration', in W. Swann (ed.) *The Practice of Special Education*, Oxford: Blackwell, in association with The Open University Press, ch.5.1. Especially relevant is page 301 in which Booth discusses the survey of Jessie Parfitt (1975) *The Integration of*

Handicapped Children in Greater London, London: Institute for Research into Mental and Multiple Handicap.

6. J. Todman, S. Justice and I. Swanson (1991) 'Disruptiveness and referral to the Educational Psychology Service', *Educational Psychology in Practice*, 6 (4): 199–202.
7. Department of Education and Science (DES) (1978) Special Educational Needs, The Warnock Report, London: HMSO.
8. J. Lawrence (1984) 'European voices on disruptive behaviour in schools: definitions, concern, and types of behaviour', *British Journal of Educational Studies*, 32(1) pp.4–17.
9. R.M. Povey (1972) *Exceptional Children*, London: Hodder and Stoughton.
10. S.L. Bull and J.E. Solity (1987) *Classroom Management: Principles to Practice*, Beckenham: Croom Helm.
11. For a useful checklist see D. Coulby and T. Harper (1985) *Preventing Classroom Disruption Policy, Practice and Evaluation in Urban Schools*, Beckenham: Croom Helm, pp. 69–72. (Reproduced in Appendix 2.)
12. Another useful checklist which includes suggestions for a management programme is that of P. Galvin and R. Singleton (1984) *Behaviour Problems: a System of Management*, Windsor: NFER-Nelson.
13. D.L. Leach and E.C. Raybould (1977) *Learning and Behaviour Difficulties* London: Open Books, ch. 3.
14. S.L. Bull and J.E. Solity (1987) op. cit. (see note 10).
15. P. Cooper (1989) 'Emotional and behaviour difficulties in the real world: a strategy for helping junior school teachers cope with behavioural problems', *Maladjustment and Therapeutic Education*, 7(3): 178–85.
16. D. Coulby and T. Harper (1985) op. cit. (see note 11).
17. C. Kyriacou (1986) op. cit. (see note 3).
18. J. Lawrence and D. Steed (1983) 'Coping with Disruptive Behaviour', *British Journal of Special Education*, 10(1).
19. M. McManus (1989) *Troublesome Behaviour in the Classroom: a Teachers' Survival Guide*, London: Routledge.
20. M. Saunders (1979) *Class control and behaviour problems*, Maidenhead: McGraw-Hill.
21. J.W. Docking (1980) *Control and Discipline in Schools*, London: Harper and Row.
22. K. Wheldall, F.E. Merrett and H. Russell (1983) *The Behavioural Approach to Teaching Package* (Birmingham: Centre for Child Study, University of Birmingham).
23. Department of Education and Science (DES) (1989) Discipline in Schools, Elton Report, London: HMSO.
24. S. Houghton, K. Wheldall and K. Merrett (1988) 'Classroom behaviours which secondary school teachers say they find most troublesome', *British Education Research Journal*, 14: 295–310.
25. See review by J. Docking (1989) 'Elton's four questions: some general considerations', in N. Jones (ed.) *School Management and Pupil Behaviour*, Lewes: Falmer Press, pp.10–12.
26. See also D. Galloway, T. Ball, D. Blomfield and R. Seyd (1982) *Schools and Disruptive Pupils*, London: Longman.
27. D. Fontana (1985) *Classroom Control: Understanding and Guiding Classroom Behaviour*, Leicester: BPS British Psychological Service in association with Methuen, ch. 3.

28. DES (1989) op. cit. (see note 23).
29. B. Burden (1990) 'The Elton issue: an introduction', *Educational Psychology in Practice*, 5(4): 171.
30. For a comparison of norm versus criterion-referenced assessments see D. Slatterly (1989) *Assessment in Schools*, 2nd edn, Oxford: Blackwell. It should be noted, however, that such comparisons relate generally to performance in *cognitive* skills. Although behaviour check lists are criterion-referenced to some extent, they tend to relate to 'problem behaviours' and not to degree of 'skill mastery' which is the predominant characteristic of criterion-referenced achievement tests.
31. D.H. Stott and N.C. Marston (1974) *Bristol Social Adjustment Guides*, 5th edn, Sevenoaks: Hodder and Stoughton.
32. M.L.K. Pringle, N.R. Butler and R. Davie (1966) *11,000 Seven Year Olds*, Harlow: Longman.
33. R. Davie, N. Butler and H. Goldstein (1972) *From Birth to Seven: a Report of the National Child Development Study*, London: Longman, in association with The National Children's Bureau.
34. C. Gilmore, S. Mattison, G. Pollack and J. Stewart (1985) 'Identification of aggressive behaviour tendencies in junior age children: first stage in a study of aggression', *Educational Review*, 37: 53–63.
35. D. Coulby and T. Harper (1985) op. cit. (see note 11).
36. D.H. Stott and E.G. Sykes (1956) *The Bristol Social Adjustment Guides* London: University of London Press.
37. R. Davie, N. Butler and H. Goldstein (1972) op. cit. (see note 33).
38. D.H. Stott and N.C. Marston (1974) op. cit. (see note 31).
39. D.H. Stott (1966) *Studies of Troublesome Children*, London: Tavistock.
40. D.H. Stott, N.C. Marston and S.J. Neill (1975) *Taxonomy of Behaviour Disturbance*, Sevenoaks: Hodder and Stoughton.
41. P.A. McDermott (1980) 'Principal components analysis of the revised Bristol Social Adjustment Guides', *British Journal of Educational Psychology*, 50: 223–8.
42. M.L.K. Pringle (1965) in O.K. Buros (ed.) *The Sixth Mental Measurement Year Book*, New Jersey: The Gryphon Press.
43. M. Rutter (1967) 'A children's behaviour questionnaire for completion by teachers: preliminary findings', *Journal of Child Psychology and Psychiatry* 8: 1–11.
44. M. Rutter, J. Tizard and K. Whitmore (1970) *Education, Health and Behaviour*, London: Longman.
45. W. Yule, M. Urbanowicz, R. Lansdown and I.B. Millar (1984) 'Teachers' ratings of children's behaviour in relation to blood levels', *British Journal of Development Psychology*, 2: 295–305.
46. M. Rutter, et al. (1970) op. cit. (see note 44).
47. M. Rutter, et al. (1970) op. cit. (see note 44).
48. M. Rutter, et al. (1970) op. cit. (see note 44).
49. C. Kyriacou and H. Roe (1988) 'Teachers' perceptions of pupils' behaviour problems at a comprehensive school', *British Educational Research Journal*, 14(2): 167–73.
50. J. Tizard (1968) 'Questionnaire measures of maladjustment', *British Journal of Educational Psychology*, 38: 9–13.
51. P. McMichael (1981) 'Behavioural judgements: a comparison of two teacher rating scales', *Educational Studies*, 7(1) 61–72.
52. P. McMichael (1981) op. cit. (see note 51).

53. J.C. Moreno (1934) *Who Shall Survive?* Washington: Mental Diseases Publishing Co.
54. N.E. Gronlund (1959) *Sociometry in the classroom*, New York: Harper and Row.
55. K.M. Evans (1962) *Sociometry and Education*, London: Routledge and Kegan Paul.
56. M.L. Northway and L.W. Weld (1957) *Sociometric Testing: a Guide for Teachers*, Toronto: University of Toronto Press.
57. K.C. Thomas (n.d.) *Sociometric techniques. Rediguide No. 18*, Maidenhead: TRC Rediguides.
58. D.H. Hargreaves (1967) *Social Relations in a Secondary school*, London: Routledge and Kegan Paul.
59. J.C. Barker-Lunn (1970) *Streaming in the Primary School*, Windsor: NFER.
60. E.M. Anderson (1973) *The Disabled Schoolchild*, London: Methuen.
61. F. Maltby (1984) *Gifted Children and Teachers*, Lewes: Falmer.
62. K.C. Thomas (n.d.) op. cit. (see note 57).
63. M.L. Northway and L.W. Weld (1957) op. cit. (see note 56).
64. K.G. Rowley (1967) 'Social relations between British and immigrant children', *Educational Research* 10(2) 145–9.
65. A.G. Davey and P.N. Mullin (1982) 'Inter-ethnic friendship patterns in British primary schools', *Educational Research*, 24(2) 83–92.
66. N.E. Gronlund (1959) *Sociometry in the Classroom*, London: Harper and Row.
67. J.S. Moulton, R.B. Blake and B. Fruchter (1960) *Sociometric Reader*, Glencoe: Free Press.
68. K.C. Thomas (n.d.) op. cit. (see note 57).
69. S. Oden and S.R. Asher (1977) 'Coaching children in social skills for friendship making', *Child Development*, 48: 495–506.
70. M.L. Northway (1968) 'The stability of young children's social relations', *Educational Research* 11(1): 54–7.
71. L.J. Cronbach (1970) *Essentials of Psychological Testing*, 3rd edn, New York: Harper and Row.
72. See D. Coulby and T. Harper (1985) op. cit., pp. 69–72. (see note 11).
73. J. Battle (1977) 'Test-retest reliability of the Canadian self-esteem inventory for children', *Psychological Reports* 40: 157–8.
74. Details of the original 60-item scale are provided in J. Battle (1976) 'Test-retest reliability of the Canadian self-esteem inventory for children', *Psychological Reports*, 38: 1343–5.
75. Other useful measures of self-esteem and self-concept can be found in R.B. Burns (1979) *The Self-Concept: Theory, Measurement, Development and Behaviour*, Harlow: Longman and L. Cohen (1976) *Educational Research in Classrooms and Schools: a Manual of Materials and Methods*, London: Harper and Row.
76. For older students (16–21 years) a useful scale is Berger's 'Acceptance of Self' scale (in E. Berger (1952) 'The relation between expressed acceptance of self and expressed acceptance of others', *Journal of Abnormal and Social Psychology* 47: 778–82). Emms, et al. (1986) have developed a modified version of this scale together with some normative data. See T.W. Emms, R.M. Povey and S.M. Clift (1986) 'The self-concepts of black and white delinquents: a comparison within an English youth custody centre', *British Journal of Criminology*, 26(4): 385–93.

Appendix 1:   A children's behaviour questionnaire for completion by teachers

Child scale B

to be completed by teachers

Below are a series of descriptions of behaviour often shown by children. After each statement are three columns: 'Doesn't Apply', 'Applies Somewhat', and 'Certainly Applies'. If the child definitely shows the behaviour described by the statement place a cross in the box under 'Certainly Applies'. If the child shows the behaviour described by the statement but to a lesser degree or less often place a cross in the box under 'Applies Somewhat'. If, *as far as you are aware*, the child does not show the behaviour place a cross in the box under 'Doesn't Apply'. Please put *one* cross against *each* statement. Thank you.

Statement	Doesn't apply	Applies somewhat	Certainly applies
1. Very restless. Often running about or jumping up and down. Hardly ever still	☐	☐	☐
2. Truants from school	☐	☐	☐
3. Squirmy, fidgety child	☐	☐	☐
4. Often destroys own or others' belongings	☐	☐	☐
5. Frequently fights with other children	☐	☐	☐
6. Not much liked by other children	☐	☐	☐
7. Often worried, worries about many things	☐	☐	☐
8. Tends to do things on his own – rather solitary	☐	☐	☐
9. Irritable. Is quick to 'fly off the handle'	☐	☐	☐
10. Often appears miserable, unhappy, tearful or distressed	☐	☐	☐
11. Has twitches, mannerisms or tics of the face or body	☐	☐	☐
12. Frequently sucks thumb or finger	☐	☐	☐
13. Frequently bites nails or finger	☐	☐	☐
14. Tends to be absent from school for trivial reasons	☐	☐	☐
15. Is often disobedient	☐	☐	☐
16. Has poor concentration or short attention span	☐	☐	☐
17. Tends to be fearful or afraid of new things or new situations	☐	☐	☐
18. Fussy or over-particular child	☐	☐	☐
19. Often tells lies	☐	☐	☐
20. Has stolen things on one or more occasions	☐	☐	☐
21. Has wet or soiled self at school this year	☐	☐	☐
22. Often complains of pains or aches	☐	☐	☐

23. Has had tears on arrival at school *or*   ☐   ☐   ☐
    has refused to come into the
    building this year
24. Has a stutter or stammer   ☐   ☐   ☐
25. Has other speech difficulty   ☐   ☐   ☐
26. Bullies other children   ☐   ☐   ☐
    Are there any other problems of behaviour?

....

....

Mr/Mrs/Miss ....

How well do you know this child? Very well ☐

Moderately well ☐   Not very well ☐

Source: M. Rutter (1967) 'A children's behaviour questionnaire for completion by teachers: preliminary findings', *Journal of Child Psychology and Psychiatry*, 8?.

Appendix 2: *The Behaviour Checklist.*
Schools Support Unit

Checklist of potentially disruptive classroom behaviour

This information is to help with our assessment procedure and will also form part of the data used in the ongoing evaluation of the Schools Support Unit project. Please circle each of the following behaviours in the appropriate column. Your decision will depend on:

  a) whether or not it is disruptive in a given situation;
  b) the number of times you would expect an average child to do such a thing;

0 would mean occurs a usual number of times compared to an average pupil; 1 occurs more than a usual number of times compared to an average pupil; 2 occurs much more frequently than average.

nn – please circle if this behaviour does not apply to any pupil in the class.

Thank you very much for your co-operation.

Name of pupil:

A 1. Turns round in seat   nn   0   1   2
   2. Rocks in chair   nn   0   1   2
   3. Sits out of position in seat   nn   0   1   2
   4. Fidgets   nn   0   1   2
   5. Plays with toys or possessions   nn   0   1   2
   6. Shuffles chair   nn   0   1   2
   7. Stands up   nn   0   1   2
   8. Changes seat   nn   0   1   2
   9. Moves from seat   nn   0   1   2
  10. Walks about class   nn   0   1   2
  11. Runs about class   nn   0   1   2
  12. Leaves classroom   nn   0   1   2
  13. Climbs on furniture   nn   0   1   2
  14. Lies on floor   nn   0   1   2
  15. Crawls on furniture   nn   0   1   2

B	1. Moves furniture	nn	0	1	2
	2. Throws pellets/paper	nn	0	1	2
	3. Throws equipment/books	nn	0	1	2
	4. Throws furniture	nn	0	1	2
	5. Bangs furniture	nn	0	1	2
	6. Stamps feet	nn	0	1	2
	7. Taps hand on furniture	nn	0	1	2
	8. Taps pencil/ruler	nn	0	1	2
C	1. Cries	nn	0	1	2
	2. Laughs/giggles inappropriately	nn	0	1	2
	3. Makes non-verbal noises	nn	0	1	2
	4. Whistles	nn	0	1	2
	5. Sings	nn	0	1	2
	6. Tells lies	nn	0	1	2
	7. Pulls funny faces	nn	0	1	2
	8. Makes inappropriate gestures	nn	0	1	2
	9. Talks to self	nn	0	1	2
D	1. Damages own work	nn	0	1	2
	2. Damages own property	nn	0	1	2
	3. Damages class furniture	nn	0	1	2
	4. Writes on furniture	nn	0	1	2
	5. Writes on wall	nn	0	1	2
	6. Spits on floor	nn	0	1	2
	7. Deliberately disarranges dress	nn	0	1	2
	8. Hurts self	nn	0	1	2
	9. Feigns illness	nn	0	1	2
	10. Feigns need to go to the toilet	nn	0	1	2
	11. Plays with or strikes matches	nn	0	1	2
	12. Plays with or smokes cigarettes	nn	0	1	2
	13. Moves others' property	nn	0	1	2
	14. Damages others' property	nn	0	1	2
	15. Takes others' property	nn	0	1	2
	16. Interferes with teacher's property	nn	0	1	2
E	1. Carries on distracting conversation with other pupil	nn	0	1	2
	2. Shouts to other pupil	nn	0	1	2
	3. Verbally abuses other pupil	nn	0	1	2
	4. Spits at other pupil	nn	0	1	2
	5. Obliquely assaults another, e.g. drawing pin on chair	nn	0	1	2
	6. Mimics other pupil	nn	0	1	2
	7. Passes food/drink to another pupil	nn	0	1	2
	8. Strikes with hand another pupil	nn	0	1	2
	9. Strikes with weapon another pupil	nn	0	1	2
	10. Pokes another pupil	nn	0	1	2
	11. Kicks another pupil	nn	0	1	2
	12. Pushes another pupil	nn	0	1	2
	13. Trips another pupil	nn	0	1	2
	14. Bites another pupil	nn	0	1	2
	15. Scratches another pupil	nn	0	1	2
	16. Pinches another pupil	nn	0	1	2
	17. 'Strangles' another pupil	nn	0	1	2
	18. Clings to other pupil	nn	0	1	2

	19. Verbally threathens other pupil	nn	0	1	2
	20. Physically threatens other pupil	nn	0	1	2
F	1. Fails to bring equipment	nn	0	1	2
	2. Fails to bring correct book	nn	0	1	2
	3. Fails to do homework	nn	0	1	2
	4. Fails to do punishment work/attend detention	nn	0	1	2
	5. Carries on distracting conversation with teacher	nn	0	1	2
	6. Calls out to teacher	nn	0	1	2
	7. Shouts at teacher	nn	0	1	2
	8. Mimics teacher	nn	0	1	2
	9. Verbally abuses teacher under breath	nn	0	1	2
	10. Verbally abuses teacher directly	nn	0	1	2
	11. Clings to teacher	nn	0	1	2
	12. Assaults teacher obliquely, e.g. practical joke	nn	0	1	2
	13. Assaults teacher directly	nn	0	1	2
	14. Verbally threatens teacher	nn	0	1	2
	15. Physically threatens teacher	nn	0	1	2
	16. Silently fails to follow teachers' instructions	nn	0	1	2
	17. Silently refuses to attempt work	nn	0	1	2
	18. Arrives late	nn	0	1	2
	19. Leaves coat on	nn	0	1	2
	20. Packs away early	nn	0	1	2
	21. Fails to leave classroom	nn	0	1	2
	22. Eats/drinks	nn	0	1	2
G	*Any other*				
	Please specify and circle	nn	0	1	2

Source: D. Coulby and T. Harper (1985)
Preventing Classroom Disruption Policy, Practice and Evaluation in Urban Schools,
Beckenham: Croom Helm, pp. 69–72.

Management of curriculum and teaching methods and pupils' behaviour in school

TIM BRIGHOUSE

Context of the school and the school itself

Context is all. Too easily, especially in staff rooms, we nod wisely to each other and subscribe to the proposition that children are 'the same the whole world over': we dispel any personal doubts we may have because it is a topic about which we have opinions but precious little data beyond the anecdotal and even less research to begin to back up those opinions. We know, however, that we have never had a fourth year like this lot. 'They are impossible'. We find no difficulty in contradicting ourselves. Context indeed is important. More general rules and principles are to be tempered by some consideration of it. By context I imply differences in teachers, children, schools and localities. Consider.

- Jane is 55 and has been teaching classes of fifteen youngsters aged from about 3½ years to 8 years in a two-roomed primary school in Ullswater in Cumbria, for the last twenty-eight years. She is a pillar of the local church and is married to a farmer. She knows not only the children but their parents. Her room is barn-like, it has high windows and she has accumulated ample materials. All the children in her class learn to read and leave her care with no problems with number. She gets on well with Kath, the head-teacher of ten years standing, who is a year or two younger and who is glad to have Jane as a colleague. They talk easily together about work and have an established rhythm to their school day with a start before 8.0 o'clock and a comfortable finish by 4.0 o'clock or so. They often go home to prepare more work but as often as not, to their various social business. Their preparation for the task ahead lies in the sifted wisdom and well-tried practices of the many years in the locality with the children and their folk.

- David is 28 and has been teaching for one year. He has a full maths timetable which means 36 periods out of 80. He teaches eight different classes from the first (year 7) to the fifth (year 11): some are mixed ability (year 7) and 'set' by ability for maths thereafter. Dave, disillusioned with the rat race of the retail world, has arrived in teaching with a mission and with a wish to teach science. His initial degree was in biology. His large secondary school is in Tower Hamlets in London's East End. It has a transient population, both of teachers and pupils, with a turnover from one year's end to the next of about 40 per cent in both in a good year. Many of the children in Dave's classes seem to have enormous difficulty with English language for which he has been ill-prepared. In his evenings he goes to the local Teachers' Centre to learn more about the issues involved and spends his nights until 2.00 a.m. preparing maths. He aims to have two good lessons a day. There are 60 staff and 900 pupils in the school.

- Helen is 34 and head of the English Department in a Shropshire comprehensive school. The school is one of HMIs *Ten Good Schools* and the local community accept that they are lucky although in order to keep the school on its toes they never show it. House prices are high in this rural/commuter area and the school is a selling feature in the local estate agents. Helen is anxious to ensure that any good academic performance of many of the pupils in English is matched by a stretching and motivating experience for each and every one of them. She is active in extra curricular activities like so many others among her 50 colleagues on the staff, most of whom live in the school's catchment area. Along with most of the staff she knows at least three-quarters of the 700 pupils, one way or another: she takes it for granted that the deputies seem to know everyone. Helen has been at the school seven years, having come as second in department: she would like to become a deputy head in the not too distant future but knows that it will be difficult to find somewhere as good or fulfilling in which to practise the profession she loves.

- Wendy is 32 and is happy when her junior classroom door closes behind her. She knows that she can work wonders with a class of 33 8 year olds, from 'the worst council estate in Wolverhampton', according to the head and the rest of the staff. Wendy, however, privately thinks it is down to teacher expectation and not the families and remembers wistfully her last school in a similar area in another part of the country where the head had transformed from resigned pessimism to brisk optimism the working lives of junior teachers, many of whom would have previously said exactly what she hears in her present staff room. She keeps her counsel, however, and she reflects sadly that her scale C allowance wasn't worth it. She has had no effect on the language work of others because there is no structure to do so and she can't persuade anyone that the National Curriculum and Key stage 2 could be any sort of fun or opportunity. The school is full of problems. Happiness for her is in her classroom but she notices with regret that the children's behaviour there does not spill over into the corridors or the playground. She reckons she will need to move if she is to sustain her professional enthusiasm.

- Jan is 35 and works in Southern Hall School for thirty behaviourally disturbed children between the ages of 3 and 14 in Cambridge. Most of the children are suspected of having been physically or sexually abused and most have reached 'the end of the line' early in their mainstream schools. Jan, like all the staff, respects, is rude to and worships Fred, the eccentric headteacher, who is in his late forties and has devoted most of his teaching career to children such as these. Jan has seven children in her class aged 9, 10 and 11. Occasionally one of them 'blows' at the staff. Jan has learnt to handle that and the occasional violence with subtle skill. The school has merits for the children's good behaviour and is heavily into positive behaviour modification. The day starts with assembly and the week closes with whole school performances at which most of the children receive some sort of praise and recognition.
- John is a PGCE student at Keele looking for a job. He has the promise of two interviews in comprehensive schools in the same town. He asks to visit in order to take a look at each before the day of the interview. He brings back from the schools staff handbooks from which I present some extracts.

The first school provided the following:

NOTES FOR THE GUIDANCE OF STAFF
1. Time-keeping throughout the day must be initiated by the Staff. NO MEMBER OF STAFF SHOULD BE IN THE STAFFROOM AFTER 8.45 a.m., you are either registering a Form or are acting in the support of a Form Teacher by signing Diaries, etc.

    THE KEY TIMES ARE:

8.45 a.m.	Whistle
8.50–9.15	Registration and Form period on Monday for the whole school; Weds also L/S period.
8.55	FULL SCHOOL ASSEMBLY on Tuesday and Thursday. UPPER SCHOOL ASSEMBLY on Wednesday. Form teachers escort pupils to the Hall and sit with them where possible.
10.25	Morning break
13.00	Lunch break
14.00	Registration
14.05	Afternoon timetable
15.15	SCHOOL DISMISSAL

2. Lateness to lessons should be positively discouraged. Know the seating plan of your study group in order that absentees are identified easily. Inform the Head of Year of any pupil known to have registered who then absents him/herself from your lesson.
3. Pupils taken, or allowed outside the classroom for open-air activities must be fully supervised. PE Staff obviously have priority over the 'all-weather' pitches and playground areas.
4. Except in cases of extreme emergency, no pupil should be allowed to go to the toilets and then only ever singly. Pilfering does occur if pupils wander between lessons.

5. Please do not stand pupils outside your classroom as a punishment. If necessary place a desk outside and provide work to do. Check the pupil's progress.

6. No pupil should be sent to the Staffroom to collect books, etc. during lessons. The Staffroom is private and there may not be a member of Staff there.

7. School Detention is held from 3.20 p.m. to 4.20 p.m . on Wednesday evenings in Room 25. It is supervised by two members of Staff on a rota basis which occurs once a year. During the hour, written work is set. A box kept in the Deputy Head Executive's office has pencils, paper, etc. if needed. The Detention Book should be collected from the same office, the detainees checked and their attendance initialled. The book should be returned to the office at the end of the session.

    If you award a detention, firstly notify the pupil stating the reason and enter this in his/her Homework Diary. As soon as possible enter the details in the Detention Book and complete a Proforma Letter to parents, both found in the Deputy Head Executive's office. The letter will be posted to the parents by the Head of Year. Note: Each Monday to Friday is one session. A detention awarded in any one week will normally be served on the following Wednesday. Only the Deputy Head Executive may excuse a pupil.

8. Staff may award a Personal Detention but a pupil may only be retained in school for a statutory 20 minutes without 24 hours notice to parents. Staff should try to avoid retaining pupils during the lunch-hour. Under no circumstances should a pupil miss having lunch.

9. If you wish to place a pupil 'On Report' please refer to the Head of Year for advice. A pupil who is 'On Report' should present the Form to you during your teaching session at the *beginning* of the lesson. This gives you an opportunity to scrutinise work, homework, attitude, etc. before you sign the Form at the end of the lesson. The pupil presents the completed Form at the end of the day to the Head of Year. The 'On Report' system is shown to be most efficient if used for short periods although this may be done repeatedly. You may find that a pupil has requested to be placed 'On Report' him/herself. This is usually when the pupil wishes to convince his/her parents that all is well.

10. Staff may, of course, write letters to parents but all such letters should first be shown to the Head of Year for information and a copy must be placed in the pupil's Personal Record Card kept in the Section Office. Letters should not be hand-written but presented on headed notepaper, typed by the Secretary.

11. Staff may wish to invite parents into school to discuss a problem. Please inform the Head of Year who may wish to be present. Use the Homework Diary to make the appointment. Any parent may attend our surgery held on Wednesday from 3.20–4.00 p.m. by telephoning the office. All such appointments are entered in a book in the Secretary's office. Staff should, therefore, check this book before leaving the school premises on Wednesday evenings. Normally the Secretary will attempt to inform you.

12. On request to the Head of Year, a pupil may be removed from your teaching session/s for a period of time. The pupil will work under the supervision of a Senior member of Staff but you are responsible for setting the work to be done in your subject. Parents are informed of this

action and invited into school to discuss the matter with you and the Head of Year. Upper School pupils are expected to sign a covenant of behaviour and cooperation in the presence of their parents.

13. In extreme circumstances it may be necessary to exclude the pupil from school. Suspension is our ultimate deterrent. In such cases the Chairman of Governors' permission is sought and the Education Office informed.

14. If an accident occurs within your classroom or whilst on duty please refer the pupil immediately to the School Secretary who is trained in First Aid. She will ensure that the pupil's possessions are passed to her. She will raise an Accident Form and you will be asked to write a statement. This is forwarded to the Education Officer for insurance purposes.

DISCIPLINARY PROCEDURES–SANCTIONS AVAILABLE TO STAFF
Will you please make use of the established procedure for dealing with misbehaviour or laziness in your classes. NO TEACHER SHOULD STRUGGLE ALONE AGAINST PERSISTENT NON-COOPERATION FROM ANY PUPIL OR GROUP OF PUPILS.

The system is designed to support you in your efforts to deal with difficult pupils. If you follow the steps described below, the experience of your Head of Departent and the authority of Senior Pastoral Staff will be brought to bear on your difficulties.

A. *ACTION BY THE TEACHER AND THE HEAD OF DEPARTMENT*
   1. Give the pupil a verbal warning.
   2. Enter the offence in the Homework Diary.
   3. Use a personal detention or written imposition, such as extra/missed work in your own subject.
   4. Discuss the problem with your Head of Department. A change of teaching method may gain a better response and improve discipline.
   5. Ask for your Head of Department's help in effecting a personal detention, etc.
   6. Enter a School Detention in the book in the Deputy Head Executive's room. This should only be done if, with the help of your Head of Department, you have been unable to make your own punishment effective. You must be prepared to take the trouble to do this first.
   7. Report the problem to the Head of Year, also keeping the Form Teacher informed.
   8. If a pupil is *SERIOUSLY DISRUPTIVE* or *DEEMED TO BE A SOURCE OF DANGER* within the classroom making the learning situation impossible for the other pupils then the culprit should be sent to ROOM X. If the pupil refuses to go, send a responsible pupil to fetch the NEAREST SENIOR COLLEAGUE. Please see further notes of guidance below.

B. *ACTION BY HEAD OF YEAR, SECTION HEAD OR DEPUTY HEAD EXECUTIVE*
   1. An investigation will be made into your complaint against the pupil. The following action or combination of actions will then be considered:

   Counselling the pupil
   Placing the pupil 'ON REPORT'
   Punishing the pupil
   Writing to the pupil's parents

Requesting the parents to come into school

Excluding the pupil from certain lessons

Preparing a dossier on the pupil for the Section Head/Deputy Head Executive

2. THE SECTION HEAD will reinforce the work of the HEAD OF YEAR. If necessary he may refer the case to the DEPUTY HEAD EXECUTIVE providing him with the pupil's dossier.
3. THE DEPUTY HEAD EXECUTIVE/SECTION HEAD may suspend the pupil, having previously given him/her formal warning of suspension. If they wish the suspension to be of an indefinite duration (i.e. expulsion), they will ask for a Case Conference to be convened at which the Education Authority is represented by several of its Officers.

ROOM X. NOTES FOR THE GUIDANCE OF STAFF

Exclusion from a lesson is a very serious measure which should only be used in EXTREME cases, i.e. where a pupil's continued presence is so disruptive or dangerous that it prevents other pupils from learning. ROOM X SHOULD *NEVER* BE USED FOR PETTY REPEATED OFFENCES SUCH AS HAVING NO BOOKS/EQUIPMENT/APRON/P.E. KIT. Although such offences may annoy Staff, using ROOM X as a punishment detracts from its intended role. ROOM X, similarly, should never be used to off-load a number of pupils from your class.

Any pupil sent to ROOM X should have a completed ROOM X slip. Wherever possible, the pupil should have relevant work to complete.

The member of Staff on duty in ROOM X should check the details on the slip and enter these details into Upper/Lower School Record Book housed in the Staff Room. This entry should be checked and countersigned *as soon as possible* after the offence by the subject teacher. This ensures that the pupil arrives. If a pupil arrives without work, the Duty Staff members should provide paper so that some written work is done.

It is not the role of the Duty Staff member to investigate the offence. At the end of the session the note from the offended teacher should be placed in the appropriate Section Head's basket in the Secretary's Office. The Section Head/Head of Year will then investigate the offence. They will then decide whether to contact the parents and invite them into school to discuss the problem in the presence of the offended teacher.

Staff on duty in ROOM X are free to mark books there. ROOM X should be manned for all 40 lessons per week and Staff should feel secure in that knowledge when sending pupils there.

The second school provided the following:

SCHOOL CODE OF CONDUCT

This Code of Conduct has been produced after full consultation with students, staff, parents and governors.

INTRODUCTION

Students at Abbey have the right to an education which offers them the best opportunity to attain their potential.

Teachers are here to create the circumstances for this to happen, support staff, governors, parents and officers of the LEA to assist in the process.

It is the right of every individual at Abbey to do these things without being hindered by others.

GUIDING PRINCIPLES

In order that the foregoing should happen, it is essential that everyone of us is:

CONSIDERATE – respecting everyone else as an individual; making sure our words and actions do not cause inconvenience to anybody

COURTEOUS being polite and helpful at all times

COOPERATIVE being willing to work together

FRIENDLY being on good terms with each other

HARD WORKING – doing our best

HONEST being truthful

TRUSTING accepting that others genuinely want to help

RESPONSIBLE being reliable and responsible for our actions; behaving as part of a community.

THE PRINCIPLES IN ACTION

What this means in practice is that we should all do the following:

BE PUNCTUAL – avoid late arrival

SPEAK CONSIDERATELY – avoid shouting, swearing and offensive language

BE READY FOR LESSONS – have the necessary materials

CLEAR UP – after lessons, break and lunch

MOVE IN AN ORDERLY WAY – avoid running and use paths; hold doors open for other people

RESPECT THE ENVIRONMENT – the grass, trees, hedges, buildings and furniture.

IN LESSONS

It is the responsibility of teachers to:

prepare appropriate work for all students in the group

provide opportunities for students to be actively involved in their learning

recognise and encourage achievement and success

assess students' work regularly

maintain an orderly atmosphere in the classroom.

It is the responsibility of students to:

get on with their work to the best of their ability

be prepared to work with anyone else in the group

ask for help when necessary

be prepared to wait for their turn

accept advice and guidance from the teacher

carry out requests from the teacher.

THE BOTTOM LINE

The law of the land applies at Abbey just as it does everywhere else. So, there are some things which are forbidden, not just because we may disapprove of them, but because they are *against the law*.

These are

TRUANCY   DRINKING ALCOHOL UNDER AGE

PHYSICAL VIOLENCE   DAMAGE TO PROPERTY

THREATENING BEHAVIOUR   LEAVING LITTER

Sexist behaviour and smoking by students are not permitted.

These Jane, David, Helen, Wendy, Jan and John (with two school handbooks) are real enough cases even if I have disguised their identity. What do they tell us?

First, there is the context of the *location* of the school itself. To run a school in an area where a high proportion of the youngsters have English as a tentative and emerging second language and where the cultural expectation of their homes are different, poses different challenges to the school as a whole and the teachers within it. That is not to argue that they are necessarily more difficult challenges than many other schools and teachers face – although many with experience in different contexts would acknowledge that they are – but they are certainly different and will require different knowledge skills and attitudes in teachers both individually and collectively. Moreover, the curriculum design and teaching styles should be affected by those considerations. To ignore occupations and backgrounds of the youngsters being taught is to miss the opportunity to influence their curriculum. Nor is it simply that. The wise teacher tunes in to the local accent and dialect, local customs and habits, and makes a judgement how far they can be orchestrated to optimize each child's learning opportunity. Teachers who have experienced both will talk wisely of inner city and rural disadvantages, not as things that are equal but as factors demanding different approaches. They will also talk of the advantages!

Locality does not end there. It is generally the case that secondary schools on council house estates represent to many ambitious parents on those self-same estates, a symbol of what they wish to avoid if possible for themselves and certainly for their children. Some are inclined to make sacrifices to remove their children to schools off the estate, a process in which they are encouraged by the advent in some areas of City Technology Colleges and in all areas by open enrolment. To teach in the 'off the estate' school involved will demand different assumptions about parental interest and backing from those who are teaching in the school 'on the estate'.

The contextual matters of locality we have so far addressed are more or less out of the control of the school. Although in the past there have been examples from schools funded by city livery companies which have moved from one part of the country to the other, nowadays a school cannot very well decide *not* to be on the council estate. The school must make the best of its circumstances but the wise school will recognize the idiosyncratic and perhaps changing nature of their circumstances. So too will the teachers who are in the schools and those who seek to teach there. It is no good saying 'well what more can you expect of these children . . . look at their homes'. That is to collude.

Curriculum teaching and learning styles and of course pupil behaviour are also affected by contextual factors of the school which *are within the school's own control*. It is to those that I now wish to turn.

The above example of John who returned with staff handbooks, illustrates how the school as a whole affects the environment in which pupils and staff behave one towards another. There is no need to comment on the hidden curriculum which the extracts from the two staff handbooks imply. It will be a sufficient exercise for practising teachers, advisers and trainers of teachers, to debate the curriculum effects of school organizational factors, rules, rewards, the location of rooms and their relationship one to another even of the staffroom, to the headteacher's room and the school office, of whether staff take part in extra-curricular activities or share activities with pupils, the training and practice of the mid-day supervisor – all contribute to the *human* environment. The school can affect its visual environment too, however unpromising it is. Sandon High School in Stoke-on-Trent suffers from the disadvantage of being an unusual 1930s design. Its white facade flakes in a way that would make the worst sufferer from dandruff gasp in amazement. For good measure the LEA sold to a local contractor, the aggregate in the school playing field which as you can imagine is a difficult thing to do without rendering the field useless. And so they were at Sandon for five years. In consequence, the school suffered a near mortal blow, which only the vision, resilience and commitment of a new head, together with an amazingly professional staff, have overcome. She fought tooth and nail to win resources to transform the backdrop against which the staff arranged their curriculum and their teaching styles. The staff and their head hoped in so doing to modify the behaviour of pupils from Sandon High School. Day by day, term by tiring but rewarding term, they are doing so.

The recently arrived headteacher at Queens Park, an 11–18 comprehensive school in Chester, has used the windfall arising out of the LMS formula to carpet most of the school: the staff already acknowledge that their teaching and the children's learning at the end of a busy and stressful year, is the better for the changed environment.

Within the school's own control therefore is a substantial part of the visual and aural environment. These, moreover, are much more susceptible to painless change than other matters such as the teachers' use of material or their styles of teaching or even their beliefs. Even the organizational features which establish and regulate the rhythm of the school's everyday practices are changed only with the greatest care.

Of course as we move to the contextual factors which *are* within the control of the school itself, we are into the territory of what makes one school a more favourable backdrop against which to teach than another. Ever since HMI's 'Ten Good Schools' there has been a growing, if tentative, body of research on the issue of school 'effectiveness' or 'success'. The factors, processes or characteristics which have been found to be significant in the UK in the various ages can be summarized as follows. For nursery and infant schools we have to rely on Barbara Tizzard's work which indicates that

- preschool attainments (especially acquiring knowledge of letter sounds and the ability to use words)
- mothers' level of education
- teachers' expectations (critically too low)
- parent–teacher cooperation.

are four crucial factors which affect outcome.

Peter Mortimer also conducted an extensive longitudinal survey of school difference for the junior years in inner London and found the following factors to be significant.

- purposeful leadership by the head
- involvement of the deputy head
- involvement of teachers
- consistency among teachers
- structured sessions
- intellectually challenging teaching
- work-centred environment
- limited focus in sessions
- maximum communication between teachers and pupils
- parental involvement
- record keeping
- positive climate.

Mortimer has worked with Michael Rutter whose book *Fifteen Thousand Hours* first gave research backing to the school effect. The researchers concluded that the following were important:

- school ethos
- good classroom management
- high teacher expectations
- teachers as positive role models
- positive feedback and treatment of pupils
- pupils given responsibility
- shared staff-pupil activities.

What all this amounts to is a list of processes, all within the control of the school itself and arguably susceptible to positive influence and reinforcement from the LEA. These processes may be summarized as follows:

- leadership (at all levels)
- management and organization
- collective self-review
- staff development
- environment building and ethos
- teaching and learning

● parental involvement.

The school needs to address all these issues if individual teachers, with their chosen curriculum and particular learning styles are to have the most favourable circumstances in which their pupils may succeed. Space precludes an elaboration of any detail. The inquisitive reader will have to look elsewhere to find the elusive ways in which the processes can be addressed in a way in which positive rather than negative features can be made manifest.

But what of the classroom and the individual teacher?

The teacher's education and training – the early years.

As a teacher trainer I should be tempted to say their initial training is all important. Indeed in a previous incarnation as Chief Education Officer in Oxfordshire, I know that colleagues responsible for appointments deliberately sought primary teachers who had been trained at either Bishop Grosseteste, Lincoln, or Charlotte Mason, Cumbria, or a college in York, because it was thought the graduates from those places seemed to have a more thorough grasp, a clearer and better founded philosophy and a determination to be successful teachers, than was the case with 'beginning' teachers from other places. So too it seemed in practice to me. It was of course not always so: nor did it mean that teachers from other training institutions were not appointed. It is simply to illustrate that we thought along with others that the nature and quality of the initial training made a significant difference to the 'beginning' teacher's chance for translation into a confident practitioner.

In the light of closer experience of teacher training I am not going back on that proposition entirely although some, spotting its extraordinary stereotyping, would doubtless believe I should. It now seems to me that a teacher's career is at least as greatly influenced by the nature of the local authority and particularly the school and the department in which they start teaching. Back to the school effect! Ideally therefore teachers in training need a statement of principles and skills against which they can reflect. That is why there is a growing interest in school-focused teacher training to link more closely those in higher education who are responsible for providing the 'beginning' teachers with training and education to particular and designated schools whose staff or 'mentors' share in the process. It helps to emphasize to the teachers and the schools, the longer term nature of emerging development of the successful practitioner. Such initial education and training demands a set of clearly stated principles and some common aims. For at least one such set of teacher educators and trainers, it takes the following form:

We believe that there are different teaching styles but that those which are successful in unlocking children's talents are informed by certain common principles and attitudes. We have found it difficult to be precise or exhaustive about the common features but their flavour is perhaps best captured by saying that those involved in this initiative want to help to produce teachers who are prepared to:

- provide equal opportunities for pupils or students to help them to become confident, competent and contributing citizens
- treat children as individuals
- realize the powerful influence inevitably exerted by their own various role models
- present high expectations to pupils and emphasize their positive achievements
- become supportive team members who will contribute to creating and maintaining a successful school
- take seriously their own professional development standard and remain intellectually curious
- contribute to the greater knowledge of the profession during their career
- have a healthy sense of humour and of perspective.

This is included in a profile which also elaborates some understanding and practice which a teacher will gradually acquire. There are sections for work with the individual in the classroom, for the teacher working with the class as a whole, for a teacher as a member of the whole school community and for the teacher as a member of the profession.

Now I come to the last and vital part relating to the teacher as a practitioner in the classroom. We can take it as read that their training has been reasonably positive and enlightened and the school in which they are working has taken on board most of the lessons of the 'school effectiveness' debate. The teacher has allowed for context. She will not assume that she is teaching the motivated teenage offspring of affluent, supportive and successful parents when in reality she is teaching 5-year-olds whose lone parent is in a shelter for battered women. So all the conditions are right.

What is there in the microprocesses of successful teaching and learning that affects curriculum and teaching and teaching and learning styles? The most illuminative piece I have read on the subject is a book *Effective Teaching* published by the National Primary Centre and those in quest of the tune as well as the words of successful teaching should examine it closely. It not merely underlines but brings to life the importance of the time honoured processes of good lesson preparation, of varying style, of rhythm, pace and pitch, of open questionnaire, of positive assessment and above all of the necessity to arrange interesting material and activities which are the antidote to behavioural problems. Moreover the summaries of essential points contained in Chris Kyriacou's book (*Essential Teaching Skills*, Blackwell 1991) are as succint a guide as any one is likely to find. It covers in a persuasive way the key points to planning and preparation; lesson preparation; lesson management; classroom climate; discipline; assessing pupils' progress and reflection and evaluation.

In teachers, however, there are certain qualities without which, whatever their style, children are very unlikely to learn. Harry Ree who among other things has been a highly successful headteacher tells of his interview for the headship of Watford Grammar School in the 1950s. He was cross-questioned by Sir John Newsom, then Hertfordshire's education officer. 'Tell me Mr Ree, you were the only candidate who has not been a headteacher already. They have experience which you lack, for example in selecting new staff. What will you look for in the staff you appoint?'

Ree recalls 'At that moment an angel descended on my shoulder. "Generosity," I replied.' Indeed generosity is the first quality of successful teachers. They need to be prepared to be generous in spirit, to be prepared to treat people as they will become rather than as they are, to go far beyond duty or what is reasonable, to turn themselves inside out to find a way to unlock the children's interest and potential. The generosity needs to be tempered by the fine judgement of knowing when to press and when to hold back. It means that teachers will need to be excessively generous with their time and their energy. Such generosity implies *interest* not merely in what they are teaching but whom they teach. Ask any group of pupils the factors which contribute to 'a good teacher' and words which convey the overriding importance to the pupils of someone being interested in them, in their uniqueness as people will be in every reply.

Coupled to the 'generosity' of spirit, the teacher needs a restless intellectual curiosity about their own practice, the subject matter they teach, their methods in the classroom and the society in which they and their children live. Such a combination of 'generosity' and 'intellectual curiosity' is often evident in teachers who acquire the habit in their early years of working as a 'researcher' or 'reflective practitioner': in short they collect evidence of their own present practice the better to inform their future practice. This is admirably illustrated by the following extract from a study by a teacher of her 11 year-olds who were reckoned to be a behavioural problem.

A Case Study from a practising teacher of 15 years' experience
Two years ago I found a real problem to be solved. I was given a class of 10/11 year-old children. They had a reputation for bad behaviour, no interest in learning and a 'bad' attitude generally in schools. I had to teach them for their last year in primary school and I could see that this was going to be a real problem. Something was going to have to be done to make them want to learn and to give them some self-respect.

I looked at the reports from previous teachers and these gave me a starting point. I have listed the complaints and responses from the previous teachers as follows:

'Low reading standard generally' . . . 'an inability to communicate' . . . 'the language development is inadequate' . . . 'this class has difficulty verging on the impossible in working in groups'.

I could immediately diagnose the general feeling of failure, of defiance and lack of interest. Of course there was also the issue of who had taught the group in the previous year. Even allowing for that and the question of streaming which I describe below, I knew the group had a 'reputation': moreover, when I looked at their reading ages which had been worked out in the previous year, I could see how they generally were lagging behind their chronological ages. I was quite convinced that many of these children were underachieving. Not one child was reading to his/her chronological age.

I delved back again into the records of the class and found some interesting information which left no doubt in my mind as to some of the causes of the under-achievement of these pupils. The children along with other children of similar age, were given the 7+ screening when they entered the junior school. The results of the screening test decided which class they were to enter: this particular group were the lower scorers on the test. At the age of 7 they had been streamed. It was also interesting to note that the majority of these children were generally younger than the children in the other class, which means in fact that they had belonged to a group of children who had not started school until January, some six months after the older group of children in the same age group. This seemed to confirm to me the well-researched evidence of disadvantage to the Summer born child – compounded in this case by streaming.

Reading on I found that in its progress through the primary school the class had experienced no fewer than six different teachers. The first year was with two teachers, the second year with one and the third year with no fewer than three. The teaching that the children had received over the last three years had been at times very formal and not aimed at individual levels but at the class as a whole.

In short I had come up with reasons and causes for the lack of interest and general apathy in the class as well as the discipline problems. All I felt I had to do now was to find a cure. I tried to put myself in the position of a child in the class. I thought of the things that had interested me as a child and about the lessons that I had enjoyed most and why.

In many ways my school life was the best of any. I was educated at a village school and all my memories were fond ones. I can't remember very much about actual lessons, as so many people can't, but I do recall all the other things that we used to enjoy. I remember the long nature walks, catching sticklebacks and frogspawn, planning and making the school garden, going on visits and playing imaginative games in the yard. I had been on endless bike rides, had enjoyed dancing lessons and piano lessons. My greatest love however was to paint and draw and make things: indeed most of my learning took place when I was making and doing things. I knew my environment and I had used it. I had exploited all my senses to the full and I had never been happier than when outside exploring.

I felt sure that I could get through to these children who perhaps, as I had, favoured experiential activity and in particular activity within their local environment. From a mixture therefore of analysis, experience and intuition, I decided that I would adopt my strategy on this hypothesis.

I felt sure that I could get through to these children by taking them out of school and into their environment and decided that the whole year should be devoted to environmental work, saturating the children's sense with first-hand experiences. First I received the headteacher's permission, which was readily forthcoming, and I began to plan my campaign.

The children were from a mixed background of council and private housing and many of them in both sectors from broken homes – possibly another contributory factor to the behaviour problem.

First, I decided to take them away from the school for a week, to Stanley Head Outdoor Education Centre. I felt that a complete break with past routine was needed. We were fortunate to be accepted at short notice and although the cost was £30, we ensured that every child went. (As a school we compensated the one or two cases where the costs would be too much for the home pocket.) For some of them it was their first time away from home and they were very apprehensive. Others couldn't wait to get away.

The residential experience
They experienced just about every emotion during the week. On the first day they went rock climbing. This was a salutory experience to observe. They laughed, cried, screamed and gazed open mouthed. Those who thought they couldn't, could; and those who were over-confident, realized that maybe they shouldn't be too sure in future. Not only did the pure physical effort of rock climbing have a great effect on them but the wonderful view from the top of the moor really impressed everyone of them. That evening after dinner most of them went to the classroom and painted or sketched their impressions of the afternoon. One of two others sat and wrote about their experience.

We made several visits during the week. We visited an old lead mine and a museum of mining in Matlock. We went on a bike ride along the Manifold Valley, which really was wonderful. They thought it was marvellous to see their teacher riding a bike, little realizing that her enthusiasm for such an experience was rekindled by the nostalgia of recollected childhood.

We went on a visit to Manchester Airport and this for some was in their own words 'pure magic'. They stood open mouthed, watching the planes taking off and landing. They found it difficult to comprehend that planes were going to and coming from countries all over the world. That evening many of them found atlases and looked up the different countries that they had seen on the huge departure boards.

In the later evening, when it was very dark, the children were sent off on an orienteering course and this took them away from the camp but within the camp limits. This was quite a similar experience for them to the rock climbing as many of them had fear of the dark and it took a lot of courage for several children to venture away from the camp. All of them, however, completed the course.

Apart from the traumatic 'learning experience' which both the rock climbing and the orienteering had provided and the vivid stimulus from the various visits, they all learnt other things as members of a group. They were expected to contribute to the group as a whole by taking responsibility in sharing the tasks of living. They all had duties to perform from cleaning the dormitories to washing the pots after dinner. It was clear that as the week went on, a real team spirit was developing and they became more tolerant of one another and even volunteered to help one another out when difficulties occurred.

On the last day we tried our hands at archery and bird-ringing. The archery was a new experience for all of us and the bird-ringing was quite a surprise. Although the children knew about birds, very few of them could identify the different species and to see them close up was really a new experience for most of them.

When the time to leave came, the children were quite upset. It had been a most successful week. A lot of parents and children realized how much they missed each other and it was easy to see from the way children greeted parents and vice-versa, that both sides had gained enormously. The proof of the theory, however, would be in the everyday attitudes in the classroom.

Subsequent behaviour in the classroom

The attitude of the children once back to the normal school routine was transformed. They tackled their work with enthusiasm and interest and even though some of them were very limited academically, they produced the very best that their capabilities would allow.

This project had taken place in the Autumn term and the rest of the term was spent on geographical, environmental, language and artistic work connected with the visit.

The period in the early part of the Spring term I felt would be crucial: it was essential to sustain the spirit of teamwork and enthusiasm which had been generated. I wanted the children to go to their secondary school feeling confident and assured that they could achieve, if they would bring the right attitude to their tasks.

The children by this time were mature and responsible and I felt that another project which would use these qualities was needed to sustain the benefits and attitudes and performance which the 'residential' had introduced.

As it happened the staff of the school decided that they would introduce a school project on the Victorians during the Spring term and this, coupled with a course on involving schools with local industries and businesses, generally gave me an idea on which to work.

At the time my responsibility was for music in the school and I thought of producing some kind of concert. I discussed this with the children and they developed their project from there. They suggested for me a Victorian theatre company and actually running the company and producing a concert all on their own with a little help from me and the rest of the staff.

It was agreed that a visit to the Theatre Royal in Hanley might be useful and they appointed someone to telephone the theatre and arrange a visit for the class to look behind the scenes. This took place and from there the Victorian Theatre Company was formed. The children elected a chairperson, a secretary, a treasurer and a committee. They held meetings at which minutes were taken and various members of staff including the head-teacher, were invited. The minutes were typed on the wordpro-cessor by various members of the class and circulated in the appropriate manner. They negotiated a loan from school funds to start the company off and enlisted the help of various members of staff and children from other classes in the production. Their contribution to the performance, apart from the stage managing and backstage work, was to put on a short Victorian melodrama. The whole concert was a resounding success, running for three performances and with over 100 children involved. A profit of £100 was made and the children chose what the money was used for.

Interestingly, they decided to pay for themselves and the other fourth year class to visit RAF Cosford Aerospace museum. It seemed that they too now valued the stimulus of visits!

For one child the Victorian Theatre proved to be what Graham Greene has called 'the moment in childhood which lets in the future': for one of the girls applied to audition for a stage show and was successful. She decided that she enjoyed singing and would make her reason for living in the future a musical one. Again the children's work following the RAF Cosford visit was informed by determined application, energy and vivid outcome. Even the children who were quite poor academically, when compared with children in the parallel class, produced comparatively more descriptive and imaginative written work.

The all round development of these children was quite remarkable. I realized at the beginning of the year that I couldn't turn them into academic geniuses but I wanted to awaken feelings and emotions that hitherto had not been felt. I wanted them to be able to speak out without fear of being shouted down and to become more socially aware of other children and people about them. There was progress in their academic abilities which was quite astonishing in some cases. Five children had entered poems in an external competition and received certificates of recommendation. Another child found that she enjoyed writing poetry so much that she wrote a book of poems. She presented them to me as a gift when she left. There were also improvements in their reading ages.

The reading ages at the end of the year bear out the fact that with two exceptions the children were still under-achieving in reading but they had made more than ordinary or expected progress during the year.

The second year
Although I had been pleased with the year's work, I felt that I would like to try again with the next class, similarly streamed, although the last of such streamed classes in the school. A visit to Stanley Head was not possible on this occasion but I considered it not quite so important as I was informed that the class was calmer. I couldn't help noticing however, a significant difference between the two years as a result of their experience at the 'residential'. For example, subsequently when they left the school it was only from the first year that I received visits from the class to let me know how they were getting on.

The previous year's work of course had been very much a case of trial and error, planning lessons as I saw avenues along which the children wanted to travel. This year I intended to plan very carefully and look at all the aspects of the curriculum, already thinking in terms of the National Curriculum and at as many different ways of working as possible. I asked myself what were the objectives of the exercise. The answers were to do with giving the children as many experiences as possible but perhaps in a more focused way, evoking echoes of Bloom's Taxonomy of behavioural objectives, I itemized more closely the different ways in which children could learn as follows:

Collaborating . . . exploring . . . investigating . . . making choices and decisions . . . organizing . . . explaining . . . talking and communicating . . . sharing . . . observing . . . taking responsibility . . . asking and answering . . . recording . . . interpreting . . . predicting . . . recording and reflecting . . . planning . . . evaluating.

On looking at the list I realized with the benefit of hindsight, how much of this I had done intuitively the previous year.

On this occasion I realized that I must plan the work more precisely. I asked myself the following questions:

1. Will what I am planning develop investigative thinking?
2. Will they be developing skills for autonomous work?
3. How will the work be recorded, whether in their own topic books, group topic books, or class topic books?
4. Should we use the computer as well as handwriting?
5. Should I ensure group as well as individual work?
6. How far would it be possible to develop the work further in art, CDT, embroidery, etc?

I decided that decisions about grouping would have to be taken as the project developed and that it would be wise to let the children have some say in how they worked.

I decided to focus the year's work on the school in the local environment. We centred our studies on the church and priory about half a mile from the school.

We visited the priory on many occasions throughout the year and the children did lots of research, finding out exciting facts about its history. Many of them wrote stories about the history of the priory and one group in particular decided to write a book of stories through the different periods of history up to the present time.

The children divided themselves up into groups and I set tasks for a week at a time for the different groups to cover. The only real instruction that I gave was that I expected every group to cover all the tasks at some point. The groups told stories which were variously factual and fictitious: they sketched and painted: they researched the church: drew plans: looked at the grave-stones and came to conclusions about how people had died. They worked at the millpond, exploring the land around and observed and recorded the inhabitants. They carried out traffic surveys and even started an anti-litter campaign. Unfortunately, while their studies were going on, the priory was badly burned by fire on two occasions and this really made them very cross. They voiced their opinions loudly and when the building eventually came up for sale, they heard many stories of what was going to happen to the land. Fortunately the land was to be restored. Had it not been these future citizens would have mounted a campaign within the community.

The work over the time of the project was excellent again, although academically not particularly of a high standard. It showed imagination, presentation and initiative. The art and craft work was of a very high standard and they all used a computer at some stage through their work. Some very interesting scientific studies were made about pond life and the bird and animal life around the priory and church and they carried out experiments on water and its various properties. One group designed a large embroidery of the church whilst others made three-dimensional models of animal life in the area.

I have not included the comparative tables which underlined for the teacher concerned the value of the 'residential' and 'environmental education' in improving the reading scores of the teacher. Perhaps her most telling comment was that the children from the residential groups revisited her for years afterwards. She demonstrates the qualities and values which provide the key to classroom management.

In summary, we have seen in this chapter the importance of the school's context, of how, through 'school improvement', any school can influence its own destiny and of how those two contextual factors profoundly affect the performance of the individual teacher. So far as the latter is concerned brief reference has been made to the well-remarked processes of classroom management, lesson preparation, presentation and other methodological factors but emphasis has been placed on qualities of the successful teacher and how the combination profoundly affects the behaviour of pupils. However traumatic the child's life outside school the successful teacher creates and manages a secure environment within which all children can flourish.

PART THREE

Behaviour of specific age groups

CHAPTER 10

Discipline in nursery and infant schools

AUDREY CURTIS

Before we can begin to consider how early childhood educators introduce discipline into their classes it is essential that we identify what is meant by discipline within the school context.

The dictionary defines discipline as 'teaching rules and forms of behaviour by continual repetition and drill'. A disciplined person is defined as one 'whose obedience is unquestioning'. Such definitions, particularly when considering young children, seem unnecessarily grim and have punitive connotations reminiscent of Dickensian England and a school philosophy which assumed that children needed to have their wickedness beaten out.

Peters (1966) in *Ethics and Education*, related discipline to conformity with rules, while Wilson (1977) in *Philosophy and Practical Education*, argued that discipline involved following rules because they seem appropriate to the task in hand. He reasoned that, if we are required to follow rules under other circumstances this is a form of coercion or control and is not necessarily discipline.

More recently, Smith (1985) refuted both these views and claimed that there are three cases of discipline:

one where we follow rules willingly because we see them as right or appropriate; two, where we follow them under manipulative coercion, such as when we are persuaded that there is no alternative to the rules and three, where we follow them under what may be called punitive coercion, being threatened with punishment, or in general some unpleasant consequences if we do not.

It has also been suggested that discipline can be defined even more loosely, that it is the process designed to aid the development of social behaviours and attitudes for appropriate participation in an adult democratic society. In considering these various definitions – and these are but a few that exist – it is debatable how useful they are to teachers and nursery nurses working with young children.

There are few educators who would disagree that one of the aims of education is to help children develop into autonomous thinking individuals and for this one has to encourage children to build up self-discipline. Learning self-discipline takes time and is certainly not fully developed in the early years of schooling. However children must learn to behave in an acceptable fashion within the school/classroom setting and I would suggest that the majority of experienced workers with young children would consider that one of their most important functions is to help children develop pro-social behaviours and acceptable strategies in order to cope effectively not only in the classroom, but also in the wider social world.

Although we can argue about definitions of discipline it is important to remember that children's understanding of discipline in this phase of schooling is related closely to their understanding and interpretation of rules and commands. This understanding may be unintentionally in conflict with the views held by the adult. When the Elton report (DES, 1989) wrote about 'promoting good behaviour' one must remember that it is relative to the age of the child and that the issues arising from managing discipline in nursery and infant schools will be affected by the age of the children.

This chapter will be divided into two main sections. In the first part some of the main types of problem behaviour associated with children aged between 3 and 7 years will be looked at in the light of their overall development. There will be discussion on whether many of the 'discipline' problems and non-conforming behaviour exhibited during the period are a function of immaturity, both intellectual and social, rather than real 'behaviour problems'.

The second section of the chapter will focus upon the effect of classroom organization and constraints upon children's behaviour. The importance of consistency of adult behaviour will be stressed as will the ways in which close links between home and school can help solve behavioural problems. Finally, a few suggestions will be made as to how some children's disruptive behaviour might be managed in the classroom.

What sort of behaviour?

Many of the children who challenge the authority of the teacher at this age, do so because they lack an understanding of the rules and not because they wish to be defiant. In recent years, the literature has drawn attention to the distinction between 'problem children' and 'children with problems'. Problem children are the disruptive ones who are 'naughty' and 'troublesome' as opposed to the children with problems who may have difficulties in coping with school or have home or other personal problems. For some children entry into school is a traumatic experience worsened by difficulties in relating to other adults. Learning itself can also pose a challenge to some. However, whether we are referring to 'problem children' or 'children with problems' both are likely to cause some form of disruption within the classroom and will require to be 'managed' within the school setting.

For the majority of children coming into nursery school this may well be the first time that they have needed to cooperate and identify with children outside the family or immediate neighbourhood and to accept discipline from adults outside the family circle. Their challenges to authority may well be due to their failure to appreciate the norms of behaviour expected of them within the school setting. Such children who seem to be 'problem children' may simply be non-conforming due to ignorance.

It is only in recent years that teachers have complained that children at the nursery and infant school age are disruptive. Evidence was presented to the Elton Committee (DES, 1989) by the Assistant Masters and Mistresses Association (AMMA) pointing out that discipline was becoming a real problem among children aged 3–7 years. We will discuss some of the possible reasons for this later but first let us consider what might be termed 'common disruptive behaviours' in children between the ages of 3 and 7 years.

Common disruptive behaviours in children between 3 and 7 years

When teachers and nursery nurses refer to the need to discipline young children because of their behaviour what do they mean? What sort of behaviour can be termed disruptive in the nursery or infant classroom? Antisocial behaviour in young children can take a number of forms, but generally it falls into two main categories; non-compliant and aggressive behaviours.

Non-compliant behaviour

Non-compliant behaviour entails refusal to carry out an instruction or recognize a rule or regulation. During bouts of non-compliance the child may stand still and either ignore a request or firmly refute it with 'NO!' or 'Don't want to'. Such behaviour is quite common among 3s or young 4s at the beginning of their school career. It may stem from a lack of understanding of the request, but more likely it comes from a child who is not yet sure of the behavioural boundaries of the nursery or infant classroom. Such children may have been brought up in a very sheltered and protective environment and are accustomed to displaying emotional outbursts when asked to do something. Some children are overwhelmed by the hurly-burly of the classroom and have always been used to being centres of attention. It is very difficult to prepare a child for nursery school especially if she has never been away from her parents before. She will be overwhelmed by the rough and tumble of the nursery and may well react in a negative fashion either because she does not understand the rules, but more possibly because she wants attention. It can be argued therefore, that much of the non-compliant behaviour in the nursery school can be attributed to the developmental stage of the child, although there is no doubt that there are a few problem children in the nursery years.

A recent study of the 3-year-old children (Richman et al. 1982) found that 15 per cent of children show mild behaviour problems, 6 per cent show moderate problems and 1 per cent have severe problems. The types of behaviours contributing to antisocial behaviour were:

over active/restless	12.9%
difficult to control	10.7%
attention seeking	9.2%
poor concentration	5.7%
tempers	5.1%

In a later study, Golding and Rush (1986) found that temper tantrums in young children are more likely to be associated with adverse behaviour traits like, destructive tendencies, fighting, disobedience, telling lies and bullying. In their sample 15 per cent of boys had a tantrum at least once a week, compared to 10 per cent of girls. It is interesting to note that residence in a poor urban environment where space is often limited, was a factor in the frequency of temper tantrums.

Aggressive behaviour

Aggressive behaviour is most likely to manifest itself in terms of temper tantrums, biting, hitting, fighting, shouting, swearing and threatening and other impulsive behaviour. During such aggressive outbursts the young child may also destroy toys and break furniture, throw objects around the room and generally resort to bullying and fighting if not stopped. It is interesting to note that children do not necessarily display aggressive behaviour both at home and in the school setting. Some who are amenable and docile within the school system may be deemed as 'out of control' by parents, while others are disruptive in school but display acceptable behaviour at home.

It is crucial that 'problems' in young children are seen in the context of the child's stage of development and within the social milieu in which the child lives. Is the cultural environment of the home the same or different from that of the school? What sort of temperament does the child have? Temperament can play an important part in children's behaviour. Some children are more easily aroused than others and are labile in their emotions and impulsive. They cannot control their emotions and demand immediate attention. If their needs are not met straightaway then there is likely to be a display of aggressive behaviour.

However, Manning and Sluckin (1984) have pointed out that aggression may have a function in the preschool and primary school years. They found that there were big differences among children in the amount of aggression they displayed on entering primary school. Manning differentiated between hostile aggression and manipulative aggression. In hostile aggression it appears that the child aims to hurt. For example, a child walking past a construction made by another child, kicks it down for no apparent reason. Whereas manipulative aggression occurs when the child uses aggression as a means of pursuance of useful goals. For example, the child snatches toys from others in order to play with them. This the researchers argue, forms the major part of aggression of many children in the early years of schooling. Hartup (1978) considered that hostile aggression is used to control the environment, while manipulative aggression is used to bolster the ego. Hartup has argued that it is difficult to differentiate between the types of aggressive behaviour as the child who can intimidate others is less likely to be molested and more likely to command a better control of resources.

Manning and Sluckin found stability in the aggressive tendencies and styles of individuals during their two years in the nursery. Very aggressive children tended to show more malicious, revengeful types of aggression, whereas the 'non-aggressive' child used aggression mainly in pursuit of 'useful' goals.

Further analysis of the behaviours and characteristics of these children showed that difficult children were more physical, attention-seeking, clinging and boastful than well-adjusted children who displayed more adaptive behaviours and were more friendly and positive.

Manning and Sluckin also found that all difficult children appeared determined to interfere with the cooperative play of others and they were less able to adjust their behaviour appropriately. This meant that these children displayed the same behaviour patterns daily even though they themselves knew that the results would be disastrous and would end in tears.

Montagner (1978) has pointed out that dominant, aggressive children are usually feared in the nursery. They need to get their own way and frequently do if there is not an adult to intervene. The trouble with this situation is that such 'destructive' children are very demanding. They want and *need* loving friendships and positive attention but their very behaviour precludes them from getting what they really desire. Rather it has the reverse effect.

By the time children reach infant school there is a greater likelihood of verbal aggression occurring. The Elton Report (DES, 1989) commented that 1 in 20 children of primary school age were verbally aggressive, although it is likely that the percentage is less in the younger aged child. Between the ages of 5 and 7 most disruptive behaviour takes the form of general rowdiness, with children talking out of turn, displaying both verbal and physical abuse to others and more rarely verbal abuse to the teacher.

Some disruptive behaviour can manifest itself in a push for dominance, with the child attempting to buy favour with others. If this does not work the child tries to build up an image of toughness. (Behaviour of this kind is more usual amongst boys.) However Sluckin (1981) in his study of behaviour in the first school found that although the child liked to be seen as tough, he studiously avoided any fights, relying on winning verbal rather than physical confrontations.

As children gradually develop the use of language there is a growth in its use for controlling behaviour. It may take the form of self-discipline when the child starts to use the same controlling language as has been used on him. For example, when a child is clambering up the climbing frame he may tell himself 'careful now, up you come' or if a child is digging in a forbidden area he may say to himself, 'no Paul, not in the flower bed' just as though it had been spoken to him by an adult. Sometimes one hears a child fiercely instructing himself but disobeying his own instructions for example, 'you mustn't hurt dolly' and at the same time yanking the doll's hair out. If this happens frequently the teacher or parent needs to ask themselves whether the child is being given a stream of instructions without the reasons being made clear or making sure that some are obeyed before the next are given.

Both nursery and infant school aged children use words to control the behaviour of others. Young children are always at the receiving end of controlling talk and therefore it is inevitable that they will try out language for themselves.

Four year olds in particular tend to sound very bossy and this may well act as an irritant to a teacher with 4 year olds in a reception class, particularly if she has had little experience of the age range. At this age the child can be heard saying 'stop that at once' or 'come here' to another child, generally younger or smaller, for by now the 4 year old is beginning to appreciate her own sense of 'self' and is trying to find someone below her so that she can be boss as well as being bossed. Furthermore, the child is trying out language to see whether her language will have as much effect on other people's behaviour as the adult's has on hers.

Another characteristic of 4 year olds that can lead to classroom disruption is boasting. The child of this age is using words to boost her self-esteem. Two children of this age can often have a boasting session which to the outsider can sound awful, but which to them is just a game, for example:

My daddy's car is bigger than yours
My daddy's car is bigger
My daddy's car is as big as a tank
My daddy's car is as big as an army
My daddy's car is bigger than anything in the whole world

Although this form of boasting is normally harmless badinage, teachers need to be wary that this form of exaggeration can be reflective of the children's inner feelings. Does the child who boasts a lot and upsets her peers really mind upsetting them or is she really a very insecure person, who needs comfort and reassurance because she feels very humble and insignificant?

Children of 4 and 5 often use words to gain approval, like 'I'm a good boy'. It is a comparison situation which many teachers find odious but it is nevertheless one way in which children demonstrate that they want to be sure of themselves.

Control of inner rage and aggression

Children in nursery and infant classes experience feelings of anger so intense that they can frighten themselves. For example, when a child shouts at another 'I'll kill you' at this stage he does not realize the extent of the damage he could do to another person and really needs, not admonition, but reassurance from the adult that he would not and could not kill, but that the adult realizes that he is very angry at that particular moment. Likewise verbal abuse like 'silly old cow' from a very young child is not the same as if a teenager used the same term of insult. Some people suggest that a reply like 'if I am a silly old cow, you are an angry little calf' might be the best way to deal with the situation. However this form of verbal abuse is dealt with it is important to remember that children are probably copying what they hear at home or in the playground and are frequently trying out words without real undestanding of the implications.

By the time children are in the second year of infant education they are beginning to develop a sense of justice and the words, 'It isn't fair' become familiar cries in the classroom. Cognitively, the 6 year old is very different from the 3 or 4 year old. Her use of language is more developed and her interests are beginning to extend beyond the home. Kutnick (1988) has pointed out that by 6 years of age we can expect the beginnings of general conformity to teachers, younger children are still too concerned with feelings of self to be able to conform. They want to please the teacher but often cannot understand what is required of them.

In the first section of this chapter we discussed some of the types of antisocial behaviour that are associated with children between the ages of 3 and 7 years. From a developmental perspective it has been shown that some of the so-called 'disruptive' behaviour may be normal for young children and that with increasing maturity many of the difficulties will disappear. However as children move from non-statutory schooling into 'proper school' the anxieties and stress associated with the transition may result in temporary regression and behaviours like temper tantrums or outbursts of tears may reappear in children who seem mature for their age.

Effect of classroom organisation and its constraints

Every school and every classroom has its rules and constraints and teachers expect children on entering the class to conform to these norms. Some children learn more rapidly than others that if you do what you are told, or at least appear to conform, and keep out of the teacher's way then all will be well. Others do not learn this as quickly and are seen early on in their school careers as 'different' at best and in many cases as 'disruptive, naughty, nuisances' etc. Developmentally, the 'conformers' may be more mature and therefore have come to understand more quickly the way classroom society works, *or* they may have elder brothers and sisters or friends higher up the school who have given them advice on how to 'survive' in the classroom.

Children entering school for the first time, whether it be nursery or infant school come as active learners who will have learnt how to problem solve and investigate their own home environments. Most will have had a considerable amount of adult attention, opportunities to talk and ask questions and will have learned to cope with the routines and constraints imposed upon them by family members. They will know how to interpret the facial expressions of adult members of the family and how to manipulate situations. Their expectations of adults and the wider social world will be based upon these experiences. Their expectations of school, either positive or negative, will be based upon the impressions given to them by adults and older children.

However well prepared, entry into either the nursery or infant classroom must be a bewildering experience for the young child. The noise, the vast numbers of children, all more or less the same age, and the poor adult/child ratios (1–13 in the nursery, possibly 1–25+ or more in the infant class) and the space – no wonder so many children stand around the edge of the classroom during their first days of nursery schooling and refuse to participate in any activities.

The prepared learning environment in a nursery class is bright, inviting and filled with interesting activities. On the surface there is a great deal of choice, but in reality there are hidden constraints and restrictions. The child has to learn that only four children are allowed to play at the water tray at the same time; 'we all hang our coats on our own pegs'; 'we put back the apparatus that we have taken from the cupboard'. Early in their school careers children have to learn the rules of the classroom and some, through immaturity, or inappropriate previous learning find it difficult to keep to the rules.

Time, which plays such an important part in our lives, has little meaning for the young child, who once engrossed in an activity may be in a dream world oblivious to the adult instructions to clear away for story time, etc. In spite of comments by teachers and nursery nurses that children are free to choose and carry out their own activities, an observer in any nursery school soon realizes that times for real freedom of choice are very limited and that 'clock time' is an important part of life in many nursery classes.

Many of the 'discipline' problems arising in the nursery stem from the adult's failure to fully appreciate that it is not necessarily disobedience on the part of the child when she fails to put her things away, but rather total absorption in an activity and lack of understanding of the need to obey this particular set of instructions immediately. After all, during the day it may well be that an adult has encouraged her to 'concentrate' on a toy or stay longer with a particular activity. How is the 4 year old to deal with these conflicting messages? Children need to be warned well in advance that they have to discontinue a particular activity, in that way they will gradually develop a sense of time and furthermore will not be seen to be non-compliant when they refuse to carry out an instruction immediately.

As they mature the majority of children of nursery school age come to understand, or at least abide by, the rules and regulations of the school setting. Their relationships with adults and other children improve and many develop into independent, young people capable of making sensible decisions about the use of time, materials and space. Outbursts of non-conforming, aggressive behaviour, mainly due to frustration, become less as the child's control over the environment improves. However, there are still children who find it impossible to cooperate with others and whose means of communication is predominantly through pushing, hitting and snatching toys from their peers.

These aggressive children are very difficult to manage in nursery school settings. They are the children who regularly disrupt the working atmosphere of peace and calm and promote fights which frequently result in children getting hurt. Their presence may well prevent other children from having the opportunity to engage in prolonged bouts of cooperative play, particularly fantasy play. Teachers frequently attempt to divert these disruptive children rather than attempt to get to the bottom of their difficulties in order to help the rest of the children whose play is being disturbed.

Demanding children are another group which may give rise to concern. Their behaviour is irritating rather than disturbing, although many teachers are worried that such children do not fit in.

Children whose behaviour gives rise to concern need help if they are not to be labelled as 'disruptive' children when they leave the nursery. It may well be that in their home environments such behaviour is tolerated and the child is behaving 'normally'. As has been mentioned earlier, children who have developed these types of behaviour patterns, particularly hostile aggressors, become so unpleasant that adults and other children have given in to them for a 'quiet life'. Such children have never had an opportunity to learn that good behaviour gets rewarded whereas bad behaviour does not. For them negative behaviours will have been the means of getting attention and achieving goals. We have all been in a supermarket when a child whines for sweets and after endless refusals the frustrated parent gives in and buys them. Once more the child has learned that if you persist in being difficult you get what you want. Unfortunately, when teachers give in in these situations, usually for the sake of the rest of the group, they do so with severe consequences for the management of discipline in their classroom. Not only will the difficult child be rewarded for bad behaviour but others will note the situation and attempt to emulate the 'bad behaviour' themselves.

Research has clearly indicated that in many cases moderate behavioural problems that cause teachers difficulties in schools have been reinforced through parents and other children giving in to the disruptive child. Such children are often very unhappy as the boundaries for their behaviour have never been made clear and as they continue to test the limits of adult control; they discover that it gives way the more they push. Such a situation *must* never arise in school.

All teachers will recognize this type of child and experienced ones will know that one of the best ways of dealing with the problem is to talk with the parent(s). A frank discussion carried out in an atmosphere of trust and respect will almost certainly be received with enthusiasm by the parent who is probably coping with similar behaviours at home. When school and home decide on similar strategies and the child comes to understand that we all have to conform at times, the chance of modifying the unpleasant behaviours is high. The disruptive child above all wants to feel needed and secure. Learning to live within consistent boundaries will go a long way towards helping the child make the necessary behavioural adjustments.

The child who has adjusted well to nursery school routine has developed a great deal of social competence and may be looking forward to entering the reception class. But frequently the transition from nursery to reception class is as traumatic an experience as entry into the nursery. Children who have spent one or two years in the nursery will have learned to be independent, to get out and put away materials, will know and understand the daily routines and be familiar with the constraints of the environment. For them the nursery environment is 'school'. However, in reality there are wide differences between nursery and infant classrooms. Not only are staff ratios different, opportunities for choosing activities are even more limited and out door play takes on a very different meaning when it is restricted to two short breaks morning and afternoon with up to 200 others and no equipment. Likewise many children who have been praised for their independence and self-reliance face criticism when they enter the classroom in the morning and start taking out equipment to use. The rules and regulations of 'proper school' may well be very different. The first few days in the reception class are frequently taken up with procedures and the young child who has learnt one set of procedures may have to unlearn them and learn a new set. Adjustment to these new sets of instructions can be as bewildering to the new entrant from the nursery as for the new entrant from home. The use of space, time and choice of activities are all different in the infant classroom and the child has to learn to conform to not only the new organizational norms of the classroom but also has to learn to conform to the behavioural patterns required by the new teacher, who, if she has no helper will have even less time for the individual child than the nursery teacher.

The hidden messages about life in the infant classroom may well be different from the nursery so the young child has a considerable amount of relearning to do. Each classroom is a different social world, although there are recognizable characteristics in common. Some children by the age of 7 will have had to adjust to at least four different classroom settings. Is there any wonder that children who are developmentally immature or have insecure backgrounds often find it difficult to conform in an acceptable manner.

However, most children make sense of school and they do it primarily through language and people watching. Teachers should never underestimate the amount of learning that takes place when children are apparently standing and staring.

A factor of prime importance in managing discipline in the classroom relates to the attitudes of the staff to the children. Not all teachers are the same even though they work within similar classroom constraints. Teachers, particularly young teachers, worry about the maintenance of control in the classroom and if questioned on the subject will identify it as an area of concern and frequently complain that it was not covered effectively in their initial teacher training.

Often the expressions and mannerisms of the adult say more to the child than the words themselves. Just as young children learn to cope with the moods and behavioural idiosyncrasies of family members so they have to learn to interpret the hidden messages they receive from their teachers. Some teachers establish the minimum of rules to ensure the maintenance of safety and order in the classroom and their attitude towards minor infringements are tolerant, providing the major rules are adhered to. Others have a more authoritarian approach and expect their rules and regulations to be rigidly kept. Such teachers tend to expect much greater conformity from their pupils, however young, and this attitude can pose very real problems for some children, particularly the immature. A third, but hopefully, small group of teachers, are very permissive and inconsistent in their outlook and allow children a great deal of latitude and freedom at an age when they do not have the capacity to handle it effectively. These teachers, like highly permissive parents, tend to generate a considerable amount of discipline problems. Although there will always be children whose behaviour is unacceptable in a classroom, 'children have a need to discover where the boundaries of acceptable behaviour lie. It is natural for them to test these boundaries to confirm their location and, in some cases, for the excitement of a challenge' (DES 1989, p. 65).

Lack of conformity within the classroom may not be the fault of the child. Some teachers, like some parents, fail to give clear instructions, use inappropriate language and present the child with ambiguities. What should the child do? How should they carry out the commands? It is very important that children are not confronted with such dilemmas. Carrying out instructions should not have to develop into a problem-solving exercise! For small children with very limited life experience it is crucial that they are given adequate support and guidance in an atmosphere of trust and respect.

What about the non-conforming child? We are aware that young children may experience tension on entering and changing phases of schooling and that problems within the home background may reflect upon behavioural ability to conform. Normally, difficulties associated with transfer will disappear after a period of settling in, but there will still be some children who find it difficult to accept classroom constraints. Such non-conformity may, as we have already mentioned, be due to developmental immaturity or inappropriate learning patterns, but a few children may have disruptive personalities. It has been argued that such children may be extremely extroverted and are unable to accept that rules have any meaning. For these very difficult children schools will need to seek outside professional help.

Many of the children who are rowdy and disruptive during their first few years of schooling will become calmer as they mature and therefore it is important that they are not labelled as 'disruptive'. In labelling a child, a teacher will probably be listing all the negative characteristics – can't sit still, can't listen, cannot obey instructions, etc. Label a child as 'difficult' and she or he will fulfil your expectations. Such a label may well go with the child throughout schooling and often fails to take into account that much of early bad behaviour is characteristic of the age range.

The expectations of the teachers regarding disruptive pupils will vary according to their attitudes towards non-conformity, their experience and how they perceive their role. Teachers, like their pupils, are individuals with varying amounts of tolerance towards disobedience and non-conformity. The type of behaviour that annoys or frustrates one teacher may be looked upon with mild amusement by another. The highly experienced, self-confident teacher who has been trained to work in the early years of schooling is likely to handle a situation differently from the inexperienced teacher who is still unsure of herself and of her professional competence. Unfortunately, nowadays there are many teachers working within the 3–7 age range whose professional training was for a higher age group. Such teachers may not be fully aware of the wide developmental difficulties between children in the early years of schooling and the rapid changes that take place in their understanding in this period.

Teachers who are rather authoritarian in their approach are likely to spend a considerable amount of their time trying to 'socialize' the non-conforming child back to the straight and narrow, often at the expense of the other children in the class. For the child whose difficult behaviour was aimed at seeking adult attention, the teacher's 'socializing' attempts will be seen as strong reinforcers of disruptive behaviour. When teachers find themselves in this position they need to reappraise their own attitudes and strategies otherwise they will nearly always find themselves as the losers.

An atmosphere of calm order with clear sets of rules and instructions and each child being and feeling respected by the adult, will have a greater positive effect upon classroom discipline than any other strategies. Children will feel secure and comfortable in an atmosphere where lessons and materials are well planned, where they know exactly what they have to do when they have finished a particular task and where each and every thing has its own place. Classroom organization of this kind will encourage a harmonious learning environment. Firm, consistent behaviour, with tolerance and understanding shown to children's problems and difficulties should minimize discipline problems in the classroom. Furthermore, a set of established strategies to deal with disruptive children, which have been discussed with other members of the staff and where appropriate, with the children themselves will certainly minimize the amount of disruption and maximize the possibilities for learning within the classroom context.

In the final part of this chapter I want to look at three types of children who are to be found in many classrooms even though they are well organized.

The solitary aggressor

The solitary aggressor, who can be identified even in the nursery school, is generally a child who is unable to break into any of the friendship groups within the class. Always selected last in any group activity chosen by the children, this child is often a hostile aggressor who appears to delight in upsetting as many of his peers as possible. Such children have very poor self-concepts and often appear to be underachieving. If not helped they are very likely to become real deviants as they moved up the school. Such children can be contained and may respond well if the teacher can persuade another child or group of children to involve them in their own activities. Such involvement will necessitate great tolerance and understanding on the part of the selected children and intervention by the teacher as frequently solitary aggressors do not know how to play or how to work cooperatively. If these strategies fail, then if their problems are to be properly addressed the teacher will probably need the help of both the outside agencies and the parents.

Group aggressors

These children are often developmentally mature physically and may therefore be larger than their peers. Their main difficulty is that they do not adapt to the working atmosphere of the class. Although there are 'gang leaders' in the nursery the group aggressor generally emerges towards the end of the infant years as a member or leader of a small disruptive group. Characteristically, the children (normally boys) will be rowdy in class and fail to listen to instructions while the rest of the children are listening intently and will generally be a nuisance during this period. They come into their own in the school playground where it is likely that the group will bully the smaller boys and tease the girls. Normally the group as a whole will have very negative views on school and learning although the leader will be articulate as he can communicate his ideas to others. Group aggressors delight in displaying aggressive behaviour in the classroom and will confront and test the teacher on every possible occasion. They will also cause considerable consternation to dinner ladies who generally find them impossible.

If unchecked such children can wreck havoc in the playground and as they grow up could become the gangs of the future. Normally they abide by the decisions of their leader, therefore the sensible teacher will utilize the leadership qualities of this child and encourage him to be on the side of authority. If this succeeds, and it often does, then that teacher is unlikely to experience further discipline problems with the class as the leader and the rest of the group will help to ensure discipline. The strength of the group aggressors will change from year to year as some teachers may be more effective in handling the situation than others. Although this strategy is a containing one, it must also be remembered that if these children can be persuaded of the importance of school work then there is a possibility that genuine interest may develop.

Exceptional children

Another group of children who may be disruptive in the classroom and go unrecognized are gifted children. Without wanting to label children, with all the connotations that this may have, the very able child is one who finishes tasks early or starts the work late because she knows she can do it speedily and accurately. In the interim period such children can cause disruption with their classmates. Recognizing and stretching able children is crucial not only for their own development, but for the rest of the class who are likely to be disrupted if this exceptional child decides to take on the role of 'class clown' and keep everyone amused at the expense of the teacher. Such gifted children frequently have a wonderful command of language even during the early years of schooling and their badinage can be upsetting to teachers.

In nursery and infant classes there are ample opportunities for children to engage in absorbing tasks which will keep them positively occupied for long periods of time. It is also a useful strategy for teachers to involve very able children in group work where their talents can be used to help others. Failure by teachers to recognize the abilities of these children can produce 'able misfits' who never reach their full potential and become unhappy, frustrated and often highly disruptive.

Most disruptive children break the social rules of the classroom, and as we have seen earlier many children are disruptive at some stage in their school careers. However, few break the law in that they have a court record.

Discipline in the early years of schooling should be concerned with helping small children understand themselves and their emotions. The concept of conformity has little or no meaning for them. For many the constraints and rules of the classroom are totally alien to anything that they have experienced in their own homes and it is the role of the teacher to help them develop self-discipline and to come to appreciate that certain behaviours are acceptable and certain behaviours are unacceptable in the classroom setting. Almost every child entering school for the first time is eager to please the teacher and wants her praise and reassurance. If the teacher's behaviour is always consistent and fair and the children are treated with respect and consideration then the management of discipline in the nursery and infant classrooms should present few problems.

References

Butler, N.R. and Golding, J. (1986) *From Birth to Five: a Study of the Health and Behaviour of Britain's Five Year Olds*, Oxford: Pergamon.

Chazan, M., Laing, A.F., Jones, J., Hayer, G.C. and Bolton J. (1983) *Helping Young Children with Behaviour Difficulties*, London: Croom Helm.

Cohen, L. and Cohen, A. (eds) (1987) *Disruptive Behaviour*, London: Harper Education Series, Harper and Row.

Curtis, A. (1986) *A Curriculum for the Pre-school Child*, Windsor: NFER-Nelson.

Curtis, A. (1989) 'Emotional development and the school', in *Maladjustment and Therapeutic Education*, 7(2): 99–105.

Department of Education and Science (DES) (1989) Discipline in Schools, Report of the Committee of Inquiry chaired by Lord Elton, London: HMSO.

Douglas, J. and Richman, N. (1984) *Coping with Young Children*, London: Penguin.

Golding, J. and Rush, D. (1986) 'Temper Tantrums and other Behaviour problems in N.R. Butler and J. Golding' (1986) *From Birth to Five: A study of the health and behaviour of Britain's five year olds*. Chapter 7. Oxford: Pergammon Press.

Griest, D.L. and Wells, K.C. (1983) 'Behavioural family therapy with conduct disorders in children', *Behaviour Therapy*, 14: 37–53.

Hartup, W. (1978) Children and their friends in H. McGurk *Issues in Childhood Social Development*. Methuen: London.

Hersov, L.A., Berger, M. and Shaffer, D. (eds) (1978) *Aggression and Anti-Social Behaviour in Childhood and Adolescence*, Oxford: Pergamon Press.

Jenkins, S., Bax, M. and Hart, H.C. (1980) 'Behaviour problems in pre-school children', *Journal of Child Psychology and Psychiatry* 14: 181–200.

Johnston, M. and Munn, P. (1987) *Discipline in Schools*, Scottish Council for Research in Education (SCRE).

Kutnick, P.J. (1988) *Relationships in the Primary School Classroom*. PCP Education Series, London: Paul Chapman Publishing.

Manning, M. and Sluckin, A. (1984) 'The function of aggression in the pre-school and primary years', in Frude, N. and Gault, H. (eds) *Disruptive Behaviour in Schools*, Chichester: Wiley.

Montagner, H. (1978) *L'Enfant et la Communication*. Penoud/Stock: Paris.

Moore, S. and Cooper, C. (eds) (1982) 'The young child', in *Reviews of Research, Vol. 3*, National Association for the Education of Young Children (NAEYC).

Olweus, D., Block, J and Radke-Yarrow, M. (eds) (1986) *Development of Anti-Social and Pro-Social Behaviour*, New York: Academic Press.

Peters, R.S. (1966) *Ethics and Education*, London: George Allen and Unwin.

Richman, N., Stevenson, J. and Graham, P.J. (1982) *Pre-School to School: A Behaviour Study*, London: Academic Press.

Richman, N. and Lansdown, R. (eds) (1985) *Problems of Pre-School Children*, Chichester: Wiley.

Sluckin, A. (1981) *Growing up in the Playground: A social developent of children*. London: Routledge & Keegan Paul.

Smith, R. (1985) *Freedom and Discipline*, London: George Allen and Unwin.

Wilson, J. (1977) *Philosophy and Practical Education*, London: Routledge and Kegan Paul.

Wilson, J and Cowell, B. (1990) *Children and Discipline: a Teacher's Guide*. London: Cassell.

Wragg, E.C. (ed.) (1984) *Classroom Teaching Skills*, London: Croom Helm.

CHAPTER 11

The management of behaviour in primary schools

JIM DOCKING

When Kenneth Baker, as Secretary of State for Education, commended the Elton Report to Parliament on 13 March 1989, he told Members of Parliament that he accepted the Committee's recommendation that all initial teacher-training courses should include 'practical training in how to manage pupil behaviour'.[1] Apart from its content, this statement is interesting for its reference to 'managing behaviour' rather than 'controlling pupils'. Indeed, in much recent discussion about discipline in schools, the former term seems to be used in preference to the latter. Is this simply semantic sport, or does it signify a change in the way we are coming to regard and respond to problem behaviour in schools? I like to think that it is the latter.

One difficulty in centering discussion about school discipline around the traditional notion of 'control' is that the debate tends to become focused on the personal shortcomings of 'problem *people*' rather than on planned strategies for preventing 'problem *behaviour*'. 'Control' connotes the outdated concepts of superordinate-subordinate teacher–pupil relationships, often with the built-in assumption that solutions to classroom behaviour problems depend upon initiative being taken by the pupils and their parents rather than the school and its teachers. The notion of 'managing pupil behaviour' concentrates the mind more on the contextual conditions associated with problem behaviour in school, and which are within the power of teachers to change, rather than on constitutional and temperamental factors which lie beyond the teachers' control. It also encourages staff to think in terms of partnership approaches which involve all relevant parties in decision-making, so that parents, pupils, helpers and governors participate in developing policies collaboratively. Further, whereas the term 'classroom control' refers essentially to adult–pupil interactions during lessons, the term 'managing pupil behaviour' also embraces relationships between the pupils themselves, and outside as well as inside the classroom.

Teachers who think in terms of 'managing' pupil behaviour recognize the pointlessness of characterizing the problem of school discipline essentially in terms of difficult personalities – the malevolent intentions of 'troublemakers', the irresponsible attitudes of the parents, or the emotional disorders of 'problem pupils'. Of course, these teachers recognize that some children do set out to make trouble, are brought up badly or in appalling circumstances, or show signs of disturbance which may require special help; and, as the Elton inquiry acknowledged, these teachers know that some localities are undoubtedly more difficult to teach in than others. But teachers who focus on the concept of 'managing behaviour' are also sensitive to the *interactive* nature of factors pertaining to the school, the home and the child, and they appreciate that the quality of relationships in schools affects the degree to which stress arising from non-school factors manifests itself in serious behaviour problems in the classroom. From their conversations with parents, or even as parents with schoolchildren of their own, these teachers can readily believe the research evidence that children by no means necessarily behave the same way at home and at school,[2] with different teachers in the same school,[3] or in different schools with similar types of intake[4]. All these factors are taken to signify that the quality of behaviour in school is not simply a function of factors within the child and the home, but is materially affected by features of the school and classroom environment and the quality of home–school relationships.

The way we conceptualize behaviour problems in school is not just an academic matter: it affects our *response* to the problems. Inappropriate attributional tendencies can even encourage counterproductive practices. Any tendency to assume that behaviour problems are generally due to 'troublemakers', for instance, too easily leads to a teaching style which is characterized by nagging and scolding on the grounds that, because the behaviour is intentional the perpetrators can control it; but, since the pupils often regard this interpretation of their motives as unfair, the effect is often to maintain rather than suppress the unwanted behaviour. Attributing problem behaviour to 'problem parents' also encourages regular reprimand – though not, in this case, because the children are seen to deserve it, but as compensation for the lack of rules and discipline in their homes. By contrast, regarding problem behaviour as a symptom of 'problem pupils' encourages the belief that reprimanding is a waste of time since the culprits are in need of 'treatment'. But teachers who hold this view can then too easily assume a state of helplessness, believing that they are incapable of changing a child's behaviour since help can only be given by 'experts', to whom problem children must be referred. The problem of discipline is then seen to turn on inadequate facilities for referring pupils to appropriate agencies outside the school.

Each of these standpoints is understandable. Teachers wish to be successful in helping children to learn, and behaviours which frustrate this process are easily interpreted as arising from factors beyond the teachers' control. Taking this position, however, can be counterproductive in effectively deskilling teachers, leading to conditions of stress which contribute further to the problem. For while a teacher is likely to feel anxious if a class is disruptive, so also may a teacher's simplistic

Table 11.1   **Focusing on 'problem people' and 'problem behaviour'**

Focusing on 'Problem People'		Focusing on 'Problem Behaviour'
Re-active	v.	*Pro-active*
An emphasis on ad hoc measures to cope with culprits whenever trouble arises ('crisis management')		An emphasis on planned strategies to pre-empt behaviour problems
Confrontational	v.	*Positive*
Frequent reprimand, labelling and punishment		An emphasis on the promotion of acceptable behaviour, thus marginalizing unacceptable behaviour
Fault-finding	v.	*Initiating*
An assumption that change in behaviour depends on initiative being taken by the culprits or their parents		A conviction that the school must take the initiative
Individualist	v.	*Collaborative*
Teachers are left to depend on their own resources		Whole-school policies are developed
Authoritarian	v.	*Incorporative*
Staff do not consult parents or pupils		Staff involve pupils, parents helpers and governors in addressing the issues
Status-focused	v.	*Welfare-focused*
The concern is essentially with behaviour which threatens staff authority		The concern is not only with teacher–pupil interaction but relationships between pupils

beliefs about the causes of pupil behaviour prompt actions which are not in the interests of effective class management.

The strength of the Elton Report is that it acknowledges the impact of the school whilst not shifting the blame from 'problem pupils' and 'problem parents' to 'problem teachers'. It sees ineffective management of pupil behaviour not in terms of teachers' personal inadequacy or negligence, but in their lack of training in classroom management skills: 'Group management skills are probably the single most important factor in achieving good standards of classroom behaviour.'[5]

The standpoint taken in the present chapter is that effective behaviour management in schools depends upon a willingness to focus on the nature of the problem *behaviour* and appropriate *intervention*, rather than the nature of problem *people* (be they pupils, parents or teachers) and why they should be *blamed*. The contrasting outcomes of focusing on 'problem people' and 'problem behaviour' might be expressed as shown in Table 11.1.

The Elton Report draws attention to all these matters, but, to my mind, does not give sufficient emphasis to the last two. Later in this chapter I would like to redress this balance.

Key issues in the management of pupil behaviour

One does not need to be committed to a hard behaviourist perspective, or to deny the influences of innate or predetermined dispositions, to recognize that behaviour can often be changed by paying attention to features of the context in which it occurs. There are two sets of factors here. One relates to the physical and human features of the school and classroom setting. This is often referred to as the antecedents of behaviour, an understanding of which provides the teacher with a means of pre-empting many kinds of everyday behaviour problems by changing the conditions which contribute to the unacceptable conduct. The other set of factors relates to the consequences of misbehaviour in terms of the way teachers and other children respond to it. An understanding of the impact of response styles should help the teacher to encourage patterns of acceptable behaviour rather than inadvertently help to maintain the unwanted behaviour.

It seems to me that one can accept this behavioural model as one which often works very well, even if one should also recognize that pupil behaviour is not infinitely plastic according to the vicissitudes of the school environment. Using this model helps to avoid the practice whereby discipline problems are facilely attributed to 'within child', 'within home' or 'within society' factors without an honest examination of 'within classroom' or 'within school' and 'home-school' factors. At the same time, an analysis of the antecedents of behaviour and its consequences should not be limited to those of the classroom: an event or circumstances in the home, for instance, can help to precipitate behaviour problems in school, which in turn can be maintained through inappropriate responses by parents when the school makes a complaint. Pupil behaviour is the result of many interacting elements, not least the interaction between those pertaining to the child, the home and the school. It is therefore important not to pay exclusive attention to 'within school' factors. However, the involvement of parents needs to be more concerned with giving constructive guidance and inviting participation in decision-making than with accusations or irresponsibility and simply relaying the school's decisions.

Table 11.2 offers a framework for reviewing practices in primary schools in the management of pupil behaviour. Preventive, pro-active strategies and styles of response to pupil behaviour are clustered around five management principles, defined briefly in column 1: foreseeability, purposefulness, accountability, constructiveness, and collective responsibility. The divisions between sections of the table, however, are not intended to be rigid, and some items could easily

Table 11.2 **Some key issues affecting the successful management of pupil behaviour**

Management principle	Preventive, pro-active strategies	Styles of response to behaviour
Foreseeability (Identifying and addressing 'at risk' behaviour circumstances)	rules reminders smoothness in management of critical points	manner of reprimand avoidance of confrontation
Purposefulness (Communicating confidently and giving pupils a clear sense of direction)	body language use of voice lesson beginnings variety of activities access to materials classroom layout	
Accountability (Helping pupils to develop feelings of commitment and responsibility)	with-it-ness allerting and accountability cues	types of punishment self-monitoring charts
Constructiveness (Giving pupils the means by which they can become more effective learners)	opportunities for success feedback on achievements positive teacher expectations promoting feelings of confidence and competence promoting cooperative behaviour	reinforcement of good behaviour helping parents and pupils to respond constructively to problem behaviour
Collective responsibility (encouraging a sense of ownership and feelings of community)	involvement of all staff, parents, pupils and helpers in behaviour policy	

appear in alternative cells. What now follows is a discussion of some strategies and response styles related to each of the management principles. In the space available, comment must be selective and brief,[6] but I wish in the last two sections to give special attention to ways in which pupils and parents can be actively involved in the management processes.

Foreseeability

The first requirement of effective behaviour management is that predictable problems are identified and addressed by drawing up appropriate rules. Although most schools have general rules, life in the classroom often proceeds in the absence of clearly articulated regulations. It seems perverse, however, to put young children in the position of having to find out what a particular teacher expects and will tolerate through a process of trial and error. The children's sense of security depends on a clear understanding of what is to count as appropriate and inappropriate behaviour; and both children and teachers need a set of criteria by which reward and reproof will be regarded as fair and deserved.

For rules to be manageable and effective, however, certain conditions need to be observed. With young children especially, the rules need to be:

- few in number (four or five is plenty)
- relating to specific matters (e.g. not just about 'considerate behaviour': young children need the experience of concrete instances in order to grasp the idea of a rule, though it is important developmentally for the teacher to draw attention to the general principles on which the rules are based and which give them justification)
- realistic (e.g. avoiding a blanket rule which insists on silence at all times, regardless of the activity)
- phrased positively, to encourage acceptable behaviour rather than just suppress that which is not wanted
- expressed as a communal commitment, rather than as a command, to encourage feelings of accountability (e.g. 'We will try to listen carefully when the teacher is explaining' rather than 'No talking when the teacher is talking')
- enforced through public display of the rules and reminders before the start of 'at risk' activities (e.g. 'Now, let's remember our rule about listening carefully so that you all know what to do').

With all age phases, the reasons for rules need to be brought out, but especially with older primary children rules can be profitably negotiated rather than just 'explained'. This is discussed below under 'Collective responsibility'.

It is also important to anticipate the sorts of problems which can arise when responding to infringements of classroom rules. For instance, there is less risk of damaging relationships if reprimand is not made a personalized matter. Sometimes, of course, teachers need to assume a 'Do as I say' voice, but not habitually. One advantage of having a clear set of rules is that it provides the means whereby discipline is more about submitting to an agreed code ('Remember we agreed that . . .') than deference to personal authority ('You'll do as I tell you'). Again, some teachers are less labelling than others because they make clear that what is 'naughty' is not the child as a person ('As usual, it's Daren who's playing around') but the child's disregard for the rule ('Remember our rule about listening when I'm explaining, Daren').

In many lessons there are critical points which can be foreseen and therefore planned for. As a result of analysing video-tapes of classes of 5 to 11 year olds, the American educationalist Jacob Kounin used the term 'smoothness' to describe the success of some teachers in sensitively managing occasions when misbehaviour was most likely to arise. Moments of this kind include transitions from one type of activity to another, explanations about what children are going to do and how they are to get started, putting children into groups, preparing the class to move to a different room, and children finishing at different times. Smoothness is also a function of the manner in which the teacher responds to behavioural incidents. Making a public issue of incidents, impetuous reactions, shouting at pupils and refusing to back down over misunderstandings are examples of teacher behaviour which militate against smoothness. Apart from creating an unpleasant atmosphere, they counterproductively focus on the teacher's personality instead of drawing the children's attention to the nature of the task and the kinds of behaviour which this requires.

Teachers who are least vulnerable to confrontation seem to be those who:

- understand that some pupils confront because they have yet to learn the social skills of apologizing, or of explaining extenuating circumstances without implying an unwillingness to accept responsibility
- are sensitive to the risk of labelling individuals as 'troublemakers'
- are careful to verify the identity of culprits in cases of incidents not personally witnessed
- avoid shouting, losing their temper, sarcasm, physically prodding the pupil, or insisting on obedience for its own sake
- try to deflect attempts to confront by refusing to make a public issue out of matters that can wait (and so deprive the culprit of public status) and instead deal with them later and privately
- are prepared to apologize when they know there has been a misunderstanding.

Purposefulness

Successful class managers seem to be those who generate a classroom atmosphere which, whilst relaxed, is purposeful and explicitly directed to the children's learning needs.[7] This point has been picked up recently in the survey of 50 London junior schools, where Peter Mortimore and his colleagues speak about the correlation between good behaviour and what they call a 'work-centred environment'.[8] As the authors point out, such a classroom ethos may appear to the casual observer to be natural order easily maintained, but in fact it is the product of skilful management which reflects meticulous preparation and regular self-appraisal.

How, then, can purposefulness be engendered in a classroom? The following are some possibilities:

Body language and use of voice

Teachers who manage to communicate a sense of purpose tend to be those who are assertive without being threatening, and flexible without being indecisive. Some of the key factors here appear to be:

- a projected and modulated voice, but not shouting. New teachers can help themselves by carefully rehearsing their explanations and instructions, and listening to tape-recordings of their efforts
- standing in a relaxed way, avoiding hunched shoulders, or clasping hands in front of the body, or having arms folded defensively
- moving into the group to reduce social distance
- focusing on different parts of the room when addressing the class
- nodding, smiling, maintaining eye contact and showing interest when a child is speaking
- sitting or squatting at child's level when helping an individual so that friendly face-to-face communication is more easily ensured.

Lesson beginnings

Administrative chores and lack of appropriate preparation often impede purposefulness at the start of timetable sessions. The more successful class managers whom I have observed have well-established routines which children follow in the absence of other instructions at the beginning of a period. They also resist the temptation to begin lessons by criticizing the class or individuals. Instead, as the class enters the room, they make a point of talking to a few individuals about their personal interests and concerns, and then start the lesson with some positive statements about children's behaviour or work, sometimes relating favourable comments picked up from other teachers.

Variety of activities

By variety is not meant a large number of diverse activities being simultaneously pursued. As the authors of the London junior school project point out, only the most skilful teachers can successfully cope with more than two or three sorts of activities going on at once since otherwise the myriad demands force attention to be given to management considerations at the expense of teaching.[9] At the same time, children will respond more positively if, during the course of a session, they are not expected to work in the same mode for too long but are subjected in turn to different kinds of demands and challenges. Put simply, they then do not have time to get bored.

Access to materials

Behaviour problems are virtually elicited if the children need to make constant enquiries about materials and resources. Having these available in clearly labelled carrels, with those needed immediately laid out ready at the start of a period, not only minimizes movement problems and frustration by facilitating access, but also sets the right tone by *symbolizing* purposefulness.

Classroom layout

The Plowden Report in 1967 advocated sitting children round tables to facilitate constructive interaction. However, this arrangement may not be the most conducive for all kinds of classroom activity. When working on individual tasks, children may work better when not facing each other in close proximity;[10] and when engaging in class discussion, children will interact better with each other, as well as with the teacher, if they are seated in a circle.[11] What is important here is a willingness to experiment and to involve the children in discussion, thus giving them a sense of 'ownership' of their classroom layout.

Accountability

Amongst his list of classroom management concepts, Kounin also identified accountability as particularly important. It is not just that the teacher demonstrates 'with-it-ness', or vigilance, scanning the classroom and thus being in a position to intervene early and effectively, though this is tremendously important. It is also a matter of giving accountability cues which gently and unfussily remind individuals what is expected of them and keep them on task. Examples would be inducing a 'ripple effect' by saying publicly, but supportively, 'John, could you just hold up your work so I can see how you're getting on', or 'Tracy and Karen, I'll be with you in a moment to see what you've done'; or towards the end of some group discussion, 'Listen everybody – I shall be asking you to stop in three minutes so we can hear the suggestions from each group.'

Another means of encouraging feelings of accountability involves the use of charts by which individuals with behaviour problems can monitor their own progress in meeting target behaviours. It is probably best if the child and teacher negotiate just one or two well-defined goals (e.g. 'I will try to stay in my seat and work quietly'). Some teachers draw up a written contract to reinforce the idea of keeping to commitments. During certain parts of the day the child records success at intervals of, say, five or ten minutes, on a tally sheet. Then, after so many tallies, the child can record sustained improvement by colouring in part of an illustration divided into segments for the purpose. Motivation is generally higher when the illustration has been tailor-made to reflect the child's favourite interest or pastime. Experience shows that children usually engage in self-monitoring honestly, provided that verbal reinforcement is given as progress is maintained.

The type of punishment or style of reprimand also contributes to, or militates against, children's feelings of accountability. Sensitively handled, punishment can make an important contribution to a child's emerging sense of moral responsibility; clumsily handled, or meted out as a standard control strategy, it simply induces feelings of alienation. Punishment needs to be unpleasant enough to prompt the offender to 'think again' and thus feel more accountable for his or her actions, yet not so unpleasant that it is perceived as unjust and the child feels victimized. Severe tellings-off, for instance, though appropriate on occasions, run the risk of setting up inappropriate adult models of aggressiveness, and making the child feel humiliated rather than remorseful. Children are probably more likely to develop feelings of 'being accountable' if the consequences of disregarding the feelings of others involve losing privileges, being asked to do socially useful tasks, or being segregated from friends for a short time. Carefully worked-out whole-school policies are particularly important in this area not only to ensure consistency of approach but also a policy which is educationally, morally and developmentally sound.

Constructiveness

So often, the actions which promote good behaviour in school are precisely those which promote effective learning. This is not surprising since children who believe that they can succeed at school and achieve status legitimately are less likely to want to misbehave. One sure way by which teachers can pre-empt misbehaviour, therefore, is to 'match' tasks to children's attainment levels and so provide opportunities for success. Yet HM Inspectorate has recently reported that, among children with special needs, differentiation of work was unsatisfactorally addressed in about half the lessons observed.[12] An equally important measure is setting aside time to give constructive feedback about achievement, a strategy which the junior school project highlighted for its special effectiveness.[13]

The key issue here concerns the teacher's ability to generate a classroom ethos of confidence, cooperation and competence. Recent evidence from teacher observation studies[14] suggests a number of reasons why some teachers are more successful than others in these respects:

Communicating positive expectations

The self-fulfilling prophecy phenomenon in the classroom is well known, but less understood are the processes involved. It seems that low expectancy levels are noticeably less manifest in classrooms in which the teacher:

1. does not allow her view of a child to be coloured by experiences of former brothers and sisters, negative generalized comments from other teachers, or stereotypic beliefs based on race, gender or social class. Comments on school records are sometimes responsible for communicating negative or positive expectations to succeeding teachers; and now that records are open to parents, the quality of comment can also play an important role in setting expectancy levels amongst members of the child's family.
2. avoids making overt comparisons of achievement between pupils and instead draws attention to progress relative to the individual's past performance. Specifically, it seems that children are likely to exaggerate teachers' expectations of them, and to worry unduly about how they are doing compared with others, if they are permanently seated according to ability and if competitiveness is encouraged by their levels of achievement being compared in front of the class.[15] This will be an important factor to monitor in the wake of National Curriculum assessments.
3. is sensitive to the dangers of signalling low expectations through verbal and non-verbal cues. Negative cues include not calling on certain pupils (perhaps because it is predicted that their response will be difficult to handle, or will pose a threat to class order), giving low-attaining pupils little time to answer before re-directing the question to a high-attaining pupil, and using labelling language. By contrast, positive expectations are communicated by asking questions to which the pupil can realistically respond, and treating pupils equally in re-phrasing questions to encourage an appropriate response, making positive comment on appropriate answers, and giving encouraging body signals by smiling, nodding and maintaining eye contact.
4. is concerned to set activities which, although differentiated according to the individual's attainment levels are none the less challenging even for lower-attaining pupils. 'Stretching' should not be the prerogative of the evidently more able children.

Encouraging children to recognize their successes

A second means by which some teachers communicate competence and confidence is through devising structures whereby children are helped to acknowledge their skills and achievements. One strategy, suggested by Peter Gurney,[16] is to get each child to keep a diary of Good Things, or a regularly updated list of their positive assets. Here it is important to encourage children to think in terms of their personal life as well as formal school activities. Another idea, described by Jacquie and David Coulby,[17] involves the construction of a 'success book', by which children, at a regular time each week, use self-report sheets to rate each of their main endeavours against a checklist and discuss progress with their teacher and parents. More generally, children can be helped to identify their successes, both in their work and behaviour, through the effective use of praise and the provision of regular feedback. Except with the youngest children, who seem buoyed-up by almost any form of praise, general approval is unlikely to be reinforcing since it does not inform. As HMI have observed, if children are to learn from praise, the remarks need to specify in exactly what respects the child deserves commendation.[18]

Encouraging constructive self-attributional tendencies

Some primary children get into self-denegratory habits through attributing lack of success to lack of inherent ability. They may say 'I think I must be stupid', or 'I'm just no good at sums'. As Colin Rogers has suggested, it is important for teachers to be sensitive to their pupils' attributional styles since these have important consequences for their success later on, if not immediately.[19] The objective should be to encourage the belief that persistent effort will bring about success: this helps children to remain optimistic about the chances of succeeding since, compared with ability, levels of effort are changeable and within their personal control. Even though children at the infant stage often fail to differentiate between 'trying hard' and 'being clever', Rogers urges teachers to encourage children to get into a habit of explaining personal failure in terms of low effort and not poor ability. Then, in later years when the children come to hold differentiated attributional concepts, they will not be discouraged about the prospects of success through having habitually explained their failures in terms of ability factors which they believe are fixed. Schunk suggests that once children *begin* to show improvement in a task, that is the time to switch from encouraging positive self-attributions in terms of effort to those of ability – for example, by saying 'There, I knew you could do it!' – since the child is then encouraged to believe that he or she has the wherewithal to maintain that improvement.[20]

Enhancing cooperative dispositions and skills

Another kind of pro-active strategy which is relevant in this discussion about being constructive involves setting up activities by which children can learn to become more cooperative and less teacher-dependent. Anne Wilson has described and evaluated her work on taking over a class of poorly adjusted inner-city 5 to 6 year olds who had already earned a negative reputation among teachers. Through a special programme of weekly activities, the children gradually developed better feelings of group cohesion and a repertoire of cooperative skills.[21]

Some of the many strategies used by Wilson were as follows:

1. *Discussion with children facing each other in a circle*

The usual arrangement with this age-group involves children gathering in a carpeted area facing the teacher. Because they have their backs to each other, constructive pupil-to-pupil interaction is discouraged because the child has to concentrate on a disembodied voice. The circle arrangement helps the children to secure eye contact with each other and so concentrate on what others are saying. To discourage children interrupting each other, an object would sometimes be passed round, the rule being that only the individual holding the object is allowed to speak.

2. *Cooperative and non-competitive games*

A range of game activities was devised to promote group cohesion, turn-taking, controlled and supportive group interaction, trust, and opportunities for group leadership.[22] Each game would be introduced to part of the class, who in turn introduced it to others. The success of these activities was apparent, since often the children would subsequently play the games on their own initiative during break and lunch times.

3. *Working with a partner*

Children in pairs, with partners sometimes self-chosen but at other times by the teacher, were encouraged to help each other before seeking adult assistance. This not only contributed to cooperative effort, but relieved pressure on the teacher while she was with a group. During feedback sessions the teacher would favourably comment on successful but initially reluctant pairings.

4. *Discussion about how to cooperate and resolve conflict*

Based on the work of Duax,[23] the children and teacher shared ideas about responding to everyday situations of potential conflict, such as sharing, borrowing, and taking turns. Alternative strategies to avoid aggressiveness were tried out through role play.

5. *Feedback*

Morning and afternoon sessions always ended in a short period of reflection when examples of work were shared and children gave accounts of what they had been doing. The teacher provided feedback by drawing attention to good examples of cooperation, such as the way she had noticed a child borrowing a crayon, or helping another to clear up after something had spilt, or commenting nicely on the work of another child.

Helping parents to respond constructively to behaviour problems

Parental involvement is another factor which has an important role to play in the constructive response to behaviour problems. Home visiting before the child starts school helps staff to get to know parents' circumstances and perceptions early in the child's career, while writing to parents about progress in a child's behaviour not only provides reinforcement but also encourages parents as well as teachers to 'catch the child being good'. Home–school reading projects also play a part. In setting up a project, the school emphasizes the importance of making positive comments on the child's progress, avoiding constant criticism over mistakes, and generally ensuring that reading is a shared and enjoyable experience. These strategies help to enhance the child's feeling of self-worth, and some research evidence suggests that the experience helps to improve the child's motivation to curriculum work in general.[24]

Some schools and local education authorities have devised parent partnership schemes which specifically address persistent problem behaviour. Coulby and Harper, for instance, have related how mutual problem-solving groups for parents of children in trouble with their teacher have worked in some East London schools.[25] West Norfolk has tried a more structured scheme based on behavioural principles. The class teacher, a worker from the Behaviour Support Service and the parent(s) sit down together to discuss the problem in a non-judgemental way. The parents are then invited to enter into an agreement whereby the child receives reinforcement at home for good behaviour at school. The mechanics of this involve the class teacher and parents agreeing realistic, short-term targets for the child's behaviour in school. Progress towards reaching these targets is monitored by the child completing illustrated record sheets of the kind described earlier. On this basis the child receives a daily behaviour score which the parents use to regulate the child's favourite home activities, such as watching television or going on an outing.

Collective responsibility

The management of pupil behaviour is not just about conformist behaviour but developing concepts of social responsibility. This means helping pupils to understand their own behaviour problems and to work together in developing policies and practices to which they collectively subscribe. It takes time and some ingenuity to engage children in activities which enable them to develop a spirit of community and feelings of 'ownership', but more and more primary schools seem to be taking this on as part of their effort to improve standards of behaviour and to contribute to children's social and moral education. As the Elton Committee recognized, children feel more committed to school policies if they have initiated some of the ideas. This does not mean that the role of adults in giving direction becomes marginalized. On the contrary, young people need help in identifying issues, in formulating and explaining their ideas, in listening to each other, in discussing the usefulness of their suggestions, in prioritizing their recommendations, and in working out how best to implement them. Some examples of pupil involvement in behaviour policy now follow.

Classroom rules

Practice in rule-making makes an important contribution to children's social education and makes it more likely that the rules will be respected. With the younger classes, the teacher will need to provide more direction since the children need experience of following rules in order to develop the concept of a rule – though reasons for rules should always be explained. As children move through the junior years, increasing demands can be made upon them to discuss, explain and justify a code for regulating classroom behaviour which corresponds to the criteria described earlier.[26] It is also important for the teacher to provide opportunities for the class to revise its rules as circumstances change. This is one way of helping children develop from a stage of heteronomy to one in which rules are seen as a flexible instrument which can be altered by agreement in the light of experience and changing needs.

School rules

The Coulbys have described the way in which the staff of one multiracial inner-city junior school organized a series of stages by which the children actively participated in drawing up new school rules.[27] The project began with the head speaking in assembly about the need for rules and how the pupils were to be involved. Each class then discussed ideas for a code and displayed their suggestions in a whole-school book. Next, the class suggestions were discussed in assembly. Overlap was noted, and 14 rules were identified. Back in their classrooms, the pupils prioritized three of these rules and justified their choice to a subsequent school assembly with the aid of posters and pictures. Staff and pupil representatives then together discussed the ideas and drew up a list of four rules covering safe play, considerate treatment of people despite their differences, reporting personal worries, and listening to and cooperating with adults in authority. Further pupil activity involved poster-making and displays, letters home and dramatizations to disseminate the rules. This step-by-step procedure enabled every child to have a say and to experience the benefits and problems of engaging in participatory democracy.

Elsewhere I have described the various events and activities in which the staff and pupils of another inner-city school worked collaboratively in drawing up a whole-school policy on behaviour.[28] A key factor here was the head delegating the coordination responsibilities to a young and enthusiastic teacher who worked with staff to involve the children in the management process. Classes completed questionnaires (verbally in the case of infant classes), conducted opinion polls, tabulated and discussed the responses, and made suggestions for rules, sanctions and rewards (particularly those needed to ensure orderly playtime behaviour). Lunch and playground helpers were also brought into these discussions. These activities formed the basis of a new set of school rules, which the children then helped to disseminate through a poster competition.

What comes through both these reports is the enthusiastic and responsible way in which these young inner-city 'deprived' children respond to opportunities whereby they can participate in rule-making. Their sensitivity to the issues and their ability to make constructive comment is truly impressive. An important off-shoot is the opportunity for cross-curricular activities which, in a variety of ways, make the enterprise an educational experience, whilst the involvement of all the pupils not only helps the problems to be better understood but also helps to bring about an improved spirit of community.

Bullying and playground aggression

There is currently considerable concern about bullying amongst schoolchildren and the quality of behaviour in school playgrounds. Eight out of ten primary school teachers told the Elton inquiry that they had recently witnessed aggressive pupil-to-pupil behaviour, and Peter Blatchford's interviews with primary teachers in 13 LEAs revealed general concern not only about physical aggression but also about name-calling, verbal abuse, petty squabbling, and racist and sexist remarks.[29] Interviews among 4000 children in a project for Kidscape by Michele Elliott has uncovered widespread anxiety about bullying, including malicious teasing, harassment, ostracizing, intimidation and extortion.

Many teachers are now addressing these problems explicitly by involving the children in a direct way, both at class and school levels. Pat White, for instance, has described a project in which children in one London primary school discussed their playground experiences with the teacher, wrote and drew about them, and acted out minidramas of playground conflict to groups of parents. These events resulted in a four-point playground code.[30]

Exploratory work in this area can be carried out by individual teachers. As part of her course work for an in-service BEd degree, Elizabeth Belilios conducted a piece of action research with her class of 5 to 6 year olds.[31] Careful observations in the playground had revealed much thoughtless behaviour, aggressiveness and suffering. The incidents observed inspired various class activities, including discussion of a code for playground behaviour. But one boy, Gary, seemed impervious to all the class discussion and role play, much of which was effectively directed against him. He continued to push his way into groups and commit daily acts of physical aggression. When on one occasion he hit another boy hard on the head with a stick and appeared to have no conscience about the hurt inflicted, the teacher decided that some more drastic action must be taken to help Gary feel pressure from his peers.

Following her reading of a successful experiment by Laslett in a school for maladjusted children,[32] the teacher decided – with much apprehension – to set up a court in which the children would act as judges. The class elected three of their number to take on this responsibility. The judges received evidence in front of the class and then retired to consider their verdict. They decided that Gary's parents must be informed (a job in fact taken over by the teacher, despite the children's eagerness to do it themselves!), that Gary should lose three playtimes, and that he must be kept under surveillance, school staff being informed of any further bullying.

Although she had been persuaded by Laslett's argument that this experience gives children practice in shared responsibility, the class teacher had been concerned that the children might act coarsely and vindictively – though she remained present throughout the proceedings. In the event, these fears were allayed. Gary responded positively to the peer ruling. Moreover the class, far from ostracizing Gary, accepted more responsibility for his behaviour and made strong efforts to integrate him into the group by going out of their way to include him in their playground activities. It seemed as if the bully court had acted as a catalyst not only in chastening the culprit but in releasing incorporative energy amongst the pupils.

A school council

A number of primary schools are developing School Councils (an institution usually found only in secondary and 'progressive' schools) and the workings of the councils in four inner-London junior schools have been analysed by Richard Brading.[33] Councils typically comprise two representatives from each class (a boy and a girl), with the head acting as chairperson. Between each council meeting (usually held monthly), each class holds its own meeting chaired by one of its council representatives. This arrangement enables *all* pupils to participate, receiving reports from the previous council meeting and making suggestions for the next one. When Brading introduced a council into his own primary school, he was faced with the problem of how (if at all) to involve the infants. It was decided that they ought to be included, but that in view of their immaturity they would be represented by juniors from the top class visiting the infant classrooms to gather suggestions and report back. There is also an arrangement whereby all classes observe council meetings in rotation to learn about procedural problems and how they are dealt with.

Councils are chaired by the head, who imposes certain constraints, such as a rule forbidding negative comments about named individuals. Although they are advisory and do not interfere with major matters of policy, the councils do generate important debate and decisions which affect the social life of the school. Examples of items are name-calling, kicking and other forms of bullying, swearing, lining up procedures, playground equipment, wet play arrangements, and space for playing football. Brading believes that the forum provides an important context for furthering children's listening and speaking skills, as required in the National Curriculum, and also for developing skills in writing minutes and reports. He is currently using the Council as the structure for developing a whole-school policy on behaviour.

Conclusion

There is more to managing children's behaviour than controlling them through reactive strategies. The more effective primary schools seem to be those in which the emphasis has been put upon preventive strategies, reinforcing good behaviour (rather than just trying to eliminate unacceptable conduct), and eliciting the active involvement of the whole staff, parents, helpers and, most of all, the pupils themselves. In this way schools can at once promote better behaviour and provide valuable experiences which contribute to the children's social education.

Notes and References

1. Department of Education and Science (DES) (1989) *Discipline in Schools*. Report of the Committee of Enquiry chaired by Lord Elton, London: HMSO
2. R. McGee, P.A. Sylva and S. Williams (1984) 'Behaviour problems in a population of seven year-old children', *Journal of Child Psychiatry and Psychology*, 25: 251–9.
3. J. Kounin (1970) *Discipline and Group Management in Classrooms*, New York: Holt, Rinehart and Winston.

4. P. Mortimore, P. Sammons, L. Stoll, D. Lewis and R. Ecob (1988) *School Matters: the Junior Years*, Wells, p.195.
5. DES (1989) op.cit., p.70 (see note 1).
6. For more detailed discussion, see J. Docking (1990) *Managing Behaviour in the Primary School*, London: David Fulton Publishers.
7. L.M. Anderson, C.M. Evertson and E.T. Emmer (1980) 'Dimensions in classroom management derived from recent research', *Journal of Curriculum Studies*, 12: 343–56.
8. Mortimore et al., op. cit., p. 269 (see note 4).
9. Ibid., p. 270.
10. See N. Bennett and D. Blundell (1983) 'Quality and quantity of work in rows and classroom groups', *Educational Psychology*, 3: 93–105 and K. Wheldall, M. Morris, P. Vaughan and Y.Y. Ng, 'Rows versus tables: an example of the use of behavioural ecology in two classes of eleven-year-old children', *Educational Psychology*, 1: 171–84.
11. P. Rosenfield, N.M. Lambert and A. Black, 'Desk arrangement effects on pupil classroom behaviour', *Journal of Educational Psychology*, 77: pp.101–8.
12. Her Majesty's Inspectorate of Schools, *A Survey of Pupils with Special Educational Needs in Ordinary Schools*, London: Department of Education and Science.
13. Mortimore et al., op. cit., p. 227 (see note 4).
14. For example, H.M. Cooper and D.Y.H. Tom (1984), 'Teacher expectation research: a review with implications for classroom instruction', *The Elementary School Journal*, 85: 77–89, and P.S. Fry (1987) 'Classroom environments and their effect on problem and non-problem children's classroom behaviour and motivation', in N. Hasting and J. Schwieso (eds) *New Directions in Educational Psychology: Vol.2, Behaviour and Motivation in the Classroom*, London: Falmer Press.
15. A.L. Mitman and A.A. Lash (1988) 'Students' perceptions of their academic standing and classroom behaviour', *The Elementary School Journal*, 89: 55–68.
16. P. Gurney (1990) 'Self-esteem and personal responsibility', in J. Docking (ed.) *Education and Alienation in the Junior School*, London: Falmer Press, p. 18.
17. J. Coulby and D. Coulby (1990) 'Intervening in junior classrooms', in Docking (ed.) op.cit., p. 52 (see note 16).
18. Her Majesty's Inspectorate (1987) *Good Behaviour and Discipline in Schools*, London: Department of Education and Science, p. 17.
19. C. Rogers (1990) 'Disaffection in the junior years: a perspective from theories of motivation', in Docking (ed.) op. cit., pp. 36–7 (see note 16).
20. D.H. Schunk (1987) 'Self-efficacy and motivated learning', in N. Hastings and J. Schwieso (eds) *New Directions in Educational Psychology: Vol. 2, Behaviour and Motivation in the Classroom*, London: Falmer Press.
21. A.M. Wilson (1990) Co-operative Behaviour in Young Children, MA Dissertation, Roehampton Institute of Higher Education, London.
22. Eleven games are described in Wilson (1990) op.cit., pp. 52–8 (see note 21). Published works which describe games to promote cooperative skills include: N. Leech and A.D. Wooster (1986) *Personal and Social Skills*, Exeter; M. Masheder: Religious and Moral Education Press (1986) *Let's Co-operate*, London: Peace Education Project; and C.A. Smith (1982) *Promoting the Social Development of Young Children: Strategies and*

Activities, California: Mayfield Publishing; *Cooperation in the Classroom: A project pack for teachers*, London: Global Cooperation for a Better World.

23. T. Duax (1988) 'Fostering self-discipline in schools', *Primary Teaching Studies*, 4: 66–73.
24. Review in J. Docking (1990) *Primary Schools and Parents: Rights, Responsibilities and Relationships*, Sevenoaks: Hodder and Stoughton, ch. 9.
25. D. Coulby and T. Harper (1985) *Preventing Classroom Disruption*, Beckenham: Croom Helm, pp. 151–2.
26. Illustrative examples are given in Docking (1990) op.cit. (see note 6).
27. J. and D. Coulby, (1990) op.cit., pp. 47–8 (see note 17).
28. See note 6.
29. P. Blatchford (1989) *Playtime in the Primary School: Problems and Improvements*, Windsor: NFER-Nelson.
30. R. White (1988) 'The playground project: a democratic learning experience', in H. Lauder and P. Brown (eds) *Education in Search of a Future*, London: Falmer Press.
31. E. Belilios (1990) Playground Behaviour in a Pre-Preparatory Boys' School, BEd Case Study, Roehampton Institute of Higher Education, London.
32. R. Laslett (1982) 'A children's court for bullies', *Special Education, Forward Trends* vol. 9: 9–11.
33. R. Brading (1989) School Councils in Primary Schools, MA Dissertation, Roehampton Institute of Higher Education, London.

CHAPTER 12

The management of discipline in secondary schools

ROBERT RICHARDSON

No discussion of the management of discipline in secondary schools can fail to take into account the far-reaching implications of the Education No. 2 Act 1986 and the Education Reform Act 1988 (ERA). In March 1989 the report of the Committee of Enquiry chaired by Lord Elton, Discipline in Schools, was published. The Committee was established in March 1988, and was given the following terms of reference:

In view of public concern about violence and indiscipline in schools and the problems faced by the teaching profession today, to consider what action can be taken by central government, local authorities, voluntary bodies owning schools, governing bodies of schools, headteachers, teachers and parents to secure the orderly atmosphere necessary in schools for effective teaching and learning to take place.*

The Committee made its focus the ordinary maintained primary and secondary schools which over 90 per cent of pupils in England and Wales attend. Those concerned with the management of discipline in secondary schools have a great deal to take into account as a result both of the legislation and the report of the Committee of Inquiry.

The 1986 and 1988 Acts change fundamentally the relationships between headteachers, local education authorities (LEAs) and school governing bodies. The powers of governing bodies are enhanced and the role of LEAs diminished. Governing bodies have been given greater power and have explicit responsibilities placed upon them. Under Section 22(b) of the Education No. 2 Act 1986, headteachers have a duty to act in accordance with any written statement of general principles in disciplinary matters which may be provided by the governing body.

The 1986 Act also sets out in sections 23 to 27 the procedures for the exclusion of pupils. The provisions, which came into force for most schools from September 1988, applied also to voluntary aided schools from September 1989. Under the 1986 Act only the head-

---

* The terms of reference of the Elton Committee are set out in the DES Press Release 93/88 of 18 March 1992 which reports Kenneth Baker's response to a question in Parliament by Robert Key. They are also set out in paragraph three of page 54 of the report.

teacher has the right to exclude a pupil. If a pupil is excluded for a fixed term or indefinitely, both the school's governing body and the LEA can direct that the pupil should be reinstated. If a pupil is excluded permanently from a county or controlled school, the governing body or the LEA can direct that the pupil be reinstated, but in voluntary aided schools only the governing body can direct that the pupil be reinstated.

Provision is made for appeals. Parents can appeal against a decision not to reinstate a pupil after a permanent exclusion which is confirmed by the LEA and the governing body. Governors of county and controlled schools may appeal against the LEA's direction to reinstate a pupil who has been permanently excluded. Appeal Committees have to be set up by LEAs. They consist of members nominated by the LEA but those who are members of the LEA or of its education committee may not outnumber the other members nominated by the LEA by more than one. For aided schools the appeal committee is set up by the governing body.

For county and controlled schools the power of the LEA to direct the reinstatement of a pupil who has been permanently excluded by the headteacher and whose permanent exclusion has been confirmed by the governing body is a source of great anxiety as one of potential conflict.

The categories of school which cannot be directed by LEAs to reinstate pupils who have been permanently excluded have been increased by the introduction of grant maintained schools and city technology colleges outside LEA control. LEAs still have the responsibility of finding places for pupils but their powers to direct schools to reinstate have been diminished by decreasing the numbers of schools under their control.

The formal framework for the discipline of schools and for dealing with the exclusion of pupils from schools has been changed in that the Education No 2 Act 1986 defines the role of the headteacher, the governing body and the LEA with more emphasis upon the role of the governing body. The procedures for dealing with exclusions, formerly known as suspensions and expulsions, are set out in statute.

The Act also prohibited the use of corporal punishment in all maintained schools and in respect of all pupils not in maintained schools, in broad terms, whose fees and expenses were met from public funds.

There are other provisions of the 1986 and 1988 Acts which have a great bearing on the management of discipline in secondary schools. There appear to be three features which have great significance for the management of discipline. These are the introduction of the National Curriculum and its associated assessment arrangements; the introduction of open enrolment; and the introduction of local management of schools (LMS). Reference has already been made to the introduction of schools outside LEA control through the setting up of city technology colleges and allowing schools to 'opt out' to become 'grant maintained schools'. The implication for schools under LEA control is that they will be expected to find places for pupils who are permanently excluded from schools outside LEA control. The National Curriculum which all schools from September 1989 are expected to teach to all children aged 5 to 16 consists of ten foundation subjects and religious education. Three of the foundation subjects, English, Science and Mathematics, are known as core subjects. Secondary schools from September 1989 have been expected to introduce the programmes of study for pupils aged 11 in mathematics and science with the associated attainment targets. The National Curriculum is to be progressively introduced. From September 1990 English, Mathematics and Science are to be taught to all pupils aged 15. Attainment targets and programmes of study for pupils in technology and English are to be introduced for pupils aged 11. From September 1991 English, Mathematics and Science are to be taught to all pupils aged 16. Attainment targets and programmes of study are to be introduced in History and Geography for pupils aged 11. From September 1992 attainment targets and programmes of study in Modern Languages are to be introduced for pupils aged 11. Other attainment targets and programmes of study will be introduced for other subjects.

Traditionally, the responsibility for the curriculum of schools has been left to headteachers though legally the responsibility was that of the LEA. Under the 1986 Act the LEAs have to produce a curriculum statement and the governing bodies of schools have to embody the LEA's statement in a curriculum statement of their own which the headteacher has to take into account when discharging his/her duties in relation to the secular curriculum of the school. The headteacher also has to take into account representations by any persons connected with the community served by the school and the chief officer of police, and has to ensure that the curriculum relating to sex education is compatible with the governing body's policy except where that policy is incompatible with any part of the syllabus for a course which forms part of that curriculum and leads to public examination.

Whereas formerly headteachers had a great deal of latitude in framing a curriculum appropriate to the ages, abilities and aptitudes of their pupils, the current position is now that the headteacher has to organize the curriculum so that it takes account of the governing body's curriculum statement and delivers the National Curriculum which has programmes of study defined by legislation, i.e. Orders.

The power of the headteacher to modify the curriculum is also limited in that the National Curriculum has to be applied to all pupils unless specific steps are taken to disapply the curriculum for particular individuals.

The ERA, therefore, fundamentally affects the curriculum which in any school is the main instrument for promoting good order and for providing effective teaching and learning by ensuring that there is a good match between the pupils' needs and the curriculum offered.

Though the curriculum of schools is to be constrained in a way unknown to modern schools some benefits may arise. For example, the fact that the content of the curriculum is to be more closely defined, then a sharper focus will be given to the teaching and that teachers will share much more common ground than before. What is not defined is what the time allocation will be for each subject other than to say that a reasonable amount of time is to be spent on each one, nor is the order of topics determined.

Externally imposed syllabuses are not new to secondary teachers preparing fourth and fifth year (now years 10 and 11) pupils for public examinations. The more closely defined curriculum will make for greater consistency between teachers and between the primary and secondary stages as secondary teachers will know with more certainty the curriculum experiences of the pupils through years 1 to 6, and within schools teachers will know what the curriculum experience will have been. The sharper focus will be reinforced by the assessment arrangements. It is proposed that there shall be assessment of each pupil's progress towards the defined attainment targets using a mixture of teacher assessments (TAs) and standard assessment tasks (SATs). It is to be noted that where the TA and the SAT assessment differ the SAT result is to be preferred to that of the teacher's assessment. Pupils' progress is to be reported at ages 7, 11, 14 (and 16 for non-GCSE subjects) which are referred to as Key Stages. The detailed information will be available to parents as a profile of achievement, but schools will also have to summarize the information for publication. For this summative assessment children will be assigned to a level of attainment in each subject from one to ten, covering the school years 1–11. Level 2 will be the expected 7-year-old performance, Level 4 the expected 11-year-old performance. Schools will publish the distribution of performance on these levels at the Key Stages. The school Level results are to be published unadjusted. They will be available for comparison and therefore can be used by aspiring parents to direct their children towards some schools and not others 'creating a hierarchy of parentally preferred schools'. Such a hierarchy is likely to have a deleterious effect upon schools low in the ranking and, therefore, upon their pupils. The rawness of the data will reflect more the attainment of the pupils on entry than upon what progress the school has enabled the pupils to make. The data will, in other words, not reflect adequately the 'added value' made by the school.

The close definition by programmes of study and assessment of progress towards attainment targets and the publication of the assessments in aggregate form carries the danger that there will be a move away from the interpretation of the pupils' needs to an emphasis in covering the programmes of study and preparing for the attainment targets. Undoubtedly there will be great pressure on time to cover the programmes and carry out the assessments. Because the published assessments will be used for comparing school with school, and indeed, possibly for comparing class with class, there will be pressure upon schools and upon teachers to teach to the test and to give emphasis to those parts of the curriculum which are assessed. Schools and teachers will be adopting defensive strategies. Styles of teaching will be affected and more didactic styles may result. The forms of assessment that are to be applied are such that able pupils should be able to go through the levels more quickly than the less able, and that the less able should not hold up the more able. If schools are to facilitate this process while at the same time dealing with pressures to ecnomize on resources, particularly on the greatest and most expensive resource, teachers, there will be pressure to return to 'streaming' and the creation of as homogeneous teaching groups as possible. It is possible to anticipate that if the able are not to be held back that there will be streaming not by age but by level. The implications for maintaining discipline in teaching pupils of the same level of attainment across a wide age range at the secondary stage are great. Secondary schools know that they will be admitting pupils whose attainment level will vary from Level 1 to Level 4 and above. By the end of Key Stage 3 some pupils may still be at Level 1 and others at Level 7 and beyond. But because the results will be published unadjusted, the schools who accept pupils at low levels of attainment and progress them through the levels more quickly will not be attributed with credit for their success in raising a pupil's individual attainment if the reported level at the Key Stage is below that considered appropriate to the pupil's age.

Streaming carries with it the danger of self-perpetuating stereotypes of achievers and non-achievers, enhancing the self-image of those in higher streams and diminishing that of those in the lower streams. The Elton Report recommends that 'Schools should not use rigid streaming arrangements . . . and that they should take full account of the implications for pupil behaviour when reviewing their arrangements for grouping pupils.'

The introduction of the National Curriculum and the assessment arrangements pose several problems for the headteacher and those managing the school and its discipline. First, the National Curriculum is not the whole curriculum. The Education Reform Act 1988 states that the curriculum of the school must be balanced and broadly based and one which:

a) promotes the spiritual, moral, cultural, mental and physical development of pupils at the school and in society; and
b) prepares such pupils for the opportunities, responsibilities and experiences of adult life.

The foundation subjects and religious education do not constitute the full curriculum. Key cross-curricular competencies: literacy, numeracy and information technology skills are required as well cross-curricular themes such as: careers education and guidance; health education; other aspects of social and personal education; and coverage across the curriculum of gender and multicultural issues.

Even after allowing 27½ hours of teaching time in a week, the task of covering the National Curriculum, religious education, the cross-curriculum competences, the cross-curriculum themes and keeping with the spirit of the broadly balanced curriculum which addresses itself to the aims set out in the Act is formidable. Thought will be needed as to how this curriculum can be delivered. It is important to emphasise that the National Curriculum has to be taught to all pupils with reasonable time allocated to the subject components unless specific disapplication is allowed for any statement of special educational need under the 1981 Act or the Secretary of State modifies the curriculum of a group of pupils by regulation or a headteacher determines that for a fixed period the National Curriculum is inappropriate temporarily for a pupil.

Besides the pressure on time available to meet all the demands the requirement that all pupils follow the National Curriculum from years 7 to 11 in the secondary school is a major shift from common practice in many secondary schools. It has been a widespread practice for pupils to be given a choice at the third year stage (year 9) to take up new 'options' and to discontinue with other subjects. The 'option' system has had the merit of helping pupils to make a fresh start and to enable pupils to work to their strengths and interests. It has been a way of involving pupils and parents in real choices about subjects to be studied, and giving opportunities for choice. It has enabled some pupils to become more involved by affording them a degree of autonomy through choice and an opportunity to commit themselves more strongly to their studies because they have chosen them. It has also helped in focusing their attention on the choices which career plans require, and has enabled them to consider the longer term implications of their courses of study. There has been consultation and negotiation. The system has, of course, been criticized for allowing pupils to opt out of key areas of the curriculum and for allowing too early a specialization or for producing an unbalanced curriculum.

The implication of the National Curriculum is that there will no longer be the opportunity for an option system as has been widely practised. On the other hand, the National Curriculum does not require that the teaching has to be organized and delivered within prescribed subject boundaries but that the attainment targets have to be achieved for each subject. It may be, therefore, that headteachers on whom rests the responsibility for organizing the curriculum so that it delivers national requirements and the responsibility for supporting

LEAs' and governing bodies' curriculum policies will be able to offer some choice in the way studies are organized. However, at Key Stage 4, because it is the GCSE which will provide the assessment, scope for subject variation is limited. Moreover, the process for securing the acceptance of an examination under Mode 3 where a school devises its own syllabus, sets its examination, marks and has to be approved by the Schools Examinations and Assessment Council, is not easy. It would seem that the choice will be more between following a GCSE based course and a Technical and Vocational Educational Initiative (TVEI) one.

Headteachers and their deputies need now to be creating a climate not only among their pupils but among teachers that every pupil will follow or will be able to follow a full National Curriculum which covers the requirements of the ten foundation subjects as well as religious education by the end of their eleventh year of school. Steps need to be taken now and preparations put in hand to deal with the situation when, towards the end of Key Stage 3 (the end of the third year of secondary schooling, year 9), assessments are made and reported. There will not be the same expectation that these assessments will provide the basis for subject choice for years 10 and 11.

The National Curriculum presents a challenge to schools to keep the needs of their pupils at the forefront and to ensure that their pupils see their curriculum as relevant to their needs. The internal pressures upon schools to cover the National Curriculum whilst simultaneously providing a broad and balanced curriculum, and at the same time reporting their pupils' aggregated levels of attainment, will be intensified by external pressures. Open enrolment and local management of schools (LMS) will add to the pressures.

Open enrolment means that an LEA no longer has the power to determine the level of admissions to a school, and that a school where there is a demand must admit up to its standard number. For most schools the admission limit will be by reference to the number of pupils the school admitted in 1979. In areas where rolls have fallen there will be surplus places and the opportunity now exists for schools to admit more pupils at the expense of others.

Under LMS, school governing bodies will have delegated to them the power to make decisions over a wide range of issues including the power to appoint staff and under certain conditions to dismiss them. LEAs will be required to delegate to school governing bodies the greater part of their budget. Each LEA has to devise a formula for resourcing schools which is 75 per cent pupil number based and 25 per cent other factors.

The emphasis upon open enrolment, financing by pupil numbers and the publication of the unadjusted aggregated scores at the key stages all imply a system of competitive schools seeking to enrol as many pupils as they can or under pressure from parents to admit their children up to the standard number.

From the point of managing discipline the preferred or more popular school will start from the advantage that its pupils will already feel successful in having been admitted. Whereas the less preferred school will have fewer pupils with a higher percentage of them having parents who did not actively seek it as a preferred school, and will have pupils who were disappointed not to have got their preferred school and so already feel a sense of failure. It may well be argued that this is already the case for a good number of secondary schools. However, the policy of open enrolment negates any LEA policy which seeks to manage the reduction of rolls and which seeks to keep schools viable by restricting admissions. The degree to which schools differ will be sharpened. The more popular schools will expand while the less popular will contract. As the more popular expand, they will attract greater resources while the reverse will be true for the less popular school. The larger popular school will enjoy some advantages of scale while the less popular will come under increasing strain as it manages shrinking, while still being under the same obligation both to cover the National Curriculum and to provide a broad and balanced curriculum.

The problems of the less popular school are likely to be compounded as inevitably the attraction of the more popular school causes the more active, concerned parents to opt for the more popular school. Then if the more popular school applies an admission criteria which gives preference to pupils with the better levels of attainment at Key Stage 2, the educational problems of the less popular school in coping with the remainder will be the greater. The less popular school is likely to end up with more children with special educational needs. It will find itself in a spiral of decline from which it will find it difficult to disengage.

The more popular schools will have greater numbers, greater resources and therefore the ability to attract teachers particularly in those curriculum areas where there is a shortage. With a larger staff it will have within it a greater range of interests and skills on which to build a more varied and interesting range of school activities. It will be able to call upon a greater number of parents, and more parents of economic means and influence than the less popular school. Meanwhile, the less popular school will find itself in a situation where its pupils have greater needs but the school has even less resources to meet them because of the working of a largely number based formula for funding.

It is to be challenged that this is in the best interests of the community at large for schools to differ so widely in character. The more popular school will be under the greatest pressure from parents to maintain its academic achievements as assessed at Key Stage 3 and in the GCSE. Internally, it will be concerned with the groupings of its pupils and may be tempted to establish strict streaming to achieve its attainment levels. The less popular school will be hard put to have enough pupils to consider streaming and may have classes with the widest range of achievement but with a very high proportion of children with learning difficulties but above the level at which they might be statemented and attract extra resources. The more popular school which opts for homogenous, that is streamed teaching groups will also be tempted to allow its class sizes to rise either in order to free resources for other areas of the curriculum or to afford some special help. However, unless the funding formula provides resources for pupils with special educational needs then schools will be tempted not to attract pupils with those needs as they will cost unit-wise more in resources than they carry. Schools will be in danger of looking at pupils in terms of the resources that they bring and the costs that they will incur if admitted. It will not be an educational judgement.

The scenario just described postulates two extremes. But there will be schools in the middle – middling popular and middling unpopular. They will either have to consider whether they can provide a collective approach to the parents of their area and agree a common admissions policy which will mitigate the worst effects of open enrolment to ensure that all children have an equal opportunity to achieve and that no hierarchy of schools is established to the detriment of any one group of pupils.

There is one feature which all schools will have to guard against: that the only motivation for learning which is addressed and which the assessment process addresses is 'extrinsic', that is wanting to learn only to move up the levels of attainment rather than wanting to learn for its own sake or because of a genuine interest in the subject.

The context in which headteachers need to manage the discipline of their schools has become harsher and more demanding. The role has been extended to include tasks formerly done by the LEA, but at the same time it has been diminished as the headteacher becomes the instrument through which the curriculum policies of the LEA and the governing body are delivered. A headteacher is no longer to have the flexibility with the staff to devise a curriculum appropriate as they see it to the ages, abilities and aptitudes of the pupils.

The research literature reassures us that schools do make a difference though there is no standard formula for schools to be successful. Successful schools require headteachers who have the ability to make schools positive institutions and who can promote a sense of community.

In promoting the sense of community the headteacher will recognize that s/he cannot single-handedly achieve all that has to be done. The staff are a key element. One of the tasks is, therefore, to see how best to develop a good team spirit. One of the difficulties of the present situation is that teachers consider that they have lost a great deal of their autonomy. A style of leadership which involves them in discussion and consultation, gives a sense of direction and allows teachers to feel that they can influence the school may be best suited to the task of developing a team. A style of leadership which is autocratic, that is where all decisions are made at the top and are handed down, diminishes teachers and their contribution to the school. At the same time a *laissez faire* style, where no decisions appear to be made and no sense of direction is given is as bad.

Headteachers need to be sensitive as to how to manage change. The nature and scale of some those changes have been described earlier. There needs to be discussion of where the school believes itself to be; where the school needs to find itself in the future; and how the changes will be brought about. Change may be brought about through the school's own efforts or it may be necessary to seek help.

Change can be very threatening. The fear of the unknown may make some wish to live with the very unsatisfactory present rather than trust to some unknown future. The headteacher will need to know the staff as well as possible so that personnel implications of change are urgently recognized and the anxiety of any teachers likely to be affected are allayed.

Communications are of utmost importance. Larger schools, where it is not easy to bring staff together so that they all hear the same message at the same time and have the opportunity to ask questions so that all hear the answer, need to have well-established comunication systems which cover everyone and are as simultaneous as possible. The written word needs as careful use as the spoken word. Each member of staff needs a separate pigeon hole for messages so that there can be no excuse for a message going astray. Where the staff have to be brought together at short notice then those staff who have to remain on duty need to be seen separately and given the same information. Large staff meetings have a reputation for being of limited value as a means of consultation. It is said that the same group of people will speak on each occasion and that their contributions will be predictable. Where a specific issue needs to be consulted there are several ways this may be done. There may be an established structure where heads of departments and pastoral heads hold meetings on a regular basis with subject colleagues or form teachers or tutors. Each of these can be asked to discuss the issue and minute their conclusions and these can be drawn into a report from which some conclusions may be drawn. From there a consultative document with proposals and or alternatives can be submitted for further consideration to the headteacher or to a staff meeting. A working party with a membership representing the various interest groups of the school may be asked to consider an issue and make a report. The whole staff can be brought together and informed irrespective of subject interest or pastoral responsibility to consider an issue or part of an issue and report to a plenary session from which recommendations and opinions may be drawn.

It should be standard practice for subjects and pastoral care teams to hold meetings and for minutes to be kept and circulated and given to the headteacher.

Headteachers need, with their deputies, to be able to talk to colleagues and to structure their work so that they afford every colleague an opportunity to talk in a calm atmosphere, ensuring that they remain in touch with the feelings and opinions of the staff.

As receptive as a headteacher must be to the perceptions of the staff within a school so too must s/he be to the perceptions of the school outside. To this end the headteacher may set targets for positive publicity and seek to develop the best of relations with the local press.

The headteacher will want to build a sense of community and as far as possible to engender a sense of commitment to the school from the staff, governors, pupils and parents. S/he will want to use the assemblies to reinforce the messages of the school, to give recognition to the range of achievements within the school and to press for the standards of behaviour which are expected.

The headteacher will want to encourage the development of the widest range of extra-curricular activities to enable as many pupils as possible to identify in some way with the school as well as to reinforce the commitment of the staff in undertaking activities they particularly enjoy. S/he will want to strongly encourage staff in their efforts both in private and in public. As the aim is to create an atmosphere in which all are to be encouraged to do their best the process of encouragement must involve all members of the school community, pupils and staff alike.

Parents should be encouraged by having open evenings which should be made as rewarding as possible. Consideration should be given to giving parents the opportunity to update themselves on the curriculum and where possible they should be given assistance in helping their children, including being clear about the school's expectations about homework and the conditions under which it is done.

Governors should be encouraged and invited to participate in school events and brought in to help at assemblies in awarding recognition to achievement as well as being made familiar with the school's activities and challenges.

Where the headteacher can provide purposeful leadership and maintain the professional involvement of the staff in decision-making the discipline of the school is likely to benefit. Under Section 22 of the Education No. 2 Act 1986, the headteacher has a statutory duty to decide the standard of behaviour which is regarded as acceptable at the school insofar as it is not determined by the governing body. Where the headteacher can secure a great measure of agreement among staff, governors and parents, the chance that the standards of behaviour will improve is greatly increased.

Acceptable standards of behaviour will only come about and be maintained where they are consistently applied. If the staff have been involved in setting the standards and so feel some sense of ownership of those standards there is a greater chance of their accepting collective responsibility for them. The model provided by the teacher in the classroom is fundamental. Each must be encouraged to uphold school policy. The policy that the headteacher has to adopt is an enabling policy, helping to increase the capability of the teacher to solve her/his own classroom problems. Part of this will be to ensure that there is a proper support system in operation. The headteacher by being about the school and taking an interest in the work in the classrooms will be reminding pupils of her/his concern as well as being seen to be supporting the teacher. Headteachers should provide the opportunity for teachers to talk to them in a one-to-one situation.

Subject post-holders have a role in supporting colleagues and discussing the best ways of managing situations to improve the learning and teaching situation and may have a role as being the facilitators in convening peer support group meetings to discuss, for example, teaching particular groups or individuals.

Headteachers need to consider the implications and likely effects of their management decisions on the commitment and morale of the staff and pupils.

Emphasis has been upon the role of the headteacher who is indentified in legislation as the person responsible. Much can be shared with deputy headteachers whose relationship with one another and with the headteacher will be crucial for the harmonious working of any school. The working of the senior members of the staff will set the tone. The concentration has been upon managing the school in changing times and upon managing the staff in particular. A relevant curriculum taught by teachers with a sense of commitment to the school and its pupils affords the best basis for managing the discipline of a secondary school.

PART FOUR

Behaviour of 'exceptional' groups

CHAPTER 13

The management of discipline in special schools

HARRY DANIELS AND LORAINE CORRIE

Introduction

The title of this chapter suggests that discipline and special schooling may be considered as separate entities. The purpose of the chapter is to explore this suggestion.

The separation of special education

There is no doubt that the 1988 Act serves as a boundary between many aspects of educational development in the past and those currently taking place. However with respect to the concept of curriculum entitlement it may be seen as an act of positive reinforcement of previous commitments. Unless exemptions are made for groups or individual children all are now legally entitled to a specified set of curriculum expectations and experiences.

This chapter is concerned with children who go to special schools. The majority of these are children who have been described as having moderate learning difficulties (MLD) or emotional and behavioural difficulties (EBD). These two groups exemplify the relativist view of special educational need. The very patchiness of provision and placement practices identified by Goacher et al., 1988 testifies to the highly context bound nature of definition in practice of these two groups. The very constitution of the groups may be seen to reflect the nature and quality of mainstream practice in particular schools and local education authorities. If special schools are to complement the provision made in mainstream schools and notions of entitlement are retained then consideration must be given to the qualitative and quantitative differences in educational experiences offered.

If concern is with respect to ensuring quality of provision in special schools questions arise as to what are the essential features of these schools. Issues of curriculum modification, access and social control certainly form a large part of this discussion. Control is foregrounded in the case of MLD and EBD schools. The actual criteria of evaluation that are seen to obtain in many cases of referral to these schools relate to matters of behaviour as well as learning. Indeed the case for a causal model of referral which is dominated by social factors has been argued by Galloway and Goodwin (1987).

There is a variable degree of insulation between mainstream and special schooling. This appears to be a general case even after the implementation of the 1981 act. In a review of research, Peter (1986) reports details of three DES-funded research projects related to the implementation of the 1981 Education Act.

Despite the growing number of link schemes between special and mainstream schools Dr Seamus Hegarty, director of the NFER Project, and his colleagues found that 33 per cent of the teachers in 268 special schools who responded to their questionnaire still had no regular contact with mainstream schools, nor did 38 per cent of the pupils in those schools. Most of the children who went in groups into ordinary schools (often children with severe learning difficulties) spent less than three hours a week there. (Peter, 1986, p. 137)

Special education, by virtue of its degree of insulation from mainstream education, must be considered and analysed from a perspective that accounts for this differentiation. Special education is itself specially positioned within the educational field. It has been shown by Tomlinson (1981) that the degree of control over the practice of special education has until recently allowed the development of very diverse forms of practice. The act of placing a child outside the mainstream system and into special education has to an extent freed special educational practice from some of the constraints of mainstream schooling. Children who have been processed out of the mainstream system no longer constitute a control problem within that mainstream system. The regulation of special schools need not be the same as in mainstream schools.

The separation of classroom discipline

Frequently classroom discipline is seen as a discrete area of concern which requires particular and specialized knowledge by classroom practitioners. The basis of such an assumption is questioned. Why is the separation of knowledge concerning discipline from knowledge concerning the teaching and learning process so widely accepted as 'normal', and what effects has the separation had on pedagogic practice?

It has been shown that interpretational schemes regulate future action, and that 'a situation defined as real will become real in consequence' (Esland, 1981). The separation of discipline implies that it is an inevitable 'issue' for educators, and it has enabled certain practices to remain unquestioned in schools. The view taken here is that some of the difficulties experienced in schools result from the fragmentation in conceptualization of these educational concerns. In agreement with researchers such as Jones (1989) it is considered that when discipline is causing concern, then the school needs to focus on the teaching/learning process as a whole, rather than discipline in isolation.

Inconsistent management?

Not only is discipline seen separately from the teaching and learning process, but also frequently it is assumed that there is a consensus concerning the standard of acceptable behaviour in any classroom, and the behaviour judged to be deviant. However this is not the case because norms are not held widely between schools or often even within a school. Thus it should not be assumed that judgements concerning acts of behaviour are uniform, or that any such judgements are made on the basis of clearly defined criteria. Often notions are constructed to be 'facts', however Gergen (1985) maintains that such 'facts' are based often on rules of interpretation that are inherently ambiguous, constantly changing and vary in accordance with the person applying them.

The same rationale applies to judgements concerning both the pupils' and teachers' acts, and this has implications for those concerned with teacher evaluation.

What is the process by which notions of acceptable and deviant behaviour are constructed in schools? What might pass as acceptable behaviour in one school might be considered a violation in another. However, this is not simply a between-schools phenomenon as considerable variations in standards and expectations are evident within a school, even in those schools which have formulated a whole-school policy concerning discipline. In a current study by Corrie, interviews with staff have highlighted inconsistencies and this can be illustrated by the view of an Inner London primary school head-teacher that children learn how to behave because of the:

overall umbrella of what's acceptable in the whole school [and yet] children will be within the parameters of what's acceptable with one teacher, and outside the parameters with another teacher

This short statement is interesting as it points to the difficulties that practitioners apparently experience in consistent application of rules at the whole-school level. It is argued here that such difficulties are a consequence of the separation of discipline from the teaching/learning process. A brief look at an individual teacher will help to clarify this point.

In the same school the teacher of a class of 4, 5 and 6 year olds, stressed the importance of established rules that govern classroom behaviour, and then continued: I have rules that are flexible . . . I let the children bend those rules [because otherwise] it may be too regimented. This statement seems simple and obvious enough. However, when seen in conjunction with what is known about the learning process then inferences may be made concerning the difficulties some children evidence when learning how to behave at school. It is not difficult to envisage the type of discrepant information being assimilated by the child, who needs to make sense of many simultaneous and novel experiences. Making sense of experiences means activation of perceptual processes, reasoning skills, and functions of memory in order to form a coherent knowledge scheme. What are children to make of 'a rule' in this context? A rule that is applied by the teacher sometimes and they are allowed to 'bend' at others, and what knowledge base underlies the articulation of this statement? The same teacher talks about the importance of pupils making their own decision, and being able to reason and think about the purpose of rules. However, at face value an observer in this classroom may judge the teacher's acts to be inconsistent, and against the principles of good classroom management. Indeed this is precisely the conclusion of the Elton inquiry into discipline in schools.

This report found that some teachers had difficulties in effectively and consistently managing relatively trivial yet persistently disruptive behaviour, such as talking out of turn, and it was concluded that the 'central problem of disruption could be significantly reduced by helping teachers to become more effective classroom managers' (DES, 1989, p. 12).

However, this conclusion is reached by inferring levels of competence on the basis of performance, and it is by no means certain that a direct relationship between competence and performance exists. It must not be assumed that a teacher is incapable of a particular behaviour simply because it has not been observed in practice. The view taken here is that discipline is an integral part of the teaching/ learning process, and that teachers' acts come out of the knowledge that is constructed through interaction with others. This socially constructed knowledge is known as the collective pedagogic discourse.

Evidence of the pedagogic discourse

How do classroom practitioners evidence socially constructed knowledge that constitutes the pedagogic discourse? Pedagogic practice includes the management of time and space in the classroom.

Knowledge is reflected in the organization of the physical environment; the positioning of furniture, the tables and chairs including any designated as the teacher's space; the emphasis and use of display areas; space given to different aspects of the whole class, often known as the carpet. It includes the management and organization of time, and the inclusion of routines and rituals. This can be illustrated by a brief look at the routines for 'carpet time' when the whole class come together as a group. What is the teacher's aim for the use of this time? Does it concern housekeeping matters, such as the register and swimming money? Is the focus on meeting and greeting class members? To make plans for the day? To introduce, revise or reinforce a teaching point? What rules govern the pupils' behaviour at this time? How consistently are the rules enforced, and what strategies are implemented by the teacher?

What collective pedagogic discourse gives rise to the hundreds of decisions made by teachers every day? It is this everyday behaviour that must be investigated so that a better understanding can be achieved (Manicas and Seccord, 1983). Attention needs to be directed to the constitution of the collective pedagogic discourse as this knowledge is central to the practitioner's behaviour. How is such pedagogic discourse formed and who is involved in the process?

The individual

In order to gain a more complete understanding of practitioners' actions, the validity of examining individual teachers in individual classrooms must be appraised. It is suggested that the assumptions and deductions which give rise to conclusions concerning teacher competencies result from the rationale associated with the structural functional tradition which incorporates the 'shared psychologistic construction of individuals' (Knight et al., 1990). Indeed some theorists claim that the discipline of psychology has given rise to explanations of behaviour in terms of an individual's internal characteristics, with failure being ascribed to personal shortcomings or pathology (Henriques et al., 1984; Handy, 1987). This reasoning has permeated thinking about both pupils' and teachers' behaviour, and has provided the basis for many models of intervention (Jones, 1989). General acceptance of this view as a 'truth' has resulted in hesitation to construct and implement alternative approaches.

What alternative is there to studying the individual teacher? An emergent theory stresses the importance of the interaction between the biological, ecological, social, cultural, political and economic facets of the context wherein the individual is situated (Shotter, 1986).

It is claimed that the upsurge of interest in Vygotsky's theories has led to greater insight concerning the conception of relationships between the individual and others, and examination of the external world in which the individual has developed (Tharp and Gallimore, 1991). This constructionist framework is concerned particularly with the transmission of knowledge through interaction (Light et al., 1991).

The construction of knowledge: the collective discourse

Teachers' knowledge concerning pedagogic practice is constructed and reconstructed in a reflexive and reciprocal interactive process that occurs between the teacher and the school. It is not the case that the teacher's knowledge is being shaped by the environment, because the knowledge that is constructed results from the reconstruction of the teacher's own knowledge schema brought to the context, and the teacher is active in the process. It is important to stress this active participation. The collective pedagogic discourse is constructed because the individual has entered the process of coordinating and setting reciprocal relations in order to generate knowledge structures.

Knowledge structures are generated in the process of articulation of the pedagogic discourse, but much pedagogic knowledge is held in the store of tacit knowledge and may not be articulated easily (Giddens, 1979). Shotter (1986) emphasises that there is a general lack of understanding concerning the social construction of knowledge. In Shotter's view this is shown by the failure to characterize discourse as not only representative, but also as constitutive of what it represents.

The notion of a collective pedagogic discourse does not preclude differences between teachers. Differences will occur because knowledge is historically embedded and each person is likely to bring a different schema to the collective discourse (Jahoda, 1989). In this way the individual does not cease to be individual, and this is shown by many differences between teachers in the same school. Some of the differences may be ascribed to personality and style preferences, but this is not at issue here.

Researchers claim that not enough is known concerning how knowledge becomes institutionalized, or how this knowledge acts to structure the experiences of pupils and teachers (Esland, 1981). There is a call for energies to be expended to bridge the gap between micro and macro analyses of social phenomena, where micro analysis refers to the interactional level and macro analysis refers to the structural level of discourse (Van Dijk, 1990).

Child-centred education and pedagogic discourse

The beginning of bridge building between micro and macro analyses of pedagogic discourse will point to the fact that not only is there a general lack of understanding about the social construction of knowledge, but also that teachers have difficulty in articulating such knowledge, partly because much of it is tacit knowledge. Frequently, such articulation becomes recitation of prescriptions which lack elaboration, and simply degenerate into slogans (Bennett, 1987). Practitioners have been shown to rely on erroneous conceptions of the teaching and learning process, many of which were theorized in the Plowden Report (DES, 1967). Bennett (1987) states firmly that the Plowden model of teaching has not stood the test of time, and that it failed because teachers are human beings not super-humans required to implement the attractive but unworkable theory. So-called teacher failure reflects the ambiguity of terms used in child centred education.

It is said that there is lack of linkage between the theory and substantive practice, and the rhetoric of the proponents of the theory has been unable to inform teachers' actions (Sharp and Green, 1975).

Although the model espoused by Plowden has not been successful, it is still in place in much pedagogic discourse. Practitioners speak in Plowdenesque terms as if espousing the 'ideal', these are the aims to which they aspire but never reach, and it seems that this 'failure' is responsible for considerable guilt. They judge their failure to be super-humans in terms of failure to be 'good' teachers, and this is rationalized in several different ways.

It is Plowden's notions of classrooms that provide the basis for explanations of the type of reasoning by the teacher quoted earlier. Plowden's children are actively engaged in exploration and discovery, operating as individuals, with access to a teacher who as guide and consultant has knowledge of their intellectual, social and physical stage of development at all times. To question and discuss is to learn, therefore questioning and 'bending' the rule is seen as positive for the pupils' development, and something that is applauded. However, the ever-present conflict asserts itself even in the following quote: 'I have rules that are flexible . . . I let the children bend those rules.' Pupils are encouraged to create ways to bend the rules, yet it is the teacher who ultimately allows that to happen. The conflict is between what is considered to be 'good' primary practice where pupils are autonomous decision-makers, and a concern that teachers be seen as controlling pupils without 'control' (Bennett, 1987).

Plowden emphasized that children should 'find out' rather than being told, and teachers apply that precept to rules, with some claiming that although they have rules they prefer to let the children see what happens when they are not kept, rather than reminding children about the existence of the rules (Corrie, 1989). Galton (1987) suggests that it is time to abandon the aim of 'autonomous learning' as research has repeatedly shown that the model cannot be implemented. However, it is clear that for many teachers the Plowden model is central to the knowledge that is constructed and reconstructed within the school context.

Plowden promulgated a theory of education which was constructed out of developmental psychology and child centred progressive education. This resulted in a theory of education that was essentially naturalistic, heuristic and developmental (Bennett, 1987). The teacher was exhorted to attend to the 'whole' child, which was seen as a composite of intellectual, physical, social and emotional needs.

Each area of development must be facilitated. Thus social skills programmes would facilitate a child's social development, but only when a child had indicated 'readiness' to move into that stage. Teachers articulate the importance of beginning with the child and accepting the things that the child brings from home, and there is a strong image of young children arriving at school with a sack of problems on their backs.

This view of the 'whole' child divided into areas of needs, has fostered the notion of discipline being separable, and provides teachers with reasons to explain their apparent failure to implement the Plowden model. Teachers explain their apparent failure to be superhuman in terms of pupil deficit, with deficiencies in home background providing the most acceptable rationale. The widespread use of this reasoning has meant that thinking has not progressed beyond this point in some pedagogic discourse.

The necessity to provide for the discrete needs of the whole child has supported the inability of teachers to implement a model of education which is now considered by many to be based on dubious if not faulty theory. It is suggested here that many positive changes to thinking may be made if the notion of teachers' responsibility to provide for the needs of 'the whole child', was replaced with an alternative and simple view of the teacher providing for the child as a 'learner'.

However if changes in conceptualization are to be initiated, where will they begin? Who is responsible for innovation and change, and what is the role of the power hierarchy in the structure of the school?

The collective discourse and power hierarchy

It has been said that not enough is known regarding how knowledge becomes part of the collective discourse, and similarly, little is known about the influence of those high in the power structure of the school in the formation of pedagogic discourse. However, on a commonsense level it can be asserted that if changes are to be made to pedagogic discourse, work should begin with those in charge. It is thought that study at this level could be more appropriate than that involving the individual teacher.

The influence of those high in the power hierarchy must be examined, together with the variables that affect the degree of influence exerted. It is likely that the selection, classification, transmission and evaluation of knowledge that constitutes pedagogic discourse is dynamically influenced by the complex patterns of power within the school, and researchers have called for examination of the process whereby such knowledge is legitimized and sanctioned (Goodson and Dowbiggin, 1990; Greeno, 1989).

In order to encourage appropriate practice there needs to be clear conceptualization and articulation of pedagogical knowledge so that coherent policies might be formed. It is suggested that practical operational definitions might result, and this could mean an end to the tendency to separate issues of discipline from issues of pedagogy.

It is suggested that a change in conceptualization of pupils from 'needy children' to 'learners' may guide thinking to favour an integrated collective pedagogic discourse, rather than the current lack of coherence.

Modes of control

As has been argued above, the case for disembedding the analysis of discipline from a more general analysis of pedagogy is of doubtful validity. The analysis to be presented here is based upon a general analysis of modes of control within the pedagogy of special schools. The central theme is that modes of social control/discipline are highly related to modes of curriculum control.

The relationships between theory of instruction, special school and classroom organization and form of curriculum modification imply some ideological framework. It is suggested here that there are ideologies relating to the special school child which lie behind the theories of instruction and thus inhere in the organization of the school and the curriculum. Through these ideologies pupils become positioned in respect of knowledge acquisition.

The regulative practices of the school, including those recognized as being disciplinary, and the pedagogic practices (the forms of teaching, the selection and organization of content) vary as a function of the aim of the particular form of schooling.

It has been shown that different theories of instruction are associated with different forms of organization and these generate different criteria of communicative competence (Daniels, 1988). Some forms of pedagogic practice are *oriented* towards adult life; other forms are oriented more towards mainstream school. Different forms of pedagogic practice *focus* to different extents on processes of acquisition and transmission of specific skills. These forms of practice tend to be associated with different *aims*. Special schools do not all have the same aims, even on paper. A model is required that will generate descriptions of varieties of practice.

There have been many attempts to analyse something generally called the 'hidden curriculum', not always with success (Cornbleth, 1984; Anyon, 1980; Apple, 1980).

Bernstein's (1977) analysis follows a somewhat different route in that he suggests that there are two orders being transmitted within the school. The distinction between these orders according to Diaz (1984) has its routes in Parson's distinction between the instrumental and the expressive. In Bernstein's hands these become defined as follows:

I propose to call that complex of behaviour and activities in the school which is to do with the conduct, character and manner the expressive order of the school and that complex of behaviour, and the activities which generate it, which is to do with the acquisition of specific skills, the instrumental order (Bernstein, 1977, p. 38)

Bernstein also indicates that there is often tension between these orders. The expressive attempts to transmit a moral order which maintains unity at one level, whereas the instrumental tends to distinguish between people at another level. It was Pedro (1981) who made the distinction between specific instructional discourse (the subject to be learned) and regulative discourse (the management of social code in the classroom).

We shall distinguish between
(a) the principles of the specific discourse to be transmitted and acquired
(b) the principles whereby the social relations of transmissions and acquisition are constituted, maintained, reproduced and legitimized.
  (Pedro, 1981, p. 207)

On the one hand, in instructional discourse concern is with specific competencies and on the other, regulative discourse is concerned with principles of order relation and identity.

Regulative discourse

Whereas the principles and distinctive features of instructional discourse and its practice are relatively clear (the what and how of the specific skills/competencies to be acquired and their relation to each other), the principles and distinctive features of the transmission of regulative discourse is less clear as this discourse is transmitted through various media. Indeed, it may be characterized as a diffuse transmission.

Essentially, regulative discourse controls the concept(s) of legitimate order, relation and identity and transmits these essentially, but not wholly, through the following media.

1. *Symbolism/ritual*

Such symbolism may refer to the identity of the school (e.g. uniform), of the state (flags, national holidays), memorial plaques, ritual displays, assemblies, entrance and exit practices, controls on movement and approaches to special places, for example the head's room, staff room, library. This is not an exclusive list and, depending on the nature of the school, many other rituals may be found, for example those relating to sport, gender, regard and punishment.

2. *Interaction*

This refers essentially to the spoken (or written) communication concerned with establishing and maintaining principles and practices of expected conduct, given usually by staff.

3. Instruction

It is possible for regulative discourse to have its own instructional discourse and its own specialist transmitters: special teachers/ courses on leisure, drugs, delinquency, family life, social and life skills, and so on. It will also be argued that the form taken by instructional discourse in classroom practice itself contains important regulatory features.

Given the embedded relation of the instructional and regulative discourse, it is clearly important that both aspects of pedagogic discourse require description in order to permit an analysis of the relationship between them and the implications of this relationship for pupils.

Bernstein (1977) is very explicit about the nature of pedagogic discourse which he regards as consisting of *one* discourse created by the embedding and interpenetration of instructional and regulative discourse. However, in the case of empirical studies these two dimensions can be examined separately.

Control over instructional practice

Clearly, the 1988 Act is likely to give rise to situations in which the teacher controls the sequence, pace and criteria of evaluation of the classroom practice. Indeed the pressures arising from the combined effects of open enrolment and local management of schools may result in an increased focus on the outcomes of assessment to the exclusion of their aspects of the teaching and learning process. Special education has witnessed the effects of raising levels of teacher control over instructional practices in the past. A variety of packs inspired by sometimes very crude interpretations of operant psychology have been sold to schools and used as 'instant' remedies to teaching problems. The tragedy about many of these materials is that whilst they emphasized flexibility and a model of hypothesis testing, in the notes of guidance, they have been used in a rigid and non-reflective way.

Many evaluations of curriculum initiatives suggest that unless staff are given training that enables them to understand the conceptual base of new models of teaching then implementation often becomes partial at best. Many skills-based special needs initiatives have fallen into this trap. They have trained staff to perform a number of skills often in the absence of understanding. This criticism has been applied to instructional systems as well as those focused on discipline. This rigidity of application of teaching procedures in a situation of an uncertain or unacknowledged knowledge base can be the source of much difficulty, confusion and unintended consequences. The potential for this occurring in the case of the implementation of the National Curriculum is immense.

A continuum of practices

Two poles of a continuum of types of pedagogic practice will now be discussed. The poles are first, one in which control of the instructional practice rests firmly in the hands of the teacher, that is the sequencing, pacing and criteria of evaluation within the classroom is controlled by the teacher. The second is one in which more control over these matters rests with the acquirer, the pupil (this is the child-centred educational practice described above). If a case of a high level of teacher control over instruction, such as with direct instruction, is considered then discipline or regulation becomes a necessary consequence of the form of instruction.

The form of instruction demands certain forms of behaviour. The structure of the learning situation is such that children are disciplined by and through the instruction. In the case of lower levels of teacher control over instruction the form of social behaviour in the classroom becomes the prime focus of the teaching activity. The structure of the learning situation is such that instruction provides a social context in which competences may be acquired and evidenced through criteria of evaluation which relate to either a developmental model or a diffuse set of social criteria derived from many sources. Regulation of social behaviour is foregrounded in this kind of classroom practice. Instruction provides contexts for the acquisition of required characteristics rather than the transmission of specific skills and knowledge. These extreme forms find their expression in instructional/behavioural and therapeutic settings in special schools and units (Apter, 1982).

Clearly, discipline cannot be considered in the same way in both these settings. The application of uniform tactics, strategies or procedures would impact on these practices in different ways and yield different results. A general weakness of any continuum such as this, is that it does not explain variation in *levels of performance*.

The main focus of attention here has been on variation in *competences* across schools. However, the continuum cannot deal with discriminations between what count as good and bad *performances*. A related issue which is not fully accounted for is the effectiveness of individual teachers. The question as to how committed teachers are to the school's official pedagogic practice constitutes a potential problem. A teacher's orientation may be at variance with that of the school.

This chapter has implications for future developments in school effectiveness research. Goodman's (1985) is one of the very few articles that considers the place of the 'effective schools movement' with respect to special education. It follows very much within the practice of Rutter et al. (1979) and Galloway (1985) in identifying *instructional* variables that are thought to affect school achievement positively and directly. The claim is that the following variables are dominant in the growing literature on effective schools:

School leadership
academic engaged time
expectations for achievement
monitoring student performance
school climate
classroom management
direct instruction
parental involvement
small teacher/student ratio
consistency of curricular objectives and test content
(Goodman, 1985, p. 102)

Goodman argues that 'special education must become concerned about program effectiveness' (Goodman, 1985, p. 104). However, the analysis of the practice of special education does not enable the investigator to consider what Wertsch et. al., (1984) term the *motives* of the various *activities* that comprise the special educational field. It is important that analysis should start with a description of the organizational and pedagogic practice in which the pupils, if not the teachers, are positioned. This implies that before the question 'What is an effective school?' can be answered, the question 'What do we want schools to do?' must be addressed. Schools are clearly involving children and teachers in very different forms of practice. They aim to position their pupils in different ways, through different practices and to acquire different competencies. Ultimately, they have different intentions. The population of many special schools comprises many children who for one reason or another have what are deemed social problems. The population does not simply consist of low ability children: – it is of a complex constitution and involves children who are seen as deficient as judged against instructional and regulative criteria. Measuring school effectiveness on solely instructional criteria is not sufficient.

A continuum of outcomes?

There have been a great number of studies of teacher behaviour (e.g. Hatton, 1985) and pupil behaviour (e.g. Harrison et al., 1981) in classrooms, usually somewhat crudely described as 'open' and 'closed'. These terms are closely related to the poles of the continuum discussed here.

A major review of the identifying features of open classrooms involving a meta-analysis of 153 studies concluded that an active role for the child in learning with diagnostic evaluation, the use of manipulative materials and individualized instruction, can produce greater self-concept, creativity and a positive attitude toward schools (Giaconia and Hedges, 1982). It is important to note that the classrooms which facilitated large effects on non-academic outcomes produced smaller average effects on academic achievement:

the superior effects in self-concept and creativity are obtained with the concomitant penalty of smaller effects on academic achievement.
(Giaconia and Hedges, 1982 p. 600)

However, comparative evaluations of different forms of pedagogic practice have tended, on the whole, to report the implications of different forms of instructional practice using instructional criteria as measures.

One of the relatively few attempts to extend this form of analysis has been published in the USA. Schweinhart et al. (1986) report an evaluation of three *preschool* curriculum models in terms of behaviour at age 15 of the children who attended these Headstart nurseries in Ypsilanti, Michigan. The comparison was between the High/Schope model, the Distar model and a model in the nursery school tradition.

The Distar model involved a programmed learning approach in which the teacher initiated and the child responded. The High/Schope model involved teacher and child both planning, initiating activities and actively working together. The traditional nursery school pattern involved the child initiating and the teacher responding.

The three preschool curriculum groups differed little in their patterns of IQ and school achievement over time. According to self-reports at age 15, the group that had attended the Distar preschool program engaged in twice as many delinquent acts as did the other two curriculum groups, including five times as many acts of property violence. The Distar group also reported relatively poor relations with their families, less participation in sports, fewer school job apppointments, and less reaching out to others for help with personal problems. These findings, based on one study with a small sample, are by no means definitive; but they do suggest possible consequences of preschool curriculum models that ought to be considered.
(Schweinhart et al., 1986, p. 15)

Despite reservations about the measures used by Schweinhart et al., it would seem that they are investigating some effects of regulative discourse.

Clearly, self-reporting is not an adequate measure; however, the indication of this research echoes the suggestion of this chapter that measures of regulative discourse must be developed if school effec-tiveness questions are to be answered on a broad base of understanding.

Conclusion

Research which ignores the cultural specific nature of educational competence and ignores the effects of the various aims within special education is likely to ignore essential elements of both ability and educational difficulty. Special educational practices are not ideologically neutral, they are driven by sets of assumptions and beliefs. Teachers in special schools, may well need to be much more conscious of the explicit features of schooling and also the tacit assumptions that underlie its practice. Research may then be usefully directed to investigating the effects of these different positions when they are put into practice. Only then will researchers be in a position to investigate whether a particular school is enabling children to realize the competencies required by particular forms of educational activity.

References

Anyon, J. (1980) 'Social class and the hidden curriculum of work', *Journal of Education*, 162 (1): pp. 212–236.

Apple, M.W. (1980) 'The other side of the hidden curriculum correspondence theories and the labour process', *Journal of Education*, 162 (1): 47–66.

Apter, S.J. (1982) *Troubled children, Troubled Systems*, New York: Pergamon.

Bennett, N. (1987) 'Changing perspectives on teaching-learning processes in the post-Plowden Era', *Oxford Review of Education*, 13 (1): 67–80.

Bernstein, B. (1977) *Class, Codes and Control: Vol. 3, Towards a Theory of Educational Transmissions,* 2nd revised edn, London: Routledge and Kegan Paul.

Cornbleth, C. (1984) 'Beyond the Hidden Curriculum?' *Journal of Curriculum Studies*, 16 (1): 29–36.

Corrie, L.F. (1989) *The Meeting of Minds: Communicative Competence in the Classroom.* Unpublished Master's Dissertation, University of London.

Daniels, H. (1988) 'An enquiry into different forms of special school organization, pedagogic practice and pupil discrimination', *Collected Original Resources in Education*, 12 (2): Fiche 2–5.

Daniels, H. (1989) 'Visual displays as tacit relays of the structure of pedagogic practice', *British Journal of Sociology of Education*, 10 (2): 123–40.

Department of Education and Science (DES) (1967) *The Plowden Report*, London: HMSO.

Department of Education and Science (DES) (1989) *Discipline in Schools*, London: HMSO.

Diaz, M. (1984) 'A Model of Pedagogic Discourse with Special Application to the Colobian Primary Level of Education'. Unpublished PhD thesis, University of London Institute of Education.

Dilkes, J. and Nicholls, M. (1988) *Low Attainers and the Teaching of Geography*, London: Geographical Association and NARE.

Esland, G.M. (1981) 'Teaching and learning as the organisation of knowledge' in M. Young (ed.) *Knowledge and Control: New Directions For Sociology*, London: Collier MacMillan.

Galloway, D. (1985) *Schools, Pupils and Special Educational Needs*, London: Croom Helm.

Galloway, D.M. and Goodwin, C. (1987) *The Education of Disturbing Children: Pupils with Learning and Adjustment Difficulties*, London: Longman.

Galton, M. (1987) 'Change and continuity in the primary school: the research evidence,' *Oxford Review of Education* 13 (1): 81–94.

Gergen, K.H. (1985) 'The social constructionist movement in modern psychology', *American Psychologist*, March, 266–75.

Giaconia, R.M. and Hedges. L.V. (1982) 'Identifying features of open education', *Review of Educational Research*, Winter, 52 (4): 579–602.

Giddens, A. (1979) *Central Problems in Social Theory Action, Structure and Contradiction in Social Analysis*.

Goacher B, Evans J, Welton J, Wedell K (1988) *Policy and provision for special educational needs, implementing the 1981 Act* , London: Cassell

Goodman, L. (1985) 'The effective schools movement', *Special Education Teaching of Exceptional Children* 17, 102–5.

Goodson, I. and Dowbiggin, I. (1990) 'Docile bodies: commonalities in the history of psychiatry and schooling', in S. Ball (ed.) *Foucault and Education Disciplines and Knowledge*, London: Routledge.

Greeno, J.G. (1989) 'A perspective on thinking', *American Psychologist*, 44 (2): 134–41.

Handy, J.A. (1987) 'Psychology and social context', *Bulletin of the British Psychological Society*, 40: 161–7.

Harrison, J., Strauss, H. and Glaubman, R. (1981) 'Who Benefits from the Open Classroom? The Interaction of Social Background with Class Setting', *Journal of Educational Research* 75 (2): 36–45.

Hatton, E.J. (1985) 'Team teaching in open plan classrooms', *School Organization*, 5 (2): 203–9.

Henriques, J., Hollway, W., Urwin, C., Venn, C. and Walkerdine, V. (1984) *Changing the Subject*, London: Methuen.

Jahoda, M. (1989) 'Why a non-reductionist social psychology is almost too difficult to be tackled but too fascinating to be left alone', *British Journal of Social Psychology*, 28: 71–8.

Jones, N. (1989) 'School discipline and the Elton Report' in N. Jones (ed.) *School Management and Pupil Behaviour,* Lewis: Falmer.

Knight, J., Smith, R. and Saches, J. (1990) 'Deconstructing hegemony', in S. Ball (ed.) *Foucault and Education: Disciplines and Knowledge*, London: Routledge.

Light, P., Sheldon S., and Woodhead, M. (1991) (eds) *Learning to Think*, London: Routledge.

Manicas, P. and Seccord, P. (1983) 'Implications for psychology of the new philosophy of science', *American Psychology*. April, 399–413.

Peter, M. (1986) Editorial, *British Journal of Special Education*, 13 (4): 1–2.

Piaget, J. (1968) *Structuralism*, London: Routledge and Kegan Paul.

Rutter, M., Maughan, B., Mortimore, P. and Ouston, J. (1979) *Fifteen Thousand Hours*, London: Open Books.

Schweinhart L.J., Werkart D.P. and Larner M.B. (1986) 'Consequences of three pre-school curriculum models through age 15', *Early Childhood Research Quarterly*, 1: 15–45.

Sharp, R. and Green A. (1975) *Education and Social Control*, London: Routledge and Kegan Paul.

Shotter, J. (1986) 'A sense of place; vico and the social production of social identities', *British Journal of Social Psychology*, 25: 199–211.

Tharp, R. and Gallimore, R. (1991) 'A theory of teaching as assisted performance', in P. Light, S. Sheldon, and M. Woodhead (eds) *Learning to Think*, London: Routledge.

Tomlinson, S. (1981) *Educational Subnormality: A Study in Decision Making*, London: Routledge and Kegan Paul.

Van Dijk, T. (1990 'Discourse and society: a new journal for a new research focus', *Discourse and Society*, 1 (1):5–17.

Wertsch, J., Minick, N. and Arns, F.J. (1984) 'The Creation of Context in Joint Problem Solving' in Rogoff, B. and Lave, J. (1984) *Everyday Cognition: its Development in Social Context*, London: Harvard University Press.

Discipline in pupils excluded from school

MICK MCMANUS

At one end of a long room sit five teenage boys and their teacher. The room forms part of an old prefabricated building and was once used as a science laboratory. Now it is a unit for pupils excluded from school. The boys sit at desks near the door, their heads bent in silence over their work. Their teacher is similarly absorbed in the books and papers on his desk. Piled untidily at the other end of the room are benches, chairs, boxes of bottles and abandoned equipment.

On one of the benches among the dusty cartons sits a sixth youth. He too is silent but his expression is hostile and he does not work. In his hands he holds two long glass tubes that he has found among the boxes of junk. He taps them together rhythmically and gently but with slowly increasing force. The noise is impossible to ignore although the teacher appears to do so, fixing his other pupils with an authoritative stare when they look up to twist round at the source of the distraction. Just as it seems that the next tap will break the tubes, the tapping ceases, and then begins again gently: a series of tantalizing crescendos.

When the crash of broken glass eventually comes it brings two of the boys to their feet. What is the teacher going to do about it? He tells them to sit down. The begetter of the disturbance strolls to the door whistling with conspicuous nonchalance. The teacher calls a cheery Goodbye, telling him to return as soon as he feels like working properly. The door slams but opens again immediately: the youth returns, demands a cigarette from another boy, lights it and is gone again in an instant. After some protests the class returns to work; the teacher takes out a folder and begins to write.

This incident was one of ten examples of difficult behaviour in this exclusion unit over a seven-week period during which less than 5 per cent of the time was taken up by misbehaviour. These pupils had been excluded from secondary schools, a school for the maladjusted, and in one case from another unit for excluded pupils. Yet something like 20 random visits would have had to be made to be sure of seeing a sample of the sort of behaviour that had led to these pupils being abandoned by the mainstream school system.

It is extraordinarily difficult to find any disorder to look at in exclusion units or indeed in secondary schools. As HMI put it, 'Most pupils are generally industrious and well-behaved, although all pupils may misbehave on occasion' (DES, 1990). The inspectors note that pupils whose behaviour is consistently unsatisfactory are a small minority; and there are few schools where order is close to break-down. Violent incidents in units are rare and it is not easy for a visitor to walk into a classroom and encounter something like this:

Four lads were sitting at a window taking pot shots with inkwells at passers-by on the street below, a little group of four were sitting quietly playing cards, several were pushing chairs and desks about for fun, and two or three lads in the front row were pretending to listen to the teacher.

This visitor's note dates from 1931 (Hatton, quoted in Pearson, 1983) and the purpose of these anecdotes is to introduce two linked points that have to be understood if we are to adopt a professional approach to pupils' behaviour.

First, that misbehaviour of a serious kind is rare – as confirmed by the most comprehensive survey ever undertaken in Britain (DES, 1989b). Second, it has to be accepted that, although rare, it is always with us and always has been: all teachers must expect to encounter some seriously unacceptable behaviour in a teaching career of any length, and such trouble as they have to deal with is not necessarily evidence of a rising tide of lawlessness that will soon engulf us all. It must be accepted that no matter what policies are adopted, or rewards and punishments deployed, total cooperation and docility will not be achieved. To be ever hoping for the impossible is to condemn oneself to disappointment: worse, it leads to despair, defeat and a feeling that, having tried everything and failed, the pupil must now be excluded. Unrealistic perceptions can encourage us to abandon pro-fessional responsibilities. Our general, overriding aim must not be to abolish misbehaviour, nor even to minimize it to a tolerable level – for some teachers in some circumstances will have to cope with pupils who have defeated their colleagues: in schools and units our aim must be to satisfy ourselves that the remnant of troublesome behaviour we are left with is no greater than we must expect having regard to our policies, situation and personnel. As the Elton Committee put it: 'We conclude that any quest for simple or complete remedies would be futile' (DES, 1989b). Of course, we must always try to achieve perfection but always be aware that, on this side of the grave at least, perfection is seldom attainable.

Any discussion of excluded pupils must face the problem of definition: what, if anything, do excluded pupils have in common? Surveys indicate that most excluded pupils are male, working-class teenagers whose lives are characterized by domestic deprivation and disorder, erratic parental discipline, and poor attainment and ability (see McManus, 1989, ch. 2). This is no help whatever in formulating policy as there are many more pupils with this profile within the ordinary school system than excluded from it. Leaving aside the small percentage of excluded pupils who are too dangerous to contain in ordinary schools, we must ask how the others are selected. Exclusion rates vary widely amongst schools (see, for example, Galloway et al., 1985). I found that schools with the highest proportions of deprived working-class teenagers were often those with the lowest exclusion rates (McManus, 1987 and 1989). The Elton Committee noted this and other work and recorded one conclusion: schools with the highest exclusion rates tended to be those where misbehaving pupils were rapidly referred to senior staff rather than being dealt with at the classroom level. Lawrence et al., (1977) describe 'a fast route which, started at the level of exclusion from class . . . could lead to . . . suspension'. These findings suggest 'that exclusion rates could be reduced in some schools by reorganising their internal referral systems' (DES, 1989b, para. 38).

Referral systems, however, are only part of the answer: in recognizing that systems are constructed from the perceptions, attitudes, commitments and actions of people, we begin to close in upon the vital clues to coping with excluded pupils. Some teachers have learned to understand pupils' behaviour in a clinical and professional way, to detach themselves from confrontational situations, and to remain dispassionate and shatterproof in the face of pupils' hostility. They are able to use what might be described as disarming strategies with which they seek to maintain order through mollifying and humouring. Other teachers are less flexible, more autocratic and unbending: they use what might be described as confrontational strategies in which demands are made and compliance through domination is aimed at.

Naturally, teachers do not approach every incident with the same perspective but vary their strategies in different situations. I questioned 49 teachers from schools exhibiting very high and very low exclusion rates (other factors, including catchment, were taken into account). Responses were assessed by myself, and separately by a colleague: only those on which we both agreed were counted, the rest being unclassified. Only three teachers were assessed as confrontational, and only one disarming, in all the five situations put to them (which asked for their response to examples of common discipline problems). On the whole, teachers tended to confront problems directly. Even in the schools with the lowest exclusion rates, most responses were confrontational. Teachers in low-exclusion schools were confrontational in 52 per cent of their responses; for teachers in high-exclusion schools the figure was 54 per cent – an insignificant difference. However, the proportion of disarming responses differed by a factor of almost two: 34 per cent of responses from low-exclusion schools were disarming as compared with only 19 per cent from high-exclusion schools. Further, teachers in high-exclusion schools were much more likely to mention referral to senior staff (29 per cent as against 20 per cent); and high-exclusion staff were much less likely to hedge their responses with doubts or qualifications (8 per cent as against 15 per cent). (In passing, we might note the comparison with a sample of second-year students training to be teachers of PE, Design and Technology and Home Economics who were overwhelmingly confrontational (59 per cent), with a small proportion of disarming strategies (9 per cent), and only 4 per cent expressing any doubts about what they would do.)

There is no way of being certain about the direction of causality. Teachers may feel constrained to be confrontational or disarming: they may feel that they are reacting to circumstances (rather than initiating them) by the pressure of pupil behaviour or parental and societal demands. However, teachers in low-exclusion schools clearly have a broader menu of strategies, a confidence to tackle their problems rather than pass them to seniors, and the more cautious and scientific approach that is the mark of an experienced professional. The evidence discussed here suggests to me that change is needed at both the organizational and personal level. Chief among the former is that group tutors and year teams need allocations of both time and responsibility and need to be encouraged to use their autonomy to work cooperatively with difficult pupils. To make this latter possible some teachers need to increase their understanding of, and ability to analyse, pupils' behaviour in terms of its motives and strategies – to look at the classroom from the pupils' point of view. This is not to recommend sympathy and indulgence but empathy: understanding why some pupils feel the way they do involves understanding that their hostile feelings are primarily their problem, not the teacher's. Teachers need to explore the knowledge bases that feed optimistic approaches, flexibility and openness of mind, and lead to the high expectations characteristic of reflective professionals.

By far the simplest entry into practical psychodynamics, and the necessary understanding and analytical detachment in respect of severely difficult pupils, is provided by the work of Dreikurs (1957). He argued that we all have a need for attention and a need to be members of groups. Those whose attention-getting has been frustrated will develop pathological forms of behaviour. At the simplest level they will become attention-seekers – a popular term for those whose behaviour is irritating and tiresome. Dreikurs suggests that we can employ two ways of identifying a pupil's behaviour. First, we must examine our feelings: if we find the pupil irritating, and no more than that, then he or she is probably only an attention seeker. Second, we must observe the pupil's reaction to the normal reprimand: if he or she desists, momentarily at least, then this would further confirm the diagnosis of attention-seeking. The pupil seeks attention, is given it, and is satisfied – for a time. The procedure with such pupils is relatively easy: the teacher must try to give the pupil attention when he or she is engaged in acceptable behaviour; and, so far as is possible, unacceptable behaviour must be ignored or given minimal attention. Sometimes a direct approach can be used by disclosing to the pupil his or her motives: 'I think you are trying to monopolize my attention aren't you? How much of my time do you need – let's say ten times this morning? Okay? So that's one!' Pupils will often indicate in some non-verbal way that they realize their needs have been recognized and that they are grateful for it.

Pupils whose behaviour has led to exclusion, or is in danger of leading to it, will seldom have such elementary problems. It has to be said, however, that pupils are sometimes proposed for exclusion on such grounds. Dreikurs describes how frustrated attention-seekers can develop into those who want power or revenge – and it is these characteristics that extremely difficult pupils most often exhibit. Again, the twofold method of analysis is used. If we feel challenged (I can't let him or her get away with that) then this suggests a power-seeker; if the pupil's response to reprimand is to persist, then this would confirm the diagnosis. This would be a pupil whose attempts to get attention have been frustrated or punished until he or she is no longer satisfied with attention only: they want attention they can be certain of keeping, and that means power and domination.

A further twist in severity takes place when attempts to gain attention through power have also been frustrated – as of course they must be. The pupil now seeks revenge. Our feelings of being wounded are a clue (How could anyone be so cruel?): and the pupil's violent response to reprimands will confirm a revenge-seeking strategy. With young children the violence is often physical; older pupils are often content with violent and abusive language. An example will make Dreikurs' theory clear. Suppose a pupil is scraping his or her chair. If the teacher feels irritated, and the scraping ceases for a time on being reprimanded, then it is a simple case of attention seeking. If the teacher feels challenged, and the behaviour continues on being reprimanded, then the motive is power. If the teacher feels a sense of foreboding, and the pupil responds abusively or threatens to hit the teacher with the chair, then a revenge-seeker has been identified. Older pupils will often display all three motives at various times and with various teachers. From time to time some will adopt another of Dreikurs' strategies: the display of inadequacy (Poor me, I can't help it, I'm no good). In this case the teacher will feel helpless and the pupil will not respond to attempts at interaction.

There are no simple responses to strategies of power and revenge as there are with attention. Much of the strength that this analysis gives to the teacher is through the power of knowledge and under-standing which helps one achieve a scientific and professional detach-ment: one loses any feeling of personal failure and begins to understand one's role as that of a safe target for the pupil's problems. The teacher is more able to accept the pupil's hostile feelings and by containing them begin to contain the pupil too (see Emanuel, 1990 for a discussion of this notion). The pupil learns, however slowly, reluctantly and unappreciatively, that he or she is being taken seriously and that deeply hidden needs might some day be met. The first thing to bear in mind then is that we must reject what might be our habitual response: we must avoid a mutually unrewarding exchange, avoid suggesting that we cannot cope with the pupil's problems or suggesting that we would like the pupil to go away. Analysing our feelings in the way described creates the space for second thoughts on the part of both teacher and pupil. A potential crisis becomes an opportunity to demonstrate the teacher's personal resilience and control – proving to the pupil that hostility can be expressed and contained without destroying the relationship.

It must be emphasized that although our feelings and attitudes will change, our actions may well be much the same: pupil misbehaviour must be corrected and violence and destruction prevented. A teacher practising the Dreikurs method will still act like a normal teacher, brisk and authoritative: indeed, the feeling of power that Dreikurs' method gives to the teacher makes effective teaching possible in even the most discouraging circumstances. Being an effective manager of challenging pupils calls for great energy and an optimistic conviction that the job is worthwhile: successful teaching is not simply the putting into practice of a body of skills. For teachers, skills and attitudes are inextricably intertwined. It is hard to see how the sort of skills identified by researchers could be operated by those with less than total commitment to the job: constant monitoring of the class, sub-groups and individuals, eye contact, giving praise and feedback, reacting to and anticipating potential difficulties and troubles. Observers find that teachers typically have around 1000 interactions in a single day and some researchers find their conventional vocabulary is unmatched to the task of describing teachers' work: kaleidoscopic simultaneity, with-it-ness, multidimensionality – no wonder teaching is tiring. (See Doyle, 1986, for a review of research on classroom management.)

Some pupils seek refuge from encounters they perceive as distressing or shaming in wild and extreme behaviour. This can take many forms: straightforward fits of rage and hostility, repetitive moaning or other noises in lessons, dangerous antics on the school roof or a busy road. Some children (often in Local Authority care) who cannot face the night try to lose themselves in the dangers and bedlam of the city centre or a fairground. We are usually unaware of the immediate source of these crises: we seldom realize, for example, how often children from deprived homes are reminded of the ideal or stereotypical happy family. Observations suggest the number is at least a dozen or so every day (Delamont and Galton, 1986). It can help to regard serious aggression as possible evidence of a search for an indestructible and reliable adult. Hostility to adults is almost always a reflection of hostility to parents who have failed from the child's point of view (see Stott, 1978, 1982). Parents can fail children unintentionally or through no fault of their own. For example, chronic illness, poverty, or the lack of the support and guidance due to adults of low ability, can all help to create an insecure or harsh domestic environment. Other parents, following busy and successful careers, might fail to notice that their child feels unwanted: expensive gifts and foreign travel seldom compensate for the feeling of security that all children need. Children know the difference between things that parents value, and things that can be bought. Teachers who reflect upon their pupils' motives, speculate about the conditions that gave rise to them, and share their thoughts with colleagues are massively strengthened in their professional work. What appeared to be gratuitous hostility becomes understandable, if still unacceptable, behaviour. The agenda for group discussions includes the pupil and his or her circumstances, motives and perceptions, relationships within the classroom and school, and the therapeutic potential of the curriculum. Information is generated, and in succeeding discussions, universal characteristics of human behaviour are encountered and elaborated. It helps for staff groups who plan to work in this way to have a school-based, introductory training day: groups are usually so successful that some members look for more extensive training in psychodynamic approaches. It is often impossible to know how far improved relationships are due to the pupil's needs being identified and met, and how much is due to the support which teachers themselves receive through group analyses and discussions (for elaboration of these points see: Hanko, 1985; Caspari, 1976; McManus, 1989, ch 4 and 6).

As well as improving conventional teaching skills, analysis of pupil behaviour automatically raises teachers' expectations of their pupils' capabilities. For example: 'Usually expectations are too low' (DES, 1984); 'unstimulating work was particularly common with less able pupils where teachers' expectations are often too low' (DES, 1990). To many teachers, this criticism seems misplaced: they expect as much or as little as the evidence before them warrants. Many would claim that they ignore bad news about pupils, preferring instead to make up their own minds. Research suggests that this 'fresh start' approach differentiates experienced teachers from neophytes (see Berliner, 1987). Few teachers have the time to discover all the information that might help them re-define their perceptions of troublesome individuals, understand their problems, and raise their own and their pupils' expectations, but a beginning can be made by employing reflection in the classroom. Where severely troublesome pupils are concerned, the rewards of such analysis encourage all concerned to find additional time for shared reviewing and evaluation.

Many units adopt systematic regimes for the management of excluded pupils. For example, they often require pupils and parents to sign contracts and they may use explicit behavioural methods, progress charts, or token economies. Sometimes this is compensated by a relatively relaxed attitude towards timetable requirements: some pupils may attend for only half-days, for example. Devotees of particular philosophies can sometimes find themselves at loggerheads – though this is more common among academics than actual practitioners. Certainly, anyone fanatically committed to a particular method is unlikely to survive the setbacks and hurly-burly of life with troublesome pupils. In practice, most approaches work well together and it is normally a considerable asset for staff to represent a range of philosophies. Whatever the manifest regime adopted, the underlying message has to be one of acceptance and optimism, securely rooted in appropriate attitudes.

The debate as to whether or not excluded pupils should be offered a different curriculum, or a caring regime without any formal curricular requirements at all, is now laid to rest by the Education Reform Act, which will be discussed later. The legal obligation to follow the National Curriculum might well focus attention on methods of engaging the interest of disaffected and lower-attaining pupils in worthwhile knowledge. All pupils are aware of the manifest teaching function of schools, and know how to construe the offer of a second-rate product. Teaching the National Curriculum, or any other, and paying heed to difficult pupils' emotional and therapeutic needs are not mutually exclusive activities. All teaching demonstrates concern for pupils' worth and carries the covert message that pupils matter: time spent in the core and foundation subjects is no less important than sympathetic counselling in raising disturbed pupils' low self-esteem.

Emotional therapy cannot take place in a vacuum and it is not soaked in through the skin. It is an inescapably cognitive enterprise: everything, as it were, goes in through the mind. Like teachers and parents, education and therapy are partners. It is my view that the gap between the most and the least able is greatly exaggerated, and in consequence a large proportion of the pupil population is assumed to be incapable of learning except through elementary exercises and the tedious practice of content-free skills. It is a worthwhile thought experiment to try to imagine what our television output would be like if the programme planners worked upon the same principle. The significance of the fact that most of the population understands and is interested by most of the programmes is generally ignored. Favouring, or noticing, only a limited range of achievements and then trying to hide pejorative appraisals through such labels as 'the opportunity class' are seldom ways of retaining pupils' respect: reward systems, however covert or muted, speak loudly (Eisner, 1985).

We can learn much from the attention-commanding techniques employed by journalists, both in the newspaper and television media. First paragraphs, and therefore introductions to lesson topics, have to be arresting: descriptions or accounts of concrete phenomena or incidents, clearly related to the audience's needs and interests; the language is direct, not passive and abstract, and is intelligible to almost the entire population without appearing condescending to anyone. It is possible to explain almost any concept in language that can be read by the average 10 year old – and therefore by almost all teenagers, however limited in their attainments. The intelligibility of written text is related to its interest for the reader, the length of the sentences and the number of uncommon or multi-syllabic words. It is a common mistake, in simplifying texts, to imagine that short words and sentences are all that is required, and not to attend to the specialized use of some short words which can confuse the reader. For example, a long sentence about how people absorb water can have its 'reading age' suitability reduced by cutting it up into three short sentences (see Currie, 1990). However, retaining the word 'gain' ('We gain water in two ways') instead of substituting 'take in' leaves an unnecessary hurdle in the way of understanding for some pupils: no one, outside a science textbook, would use 'gain' in this way. Similarly, some measures of volume are more familiar to pupils than others – pints and litres rather than 1500 cubic centimetres.

HMI, commenting on The Lower Attaining Pupils' Programme, stress the importance of giving attention to practical contexts and balancing written work with oral discussion and enquiry (DES, 1989c, para. 29). They suggest that teachers' expectations are lower where lower attaining pupils are taught in separate classes – an example of how school structures can have personal consequences. Engaging and interesting teaching in mixed ability classrooms is one possible way of relieving those pressures caused by learning failure and its associated low esteem. Many teachers have little difficulty with this but there are few props to help those less certain of success. It is particularly difficult to provide tasks for pupils in which active oral work is properly integrated into the task: often, the requirement to 'discuss these ideas for 10 minutes in groups' appears to the pupils to be artificial and contrived.

I have produced materials for a Personal, Social and Health Education (PSHE) course which aim to be interesting, intelligible and relevant to a wide ability range, as well as providing pair and group work that is properly integrated into the tasks (McManus, 1991). Pupils working in pairs or threes are more likely to contribute and share the work: the larger the group, the more scope for passengers, dictators, clowns and other unwanted roles. The two sample pages from the Foundation for Life series (Figure 14.1) illustrate these characteristics: the topic is introduced through an anecdote, a recognizable slice of life; the gist of the story is repeated and its significance made clear; the reading age is around 10 years; the pair and group tasks are essential to the requirements of the task rather than being just another way of doing things; and the topic engages the full ability range without confusing some and patronizing others. The three volumes are developed from work in exclusion units and ordinary secondary schools. They cover some topics not usually thought to be within the grasp of lower-attaining pupils (for example, philosophical issues such as the problem of evil) and some which indirectly address some of the personal problems and domestic difficulties they may have themselves (for example, poor parenting and the ways in which poverty acts upon families).

In my view, the legal requirement to teach the National Curriculum to all pupils will cut away the roots of some disaffection which leads some pupils to exclusion from school. Circular 22/89 (DES, 1989a) states that the Secretary of State believes that 'all pupils, including those with Special Educational Needs (SEN), should follow the National Curriculum to the maximum extent possible'. The National Curriculum Council (NCC) document on SEN in the National Curriculum (NCC, 1989) stresses 'the principle of full entitlement to the National Curriculum for all pupils'. One of the roots of disruption in some schools has been the exclusion of some pupils from a broad curricular experience: to be fed remedial Maths and English, often through the empty medium of structured exercises in a separate class, does nothing for the emotional development of troubled children; and it produces behaviour problems in many of those who at the outset had merely learning difficulties. Further, such pupils did not have access to the full range of teaching expertise, especially in subjects other than Maths and English. If the law is obeyed, this can no longer happen, so in that respect many more pupils should get a better deal.

Pupils whose behaviour results in a Statement should find that it protects their entitlement to the National Curriculum: Circular 22/89 says, 'The Secretary of State does not expect most statements to have references to modifications or exemptions from the new curriculum'. It goes on to point out that the 1981 Act has not been superseded by ERA. LEAs retain their duty to ensure that provision for statemented pupils is made. This is not merely a requirement to treat each individual case as it arises: the LEA's duty to secure provision must be reflected in the local management scheme. The circular further emphasizes that the statement must not be distorted in order to fit what the LEA thinks will be available in respect of resources: it must detail the child's SEN 'whether or not the LEA feels able to make provision for those needs.'

The NCC document also warns against abuse of statements: 'No ordinary school should be tempted to use the statementing procedures as a pretext for transferring certain pupils to special schools or units merely because they are not expected to perform well on national assessments.' Interestingly, for the argument of this chapter, the NCC document notes that some pupils meet 'attitudes and practices in schools which do not actively encourage full participation' and points out that pupils with SEN need 'positive attitudes from school staff who are determined to ensure their fullest participation in the National Curriculum'. The specific guidance on English even warns of the dangers in over-emphasis on behaviour-management 'without attempts to understand the child's feelings'.

2.   Travel safely

Accident rules

Road accidents must always be reported to the police. Even if you think you are not to blame, you should tell a police officer what has happened. The driver of the car told Lola and Kevin not to bother going to the police. He said the accident was not serious. Later he went to the police himself. Maybe he remembered the law. Maybe he wanted to get his story in first. Maybe he wanted to make Lola and Kevin look as if they had something to hide. Maybe he just changed his mind.

Fig 14.1

DES Circular 15/89 reinforces pupils' entitlement to the National Curriculum by severely restricting the scope for directing that pupils be excepted from it: 'very few pupils only will be the subject of directions'. The document is careful to point out that pupils must not be made exceptions on the ground that their behaviour is disturbing other pupils: 'In the Secretary of State's view, the test should be whether the pupil's behaviour prevents himself or herself from benefiting fully from the National Curriculum.' Headteachers must

After an accident, you must make a statement. This is your
description of what happened – what you saw and what you did.
All those involved in an accident are asked to make a statement.
Anyone who had a good view of the accident will be asked for a
statement, too. The statements are used to help police to decide
whether someone should be charged with an offence.

1 Prepare and write down the statement you think Lola might
   make. Describe carefully what happened in about 100 words.
   You could use a sketch map to make your description clearer.
2 Read the driver's statement below. What he says has
   happened will be different from what you have written for
   Lola. Make a list of points Lola and the driver agree on. Then
   make a list of the points they disagree about.

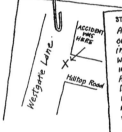

STATEMENT GIVEN BY DRIVER OF THE CAR

At approximately 7pm I was stationary and facing north
on Westgate Lane waiting to turn right into Hilltop Road. My
indicator was flashing. I checked my mirror and as the road
was clear I began to turn. Just as I did so I saw a motorcycle
in my mirror coming up behind me at high speed and
hooting its horn. I stopped to let it overtake even
though it was now on the opposite carriageway. The
motorcycle hit the side of my car knocking off a wing
mirror. The driver and passenger were not badly hurt,
even though the passenger was not wearing a helmet.
He was very abusive and threatened me. I gave
them some first aid and then left them to report
the accident to the police.

3 Both Lola and the car driver were at fault. List the mistakes
   made by each of them. Decide whether or not anyone should
   be prosecuted. Write down the reasons for your decision.
4 Lola's first mistake was to take a passenger who was not
   wearing the spare helmet. Think of the reasons for the law on
   motorcycle helmets. Consider how Lola could have persuaded
   Kevin to wear one. Write out the conversation that Lola and
   Kevin could have had before setting off. Set it out like this:

Lola: *You should wear the spare helmet.*

Kevin: *I don't need a helmet.*

Lola: *It's the law.*

Kevin: *Nobody will see us.*

Fig 14.1 continued

consult the LEA and its specialist staff before acting and, in preparing
directions, 'refer to any procedures the school has used to analyse
and monitor the pupil's needs and difficulties, and any action taken
to address them, including any special support offered.' It goes on to
point out that 'it may be more difficult to carry out assessments' if
pupils have been excepted from aspects of the National Curriculum.
Even when pupils have been excluded from school, itself a tightly
constrained and closely monitored procedure, the headteacher's duty

to implement the National Curriculum continues as long as the pupil remains on the school's register: 'It therefore extends to registered pupils being educated at home, at a hospital school or in an off-site unit.'

It is clear that if the law is obeyed in spirit and letter those pupils at risk of exclusion will be less likely to be marginalized within the school, and thereby forced inexorably towards the exit. HMI regularly point to the relatively restricted educational opportunities offered to the lowest achievers in ordinary schools. In their survey of exclusion units (DES, 19878) they found, not surprisingly, that broad and balanced curricular experiences were not on offer. In the new era of the Educational Reform Act (ERA), more pupils in difficulty will be accommodated and have their needs addressed in ordinary schools. There is a view that the parents of less troublesome children will respond by taking their children away from schools which carry out their legal responsibilities. In some cases this may be so, but this jaundiced view, often put by those who have no children in the state system, underestimates parents. It has to be remembered that the selective system was displaced at the wish of both parents and teachers: it is unlikely that a majority will wish to help it return. Perhaps most parents, tired of hectoring about educational standards and economic performance, are ready to react against such a narrow-minded, petty middle-class view of education. In the 1990s we might see the educational equivalent of the past decade's search for the natural and the real. Parents will want their children's social and educational experience to be as free from artificial preservatives and sweeteners as their breakfast; as unpurified and unbleached as whole-meal flour; as plain, fresh and wholesome as their pine floors and furniture; and full of the richness, bustle and variety of a dockside flat in a city centre. Spending money on neat uniforms and school fees will become as fashionable as buying sliced white loaves. Real education, like real bread, has the rough bits left in.

In conclusion two points need to be stressed. First, whether we hope for success, or resign ourselves to survival, we need to begin by accepting that troublesome behaviour is as much a part of a teacher's job as it is of a parent's. Teaching is one of those professions which has a responsibility to respond to uncooperative persons in intelligent and considered ways – a duty we share with solicitors, barristers, police and priests. Coming to terms with this will do much to lift morale and restore esteem to the profession: victory in the battle for recognition will be won, if won at all, by enclosing more territory, not by a retreat.

Second, in seeking to understand why some pupils behave as they do we must consider the whole context of their personal, domestic and classroom circumstances. This requires cooperation with parents and colleagues, working together to share knowledge, skills and understandings. In this way, exasperating and seemingly intractable problems are diminished; our perceptions, interpretations and expectations alter: that which appeared overwhelming looks vulnerable in the light of our professional understanding. And for some pupils, the new experience of being taken seriously, improves their self-esteem and makes possible a change in their behaviour.

Without these attitudinal changes, time spent discussing policies, rules and cases is largely wasted: procedures which do not offer quick results are likely to be abandoned in an atmosphere of despair and recrimination. For school policies to be professional, realistic and consistent, teachers must share and synthesize their views, both on teachers' responsibilities and their perceptions of individuals. This has implications for the management of schools which are a mirror image of the characteristics of a good teacher: sharing knowledge and decisions, through collective work, in a climate of acceptance and respect.

Bibliography

Berliner, D.C. (1987) 'Ways of thinking about students and classrooms by more and less experienced teachers', in J. Calderhead (ed.) *Exploring Teachers' Thinking*, London: Cassell.

Caspari, I. (1976) *Troublesome Children in Class*, London: Routledge and Kegan Paul.

Currie, H. (1990) 'Making texts more readable', *British Journal of Special Education*, 17 (4): pp. 137–9.

Delamont, S. and Galton, M. (1986) *Inside the Secondary Classroom*, London: Routledge and Kegan Paul

Department of Education and Science (DES) (1978) *Behavioural units*, London: HMSO.

Department of Education and Science (DES) (1984) *Education Observed 2*, London: HMSO.

Department of Education and Science (DES) 1989a) Assessments and Statements of Special Educational Needs: Procedures within the Education, Health and Social Services, DES/DoH Circular 22/89, London: HMSO.

Department of Education and Science (DES) (1989b) Discipline in Schools, Report of the Committee of Enquiry chaired by Lord Elton, London: HMSO.

Department of Education and Science (DES) (1989c) *The Lower Attaining Pupils' Programme*, 1982–88, London: HMSO.

Department of Education and Science (DES) 1990) Standards in Education, Annual Report of HM Senior Chief Inspector of Schools, London: HMSO.

Doyle, W. (1986) 'Classroom management', in Wittrock, M.C. (ed.) (1986)*Third Handbook of Research on Teaching*, New York: American Education Research Association/Macmillan.

Dreikurs, R. (1957) *Psychology in the Classroom*, London: Staples Press.

Eisner, E. (1985) *The Art of Educational Evaluation*, Lewes: Falmer.

Emanuel, R.B. (1990) 'Countertransference: a spanner in the works or a tool for understanding', *Journal of Educational Therapy*, 3 (2): pp. 3–12.

Galloway, D., Martin, R. and Wilcox, B. (1985) 'Persistent absence from school and exclusion from school: the predictive power of school and community variables', *British Educational Research Journal*, 11 (1): pp. 51–61.

Hanko, G. (1985) *Special Needs in Ordinary Classrooms: an Approach to Teacher Support and Pupil Care*, Oxford: Blackwell.

Lawrence, J., Steed, D. and Young, P. (1977) Disruptive Behaviour in a Secondary School, University of London.

McManus, M. (1987) 'Suspension and exclusion from high schools: the association with catchment and school variables', *School Organization*, 7 (3): pp. 261–271.

McManus, M. (1989) *Troublesome Behaviour in the Classroom: a Teachers' Survival Guide*, London: Routledge.

McManus, M. (1991) *Foundation for Life*, 3 vols: *Work and Leisure*; *Home, Health and Family*; *You and Your Community*, London: Hodder and Stoughton.

National Curriculum Council (NCC) (1989) Curriculum Guidance 2, Special Educational Needs in the National Curriculum.

Pearson, G. (1983) *Holligan: a History of Respectable Fears*, London: Macmillan.

Stott, D.H. (1978) *Helping Children with Learning Difficulties*, London: Ward Lock.

Stott, D.H. (1982) *Helping the Maladjusted Child*, Milton Keynes, Open University Press.

INDEX

ability: production of, 12–14
absenteeism, 77–9 *passim*
abuse of children, 92–3
  psychiatric examination and, 103
Achenbach's Child Behaviour
  Checklist, 26
acting out, 6
Aggressive Replacement Training, 83
aggressive behaviour, 30
  classroom organisation and, 159, 160
  physical abuse and, 92
  in the playground, 182–3
  social skills and, 74–5
  in 3–7 year olds, 154–8
  see also violent behaviour
applied behavioural analysis, 22
Argyle, Michael, 72–4 *passim*
assessment of difficult behaviour, 22–6
  baseline record-keeping, 23–4
  cognitive, 25–6
  see also psychiatric examination,
    psychological assessment
attachment theory (Bowlby), 70–1
attention disorder, 26–9 *passim*, 56–7,
  60–1
  and speed of learning, 61
attention-seeking, 221–2

bad behaviour, 66–88, 219
  classroom organisation and, 158–63
  defined, 66–9
  of excluded pupils, 218–21 *passim*
  genetic/biological accounts of, 69–70
  psychological accounts of, 70–2
  social accounts of, 72–80
  in 3–7 year olds, 153–7
  see also deviancy, management of
    difficult behaviour
Becker, H. S., 78
behaviour disorders, *see* conduct
  disorders
behaviour management in primary
  schools, 167–86
  accountability, 175–6
  collective responsibility, 180–4
  constructiveness, 176–80
  forseeability, 171–3

purposefulness, 173–5
behavioural approaches, 21–36, 170
  assessment of behaviour, 22–6
  case example, 31
  to conduct disorders, 29–32, 82
  criticisms of, 21
  to hyperactivity, 26–9
  token system, 28, 34–5
  see also applied behavioural analysis,
    cognitive behaviour therapy,
    learning theory, reinforcement,
    self-instructional training, social
    skills training
Bernstein, B., 209–10
boasting, 156–7
body language, 174
  see also non-verbal communication
boredom in school, 55–6
Bowlby, J., 70–1
Brading, Richard, 183–4
Bradley, I., 58–9
Bristol Social Adjustment Guides
  (BSAGs), 109–11, 117
Bryant, P. E., 58–9
bullying, 182–3
  see also aggressive behaviour

Carter, Bob, 49–50
Chess, S., 93–4
child-centred education, 206–8
Children's Behaviour Questionnaire,
  111–13, 117, 124–5
classroom organisation
  layout (primary schools), 175
  nursery/infant, 158–63
codes of conduct in schools, 130–4
  classroom rules, 181
  school rules, 181–2
cognitive assessment of children, 25–6
cognitive behaviour therapy, 21, 82–3
  for hyperactivity, 29
cognitive development: bad behaviour
  and, 71
Commission for Racial Equality, 42
communication skills, 73
  intra-family, 99
concentration, *see* attention disorder